Oh, Money! Money!
A Novel

by

Eleanor H. Porter

Oh, Money! Money! A Novel
by Eleanor H. Porter

ISBN: 978-93-59957-06-7

Published by

DOUBLE 9 BOOKS

2/13-B, Ansari Road
Daryaganj, New Delhi – 110002
info@double9books.com
www.double9books.com
Tel. 011-40042856

This book is under public domain

ABOUT THE AUTHOR

American author Eleanor Emily Hodgman Porter was born on December 19, 1868, and died on May 21, 1920. She was best known for her books Pollyanna (1913) and Just David (1916). Frances Fletcher Hodgman and Llewella French (née Woolson) had a daughter named Eleanor Emily Hodgman on December 19, 1868, in Littleton, New Hampshire. She learned how to sing by going to the New England Conservatory for many years. They moved to Massachusetts after getting married to John Lyman Porter in 1892. That's when she started writing and selling short stories and then novels. Her death date was May 21, 1920, in Cambridge, Massachusetts. She was buried at Mount Auburn Cemetery. She wrote several books for adults, such as The Turn of the Tide (1908), The Road to Understanding (1917), Oh Money! Money! (1918), Dawn (1919), Keith's Dark Tower (1919), Mary Marie (1920), and Sister Sue (1921). She also wrote several collections of short stories, such as Across the Years (around 1919), Money, Love, and Kate (1923), and Little Pardner (1926). Porter had a lot of success with his books. In the United States, Pollyanna was the eighth best-selling novel in 1913, the second best-selling novel in 1914, and the fourth best-selling novel in 1915 (with 47 printings between 1915 and 1920). Just David was the third best-selling novel in 1916, The Road to Understanding was the fourth best-selling novel in 1917, and Oh Money! Money! was the fifth best-selling novel in 1918.

CONTENTS

CHAPTER I
EXIT MR. STANLEY G. FULTON 7

CHAPTER II
ENTER MR. JOHN SMITH 18

CHAPTER III
THE SMALL BOY AT THE KEYHOLE 26

CHAPTER IV
IN SEARCH OF SOME DATES 34

CHAPTER V
IN MISS FLORA'S ALBUM 41

CHAPTER VI
POOR MAGGIE 48

CHAPTER VII
POOR MAGGIE AND SOME OTHERS 57

CHAPTER VIII
A SANTA CLAUS HELD UP 66

CHAPTER IX
"DEAR COUSIN STANLEY" 72

CHAPTER X
WHAT DOES IT MATTER? 82

CHAPTER XI
SANTA CLAUS ARRIVES 88

CHAPTER XII
THE TOYS RATTLE OUT 95

CHAPTER XIII
THE DANCING BEGINS 104

CHAPTER XIV
FROM ME TO YOU WITH LOVE 119

CHAPTER XV
IN SEARCH OF REST 128

CHAPTER XVI
THE FLY IN THE OINTMENT 137

CHAPTER XVII
AN AMBASSADOR OF CUPID'S 147

CHAPTER XVIII
JUST A MATTER OF BEGGING 155

CHAPTER XIX
STILL OTHER FLIES 164

CHAPTER XX
FRANKENSTEIN: BEING A LETTER FROM JOHN SMITH TO
EDWARD D. NORTON, ATTORNEY AT LAW 171

CHAPTER XXI
SYMPATHIES MISPLACED 174

CHAPTER XXII
WITH EVERY JIM A JAMES 180

CHAPTER XXIII
REFLECTIONS—MIRRORED AND OTHERWISE 190

CHAPTER XXIV
THAT MISERABLE MONEY 198

CHAPTER XXV
EXIT MR. JOHN SMITH 204

CHAPTER XXVI
REENTER MR. STANLEY G. FULTON 213

CHAPTER I
EXIT MR. STANLEY G. FULTON

There was a thoughtful frown on the face of the man who was the possessor of twenty million dollars. He was a tall, spare man, with a fringe of reddish-brown hair encircling a bald spot. His blue eyes, fixed just now in a steady gaze upon a row of ponderous law books across the room, were friendly and benevolent in direct contradiction to the bulldog, never-let-go fighting qualities of the square jaw below the firm, rather thin lips.

The lawyer, a youthfully alert man of sixty years, trimly gray as to garb, hair, and mustache, sat idly watching him, yet with eyes that looked so intently that they seemed to listen.

For fully five minutes the two men had been pulling at their cigars in silence when the millionaire spoke.

"Ned, what am I going to do with my money?"

Into the lawyer's listening eyes flashed, for a moment, the keenly scrutinizing glance usually reserved for the witness on the other side. Then quietly came the answer.

"Spend it yourself, I hope—for some years to come, Stanley."

Mr. Stanley G. Fulton was guilty of a shrug and an uplifted eyebrow.

"Thanks. Very pretty, and I appreciate it, of course. But I can't wear but one suit of clothes at a time, nor eat but one dinner—which, by the way, just now consists of somebody's health biscuit and hot water. Twenty millions don't really what you might call melt away at that rate."

The lawyer frowned.

"Shucks, Fulton!" he expostulated, with an irritable twist of his hand. "I thought better of you than that. This poor rich man's 'one-suit, one-dinner, one-bed-at-a-time' hard-luck story doesn't suit your style. Better cut it out!"

"All right. Cut it is." The man smiled good-humoredly. "But you see I was nettled. You didn't get me at all. I asked you what was to become of my money after I'd done spending it myself—the little that is left, of course."

Once more from the lawyer's eyes flashed that keenly scrutinizing glance.

"What was it, Fulton? A midnight rabbit, or a wedge of mince pie *not* like mother used to make? Why, man alive, you're barely over fifty, yet. Cheer up! It's only a little matter of indigestion. There are a lot of good days and good dinners coming to you, yet."

The millionaire made a wry face.

"Very likely—if I survive the biscuits. But, seriously, Ned, I'm in earnest. No, I don't think I'm going to die—yet awhile. But I ran across young Bixby last night—got him home, in fact. Delivered him to his white-faced little wife. Talk about your maudlin idiots!"

"Yes, I know. Too bad, too bad!"

"Hm-m; well, that's what one million did—inherited. It set me to thinking—of mine, when I get through with them."

"I see." The lawyer's lips came together a little grimly. "You've not made your will, I believe."

"No. Dreaded it, somehow. Funny how a man'll fight shy of a little thing like that, isn't it? And when we're so mighty particular where it goes while we're living!"

"Yes, I know; you're not the only one. You have relatives—somewhere, I surmise."

"Nothing nearer than cousins, third or fourth, back East. They'd get it, I suppose—without a will."

"Why don't you marry?"

The millionaire repeated the wry face of a moment before.

"I'm not a marrying man. I never did care much for women; and—I'm not fool enough to think that a woman would be apt to fall in love with my bald head. Nor am I obliging enough to care to hand the millions over to the woman that falls in love with *them*, taking me along as the necessary sack that holds the gold. If it comes to that, I'd rather risk the cousins. They, at least, are of my own blood, and they didn't angle to get the money."

"You know them?"

"Never saw 'em."

"Why not pick out a bunch of colleges and endow them?"

The millionaire shook his head.

"Doesn't appeal to me, somehow. Oh, of course it ought to, but—it just doesn't. That's all. Maybe if I was a college man myself; but—well, I had to dig for what education I got."

"Very well—charities, then. There are numberless organizations that—" He stopped abruptly at the other's uplifted hand.

"Organizations! Good Heavens, I should think there were! I tried 'em once. I got that philanthropic bee in my bonnet, and I gave thousands, tens of thousands to 'em. Then I got to wondering where the money went."

Unexpectedly the lawyer chuckled.

"You never did like to invest without investigating, Fulton," he observed.

With only a shrug for an answer the other plunged on.

"Now, understand. I'm not saying that organized charity isn't all right, and doesn't do good, of course. Neither am I prepared to propose anything to take its place. And maybe the two or three I dealt with were particularly addicted to the sort of thing I objected to. But, honestly, Ned, if you'd lost heart and friends and money, and were just ready to chuck the whole shooting-match, how would you like to become a 'Case,' say, number twenty-three thousand seven hundred and forty-one, ticketed and docketed, and duly apportioned off to a six-by-nine rule of 'do this' and 'do that,' while a dozen spectacled eyes watched you being cleaned up and regulated and wound up with a key made of just so much and no more pats and preachments carefully weighed and labeled? How *would* you like it?"

The lawyer laughed.

"I know; but, my dear fellow, what would you have? Surely, *un*organized charity and promiscuous giving is worse—"

"Oh, yes, I've tried that way, too," shrugged the other. "There was a time when every Tom, Dick, and Harry, with a run-down shoe and a ragged coat, could count on me for a ten-spot by just holding out his hand, no questions asked. Then a serious-eyed little woman sternly told me one day that the indiscriminate charity of a millionaire was not only a curse to any community, but a corruption to the whole state. I believe she kindly included the nation, as well, bless her! And I thought I was doing good!" "What a blow—to you!" There was a whimsical smile in the lawyer's eyes.

"It was." The millionaire was not smiling. "But she was right. It set me to thinking, and I began to follow up those ten-spots—the ones that I could trace. Jove! what a mess I'd made of it! Oh, some of them were all right, of course, and I made *those* fifties on the spot. But the others—! I tell you, Ned, money that isn't earned is the most risky thing in the world. If I'd left half those wretches alone, they'd have braced up and helped themselves and made men of themselves, maybe. As it was—Well, you never can tell as to the results of a so-called 'good' action. From my experience I should say they are every whit as dangerous as the bad ones."

The lawyer laughed outright.

"But, my dear fellow, that's just where the organized charity comes in. Don't you see?"

"Oh, yes, I know—Case number twenty-three thousand seven hundred and forty-one! And that's all right, of course. Relief of some sort is absolutely necessary. But I'd like to see a little warm sympathy injected into it, some way. Give the machine a heart, say, as well as hands and a head."

"Then why don't you try it yourself?"

"Not I!" His gesture of dissent was emphatic. "I have tried it, in a way, and failed. That's why I'd like some one else to tackle the job. And that brings me right back to my original question. I'm wondering what my money will do, when I'm done with it. I'd like to have one of my own kin have it—if I was sure of him. Money is a queer proposition, Ned, and it's capable of—'most anything."

"It is. You're right."

"What I can do with it, and what some one else can do with it, are two quite different matters. I don't consider my efforts to circulate it wisely, or even harmlessly, exactly what you'd call a howling success. Whatever I've done, I've always been criticized for not doing something else. If I gave a costly entertainment, I was accused of showy ostentation. If I didn't give it, I was accused of not putting money into honest circulation. If I donated to a church, it was called conscience money; and if I didn't donate to it, they said I was mean and miserly. So much for what I've done. I was just wondering—what the other fellow'd do with it."

"Why worry? 'Twon't be your fault."

"But it will—if I give it to him. Great Scott, Ned! what money does for folks, sometimes—folks that aren't used to it! Look at Bixby; and look at that poor little Marston girl, throwing herself away on that worthless scamp of a Gowing who's only after her money, as everybody (but herself) knows! And if it doesn't make knaves and martyrs of them, ten to one it does make fools of 'em. They're worse than a kid with a dollar on circus day; and they use just about as much sense spending their pile, too. You should have heard dad tell about his pals in the eighties that struck it rich in the gold mines. One bought up every grocery store in town and instituted a huge free grab-bag for the populace; and another dropped his hundred thousand in the dice box before it was a week old. I wonder what those cousins of mine back East are like!"

"If you're fearful, better take Case number twenty-three thousand seven hundred and forty-one," smiled the lawyer.

"Hm-m; I suppose so," ejaculated the other grimly, getting to his feet. "Well, I must be off. It's biscuit time, I see."

A moment later the door of the lawyer's sumptuously appointed office closed behind him. Not twenty-four hours afterward, however, it opened to admit him again. He was alert, eager-eyed, and smiling. He looked ten years younger. Even the office boy who ushered him in cocked a curious eye at him.

The man at the great flat-topped desk gave a surprised ejaculation.

"Hullo, Fulton! Those biscuits must be agreeing with you," he laughed. "Mind telling me their name?"

"Ned, I've got a scheme. I think I can carry it out." Mr. Stanley G. Fulton strode across the room and dropped himself into the waiting chair. "Remember those cousins back East? Well, I'm going to find out which of 'em I want for my heir."

"Another case of investigating before investing, eh?"

"Exactly."

"Well, that's like you. What is it, a little detective work? Going to get acquainted with them, I suppose, and see how they treat you. Then you can size them up as to hearts and habits, and drop the golden plum into the lap of the worthy man, eh?"

"Yes, and no. But not the way you say. I'm going to give 'em say fifty or a hundred thousand apiece, and—"

"*Give* it to them—*now?*"

"Sure! How'm I going to know how they'll spend money till they have it to spend?"

"I know; but—"

"Oh, I've planned all that. Don't worry. Of course you'll have to fix it up for me. I shall leave instructions with you, and when the time comes all you have to do is to carry them out."

The lawyer came erect in his chair.

"*Leave* instructions! But you, yourself—?"

"Oh, I'm going to be there, in Hillerton."

"There? Hillerton?"

"Yes, where the cousins live, you know. Of course I want to see how it works."

"Humph! I suppose you think you'll find out—with you watching their every move!" The lawyer had settled back in his chair, an ironical smile on his lips.

"Oh, they won't know me, of course, except as John Smith."

"John Smith!" The lawyer was sitting erect again.

"Yes. I'm going to take that name—for a time."

"Nonsense, Fulton! Have you lost your senses?"

"No." The millionaire still smiled imperturbably. "Really, my dear Ned, I'm disappointed in you. You don't seem to realize the possibilities of this thing."

"Oh, yes, I do—perhaps better than you, old man," retorted the other with an expressive glance.

"Oh, come, Ned, listen! I've got three cousins in Hillerton. I never saw them, and they never saw me. I'm going to give them a tidy little sum of money apiece, and then have the fun of watching them spend it. Any harm in that, especially as it's no one's business what I do with my money?"

"N—no, I suppose not—if you can carry such a wild scheme through."

"I can, I think. I'm going to be John Smith."

"Nice distinctive name!"

"I chose a colorless one on purpose. I'm going to be a colorless person, you see."

"Oh! And—er—do you think Mr. Stanley G. Fulton, multi-millionaire, with his pictured face in half the papers and magazines from the Atlantic to the Pacific, *can* hide that face behind a colorless John Smith?"

"Maybe not. But he can hide it behind a nice little close-cropped beard." The millionaire stroked his smooth chin reflectively.

"Humph! How large is Hillerton?"

"Eight or ten thousand. Nice little New England town, I'm told."

"Hm-m. And your—er—business in Hillerton, that will enable you to be the observing fly on your cousins' walls?"

"Yes, I've thought that all out, too; and that's another brilliant stroke. I'm going to be a genealogist. I'm going to be at work tracing the Blaisdell family—their name is Blaisdell. I'm writing a book which necessitates the collection of an endless amount of data. Now how about that fly's chances of observation. Eh?"

"Mighty poor, if he's swatted—and that's what he will be! New England housewives are death on flies, I understand."

"Well, I'll risk this one."

"You poor fellow!" There were exasperation and amusement in the lawyer's eyes, but there was only mock sympathy in his voice. "And to think I've known you all these years, and never suspected it, Fulton!"

The man who owned twenty millions still smiled imperturbably.

"Oh, yes, I know what you mean, but I'm not crazy. And really I'm interested in genealogy, too, and I've been thinking for some time I'd go digging about the roots of my ancestral tree. I have dug a little, in years gone. My mother was a Blaisdell, you know. Her grandfather was brother to some ancestor of these Hillerton Blaisdells; and I really am interested in collecting Blaisdell data. So that's all straight. I shall be telling no fibs. And think of the opportunity it gives me! Besides, I shall try to board with one of them. I've decided that."

"Upon my word, a pretty little scheme!"

"Yes, I knew you'd appreciate it, the more you thought about it." Mr. Stanley G. Fulton's blue eyes twinkled a little.

With a disdainful gesture the lawyer brushed this aside.

"Do you mind telling me how you happened to think of it, yourself?"

"Not a bit. 'Twas a little booklet got out by a Trust Company."

"It sounds like it!"

"Oh, they didn't suggest exactly this, I'll admit; but they did suggest that, if you were fearful as to the way your heirs would handle their inheritance, you could create a trust fund for their benefit while you were living, and then watch the way the beneficiaries spent the income, as well as the way the trust fund itself was managed. In this way you could observe the effects of your gifts, and at the same time be able to change them if you didn't like results. That gave me an idea. I've just developed it. That's all. I'm going to make my cousins a little rich, and see which, if any of them, can stand being very rich."

"But the money, man! How are you going to drop a hundred thousand dollars into three men's laps, and expect to get away without an investigation as to the why and wherefore of such a singular proceeding?"

"That's where your part comes in," smiled the millionaire blandly. "Besides, to be accurate, one of the laps is—er—a petticoat one."

"Oh, indeed! So much the worse, maybe. But—And so this is where I come in, is it? Well, and suppose I refuse to come in?"

"Regretfully I shall have to employ another attorney."

"Humph! Well?"

"But you won't refuse." The blue eyes opposite were still twinkling. "In the first place, you're my good friend—my best friend. You wouldn't be seen letting me start off on a wild-goose chase like this without your guiding hand at the helm to see that I didn't come a cropper."

"Aren't you getting your metaphors a trifle mixed?" This time the lawyer's eyes were twinkling.

"Eh? What? Well, maybe. But I reckon you get my meaning. Besides, what I want you to do is a mere routine of regular business, with you."

"It sounds like it. Routine, indeed!"

"But it is—your part. Listen. I'm off for South America, say, on an exploring tour. In your charge I leave certain papers with instructions that on the first day of the sixth month of my absence (I being unheard from), you are to open a certain envelope and act according to instructions within. Simplest thing in the world, man. Now isn't it?"

"Oh, very simple—as you put it."

"Well, meanwhile I'll start for South America—alone, of course; and, so far as you're concerned, that ends it. If on the way, somewhere, I determine suddenly on a change of destination, that is none of your affair. If, say in a month or two, a quiet, inoffensive gentleman by the name of Smith arrives in Hillerton on the legitimate and perfectly respectable business of looking up a family pedigree, that also is none of your concern." With a sudden laugh the lawyer fell back in his chair.

"By Jove, Fulton, if I don't believe you'll pull this absurd thing off!"

"There! Now you're talking like a sensible man, and we can get somewhere. Of course I'll pull it off! Now here's my plan. In order best to judge how my esteemed relatives conduct themselves under the sudden accession of wealth, I must see them first without it, of course. Hence, I plan to be in Hillerton some months before your letter and the money arrive. I intend, indeed, to be on the friendliest terms with every Blaisdell in Hillerton before that times comes."

"But can you? Will they accept you without references or introduction?"

"Oh, I shall have the best of references and introductions. Bob Chalmers is the president of a bank there. Remember Bob? Well, I shall take John

Smith in and introduce him to Bob some day. After that, Bob'll introduce John Smith? See? All I need is a letter as to my integrity and respectability, I reckon, so my kinsmen won't suspect me of designs on their spoons when I ask to board with them. You see, I'm a quiet, retiring gentleman, and I don't like noisy hotels."

With an explosive chuckle the lawyer clapped his knee. "Fulton, this is absolutely the richest thing I ever heard of! I'd give a farm to be a fly on *your* wall and see you do it. I'm blest if I don't think I'll go to Hillerton myself—to see Bob. By George, I will go and see Bob!"

"Of course," agreed the other serenely. "Why not? Besides, it will be the most natural thing in the world—business, you know. In fact, I should think you really ought to go, in connection with the bequests."

"Why, to be sure." The lawyer frowned thoughtfully. "How much are you going to give them?"

"Oh, a hundred thousand apiece, I reckon."

"That ought to do—for pin money."

"Oh, well, I want them to have enough, you know, for it to be a real test of what they would do with wealth. And it must be cash—no securities. I want them to do their own investing."

"But how are you going to fix it? What excuse are you going to give for dropping a hundred thousand into their laps like that? You can't tell your real purpose, naturally! You'd defeat your own ends."

"That part we'll have to fix up in the letter of instructions. I think we can. I've got a scheme."

"I'll warrant you have! I'll believe anything of you now. But what are you going to do afterward—when you've found out what you want to know, I mean? Won't it be something of a shock, when John Smith turns into Mr. Stanley G. Fulton? Have you thought of that?"

"Y-yes, I've thought of that, and I will confess my ideas are a little hazy, in spots. But I'm not worrying. Time enough to think of that part. Roughly, my plan is this now. There'll be two letters of instructions: one to open in six months, the other to be opened in, say, a couple of years, or so. (I want to give myself plenty of time for my observations, you see.) The second letter will really give you final instructions as to the settling of my estate—my will. I'll have to make some sort of one, I suppose."

"But, good Heavens, Stanley, you—you—" the lawyer came to a helpless pause. His eyes were startled.

"Oh, that's just for emergency, of course, in case anything—er—happened. What I really intend is that long before the second letter of instructions is due to be opened, Mr. Stanley G. Fulton will come back from his South American explorations. He'll then be in a position to settle his affairs to suit himself, and—er—make a new will. Understand?"

"Oh, I see. But—there's John Smith? How about Smith?"

The millionaire smiled musingly, and stroked his chin again.

"Smith? Oh! Well, Smith will have finished collecting Blaisdell data, of course, and will be off to parts unknown. We don't have to trouble ourselves with Smith any longer."

"Fulton, you're a wizard," laughed the lawyer. "But now about the cousins. Who are they? You know their names, of course."

"Oh, yes. You see I've done a little digging already—some years ago—looking up the Blaisdell family. (By the way, that'll come in fine now, won't it?) And an occasional letter from Bob has kept me posted as to deaths and births in the Hillerton Blaisdells. I always meant to hunt them up some time, they being my nearest kith and kin. Well, with what I already had, and with what Bob has written me, I know these facts."

He paused, pulled a small notebook from his pocket, and consulted it.

"There are two sons and a daughter, children of Rufus Blaisdell. Rufus died years ago, and his widow married a man by the name of Duff. But she's dead now. The elder son is Frank Blaisdell. He keeps a grocery store. The other is James Blaisdell. He works in a real estate office. The daughter, Flora, never married. She's about forty-two or three, I believe, and does dressmaking. James Blaisdell has a son, Fred, seventeen, and two younger children. Frank Blaisdell has one daughter, Mellicent. That's the extent of my knowledge, at present. But it's enough for our purpose."

"Oh, anything's enough—for your purpose! What are you going to do first?"

"I've done it. You'll soon be reading in your morning paper that Mr. Stanley G. Fulton, the somewhat eccentric multi-millionaire, is about to start for South America, and that it is hinted he is planning to finance a gigantic exploring expedition. The accounts of what he's going to explore will vary all the way from Inca antiquities to the source of the Amazon. I've done a lot of talking to-day, and a good deal of cautioning as to secrecy, etc. It ought to bear fruit by to-morrow, or the day after, at the latest. I'm going to start next week, and I'm really going *exploring*, too—though not exactly as they think. I came in to-day to make a business appointment for to-morrow, please. A man starting on such a hazardous journey must be prepared, you understand. I want to leave my affairs in such shape that you will know exactly what to do—in emergency. I may come to-morrow?"

The lawyer hesitated, his face an odd mixture of determination and irresolution.

"Oh, hang it all—yes. Of course you may come. To-morrow at ten—if they don't shut you up before."

With a boyish laugh Mr. Stanley G. Fulton leaped to his feet.

"Thanks. To-morrow at ten, then." At the door he turned back jauntily. "And, say, Ned, what'll you bet I don't grow fat and young over this thing? What'll you bet I don't get so I can eat real meat and 'taters again?"

CHAPTER II
ENTER MR. JOHN SMITH

It was on the first warm evening in early June that Miss Flora Blaisdell crossed the common and turned down the street that led to her brother James's home.

The common marked the center of Hillerton. Its spacious green lawns and elm-shaded walks were the pride of the town. There was a trellised band-stand for summer concerts, and a tiny pond that accommodated a few boats in summer and a limited number of skaters in winter. Perhaps, most important of all, the common divided the plebeian East Side from the more pretentious West. James Blaisdell lived on the West Side. His wife said that everybody did who *was* anybody. They had lately moved there, and were, indeed, barely settled.

Miss Blaisdell did dressmaking. Her home was a shabby little rented cottage on the East Side. She was a thin-faced little woman with an anxious frown and near-sighted, peering eyes that seemed always to be looking for wrinkles. She peered now at the houses as she passed slowly down the street. She had been only twice to her brother's new home, and she was not sure that she would recognize it, in spite of the fact that the street was still alight with the last rays of the setting sun. Suddenly across her worried face flashed a relieved smile.

"Well, if you ain't all here out on the piazza!" she exclaimed, turning, in at the walk leading up to one of the ornate little houses. "My, ain't this grand!"

"Oh, yes, it's grand, all right," nodded the tired-looking man in the big chair, removing his feet from the railing. He was in his shirt-sleeves, and was smoking a pipe. The droop of his thin mustache matched the droop of his thin shoulders—and both indefinably but unmistakably spelled disillusion and discouragement. "It's grand, but I think it's too grand—for us. However, daughter says the best is none too good—in Hillerton. Eh, Bess?"

Bessie, the pretty, sixteen-year-old daughter of the family, only shrugged her shoulders a little petulantly. It was Harriet, the wife, who spoke—a large, florid woman with a short upper lip, and a bewilderment of bepuffed light hair. She was already on her feet, pushing a chair toward her sister-in-law.

"Of course it isn't too grand, Jim, and you know it. There aren't any really nice houses in Hillerton except the Pennocks' and the old Gaylord place. There, sit here, Flora. You look tired."

"Thanks. I be—turrible tired. Warm, too, ain't it?" The little dressmaker began to fan herself with the hat she had taken off. "My, 'tis fur over here, ain't it? Not much like 'twas when you lived right 'round the corner from me! And I had to put on a hat and gloves, too. Someway, I thought I ought to—over here."

Condescendingly the bepuffed head threw an approving nod in her direction.

"Quite right, Flora. The East Side is different from the West Side, and no mistake. And what will do there won't do here at all, of course."

"How about father's shirt-sleeves?" It was a scornful gibe from Bessie in the hammock. "I don't notice any of the rest of the men around here sitting out like that."

"Bessie!" chided her mother wearily. "You know very well I'm not to blame for what your father wears. I've tried hard enough, I'm sure!"

"Well, well, Hattie," sighed the man, with a gesture of abandonment. "I supposed I still had the rights of a freeborn American citizen in my own home; but it seems I haven't." Resignedly he got to his feet and went into the house. When he returned a moment later he was wearing his coat.

Benny, perched precariously on the veranda railing, gave a sudden indignant snort. Benny was eight, the youngest of the family.

"Well, I don't think I like it here, anyhow," he chafed. "I'd rather go back an' live where we did. A feller can have some fun there. It hasn't been anything but 'Here, Benny, you mustn't do that over here, you mustn't do that over here!' ever since we came. I'm going home an' live with Aunt Flora. Say, can't I, Aunt Flo?"

"Bless the child! Of course you can," beamed his aunt. "But you won't want to, I'm sure. Why, Benny, I think it's perfectly lovely here."

"Pa don't."

"Indeed I do, Benny," corrected his father hastily. "It's very nice indeed here, of course. But I don't think we can afford it. We had to squeeze every penny before, and how we're going to meet this rent I don't know." He drew a profound sigh.

"You'll earn it, just being here—more business," asserted his wife firmly. "Anyhow, we've just got to be here, Jim! We owe it to ourselves and our family. Look at Fred to-night!"

"Oh, yes, where is Fred?" queried Miss Flora.

"He's over to Gussie Pennock's, playing tennis," interposed Bessie, with a pout. "The mean old thing wouldn't ask me!"

"But you ain't old enough, my dear," soothed her aunt. "Wait; your turn will come by and by."

"Yes, that's exactly it," triumphed the mother. "Her turn *will* come—if we live here. Do you suppose Fred would have got an invitation to Gussie Pennock's if we'd still been living on the East Side? Not much he would! Why, Mr. Pennock's worth fifty thousand, if he's worth a dollar! They are some of our very first people."

"But, Hattie, money isn't everything, dear," remonstrated her husband gently. "We had friends, and good friends, before."

"Yes; but you wait and see what kind of friends we have now!"

"But we can't keep up with such people, dear, on our income; and—"

"Ma, here's a man. I guess he wants—somebody." It was a husky whisper from Benny.

James Blaisdell stopped abruptly. Bessie Blaisdell and the little dressmaker cocked their heads interestedly. Mrs. Blaisdell rose to her feet and advanced toward the steps to meet the man coming up the walk.

He was a tall, rather slender man, with a close-cropped, sandy beard, and an air of diffidence and apology. As he took off his hat and came nearer, it was seen that his eyes were blue and friendly, and that his hair was reddish-brown, and rather scanty on top of his head.

"I am looking for Mr. Blaisdell—Mr. James Blaisdell," he murmured hesitatingly.

Something in the stranger's deferential manner sent a warm glow of importance to the woman's heart. Mrs. Blaisdell was suddenly reminded that she was Mrs. James D. Blaisdell of the West Side.

"I am Mrs. Blaisdell," she replied a bit pompously. "What can we do for you, my good man?" She swelled again, half unconsciously. She had never called a person "my good man" before. She rather liked the experience.

The man on the steps coughed slightly behind his hand—a sudden spasmodic little cough. Then very gravely he reached into his pocket and produced a letter.

"From Mr. Robert Chalmers—a note to your husband," he bowed, presenting the letter.

A look of gratified surprise came into the woman's face.

"Mr. Robert Chalmers, of the First National? Jim!" She turned to her husband joyously. "Here's a note from Mr. Chalmers. Quick—read it!"

Her husband, already on his feet, whisked the sheet of paper from the unsealed envelope, and adjusted his glasses. A moment later he held out a cordial hand to the stranger.

"Ah, Mr. Smith, I'm glad to see you. I'm glad to see any friend of Bob Chalmers'. Come up and sit down. My wife and children, and my sister, Miss Blaisdell. Mr. Smith, ladies—Mr. John Smith." (Glancing at the open note in his hand.) "He is sent to us by Mr. Chalmers, of the First National."

"Yes, thank you. Mr. Chalmers was so kind." Still with that deference so delightfully heart-warming, the newcomer bowed low to the ladies, and made his way to the offered chair. "I will explain at once my business," he said then. "I am a genealogist."

"What's that?" It was an eager question from Benny on the veranda railing. "Pa isn't anything, but ma's a Congregationalist."

"Hush, child!" protested a duet of feminine voices softly; but the stranger, apparently ignoring the interruption, continued speaking.

"I am gathering material for a book on the Blaisdell family."

"The Blaisdell family!" repeated Mr. James Blaisdell, with cordial interest.

"Yes," bowed the other. "It is my purpose to remain some time in your town. I am told there are valuable records here, and an old burying-ground of particular interest in this connection. The neighboring towns, too, have much Blaisdell data, I understand. As I said, I am intending to make this place my headquarters, and I am looking for an attractive boarding-place. Mr. Chalmers was good enough to refer me to you."

"To us—for a *boarding*-place!" There was an unmistakable frown on Mrs. James D. Blaisdell's countenance as she said the words. "Well, I'm sure I don't see why he should. *we* don't keep boarders!"

"But, Hattie, we could," interposed her husband eagerly. "There's that big front room that we don't need a bit. And it would help a lot if—" At the wrathful warning in his wife's eyes he fell back silenced.

"I said that we didn't keep boarders," reiterated the lady distinctly. "Furthermore, we do need the room ourselves."

"Yes, yes, of course; I understand," broke in Mr. Smith, as if in hasty conciliation. "I think Mr. Chalmers meant that perhaps one of you"—he glanced uncertainly at the anxious-eyed little woman at his left—"might—er—accommodate me. Perhaps you, now—" He turned his eyes full upon Miss Flora Blaisdell, and waited.

The little dressmaker blushed painfully.

"Me? Oh, mercy, no! Why, I live all alone—that is, I mean, I couldn't, you know," she stammered confusedly. "I dressmake, and I don't get any sort of meals—not fit for a man, I mean. Just women's things—tea, toast, and riz biscuit. I'm so fond of riz biscuit! But, of course, you—" She came to an expressive pause.

"Oh, I could stand the biscuit, so long as they're not health biscuit," laughed Mr. Smith genially. "You see, I've been living on those and hot water quite long enough as it is."

"Oh, ain't your health good, sir?" The little dressmaker's face wore the deepest concern.

"Well, it's better than it was, thank you. I think I can promise to be a good boarder, all right."

"Why don't you go to a hotel?" Mrs. James D. Blaisdell still spoke with a slightly injured air.

Mr. Smith lifted a deprecatory hand.

"Oh, indeed, that would not do at all—for my purpose," he murmured. "I wish to be very quiet. I fear I should find it quite disturbing—the noise and confusion of a public place like that. Besides, for my work, it seemed eminently fitting, as well as remarkably convenient, if I could make my home with one of the Blaisdell family."

With a sudden exclamation the little dressmaker sat erect.

"Say, Harriet, how funny we never thought! He's just the one for poor Maggie! Why not send him there?"

"Poor Maggie?" It was the mild voice of Mr. Smith.

"Our sister—yes. She lives—"

"Your *sister*!" Into Mr. Smith's face had come a look of startled surprise—a look almost of terror. "But there weren't but three—that is, I thought—I understood from Mr. Chalmers that there were but three Blaisdells, two brothers, and one sister—you, yourself."

"Oh, poor Maggie ain't a Blaisdell," explained the little dressmaker, with a smile. "She's just Maggie Duff, father Duff's daughter by his first wife, you know. He married our mother years ago, when we children were little, so we were brought up with Maggie, and always called her sister; though, of course, she really ain't any relation to us at all."

"Oh, I see. Yes, to be sure. Of course!" Mr. Smith seemed oddly thoughtful. He appeared to be settling something in his mind. "She isn't a Blaisdell, then."

"No, but she's so near like one, and she's a splendid cook, and—"

"Well, I shan't send him to Maggie," cut in Mrs. James D. Blaisdell with emphasis. "Poor Maggie's got quite enough on her hands, as it is, with that father of hers. Besides, she isn't a Blaisdell at all."

"And she couldn't come and cook and take care of us near so much, either, could she," plunged in Benny, "if she took this man ter feed?"

"That will do, Benny," admonished his mother, with nettled dignity. "You forget that children should be seen and not heard."

"Yes'm. But, please, can't I be heard just a minute for this? Why don't ye send the man ter Uncle Frank an' Aunt Jane? Maybe they'd take him."

"The very thing!" cried Miss Flora Blaisdell. "I wouldn't wonder a mite if they did."

"Yes, I was thinking of them," nodded her sister-in-law. "And they're always glad of a little help,—especially Jane."

"Anybody should be," observed Mr. James Blaisdell quietly.

Only the heightened color in his wife's cheeks showed that she had heard—and understood.

"Here, Benny," she directed, "go and show the gentleman where Uncle Frank lives."

"All right!" With a spring the boy leaped to the lawn and pranced to the sidewalk, dancing there on his toes. "I'll show ye, Mr. Smith."

The gentleman addressed rose to his feet.

"I thank you, Mr. Blaisdell," he said, "and you, ladies. I shall hope to see you again soon. I am sure you can help me, if you will, in my work. I shall want to ask—some questions."

"Certainly, sir, certainly! We shall be glad to see you," promised his host. "Come any time, and ask all the questions you want to."

"And we shall be so interested," fluttered Miss Flora. "I've always wanted to know about father's folks. And are you a Blaisdell, too?"

There was the briefest of pauses. Mr. Smith coughed again twice behind his hand.

"Er—ah—oh, yes, I may say that I am. Through my mother I am descended from the original immigrant, Ebenezer Blaisdell."

"Immigrant!" exclaimed Miss Flora.

"An *immigrant!*" Mrs. James Blaisdell spoke the word as if her tongue were a pair of tongs that had picked up a noxious viper.

"Yes, but not exactly as we commonly regard the term nowadays," smiled Mr. Smith. "Mr. Ebenezer Blaisdell was a man of means and distinction. He was the founder of the family in this country. He came over in 1647."

"My, how interesting!" murmured the little dressmaker, as the visitor descended the steps.

"Good-night—good-night! And thank you again," bowed Mr. John Smith to the assembled group on the veranda. "And now, young man, I'm at your service," he smiled, as he joined Benny, still prancing on the sidewalk. "Now he's what I call a real nice pleasant-spoken gentleman," avowed Miss Flora, when she thought speech was safe. "I do hope Jane'll take him."

"Oh, yes, he's well enough," condescended Mrs. Hattie Blaisdell, with a yawn.

"Hattie, why wouldn't you take him in?" reproached her husband. "Just think how the pay would help! And it wouldn't be a bit of work, hardly, for you. Certainly it would be a lot easier than the way we are doing."

The woman frowned impatiently.

"Jim, don't, please! Do you suppose I got over here on the West Side to open a boarding-house? I guess not—yet!"

"But what shall we do?"

"Oh, we'll get along somehow. Don't worry!"

"Perhaps if you'd worry a little more, I wouldn't worry so much," sighed the man deeply.

"Well, mercy me, I must be going," interposed the little dressmaker, springing to her feet with a nervous glance at her brother and his wife. "I'm forgetting it ain't so near as it used to be. Good-night!"

"Good-night, good-night! Come again," called the three on the veranda. Then the door closed behind them, as they entered the house.

Meanwhile, walking across the common, Benny was entertaining Mr. Smith.

"Yep, they'll take ye, I bet ye—Aunt Jane an' Uncle Frank will!"

"Well, that's good, I'm sure."

"Yep. An' it'll be easy, too. Why, Aunt Jane'll just tumble over herself ter get ye, if ye just mention first what yer'll *pay*. She'll begin ter reckon up right away then what she'll save. An' in a minute she'll say, 'Yes, I'll take ye.'"

"Indeed!"

The uncertainty in Mr. Smith's voice was palpable even to eight-year-old Benny.

"Oh, you don't need ter worry," he hastened to explain. "She won't starve ye; only she won't let ye waste anythin'. You'll have ter eat all the crusts to yer pie, and finish 'taters before you can get any puddin', an' all that, ye know. Ye see, she's great on savin'—Aunt Jane is. She says waste is a sinful extravagance before the Lord."

"Indeed!" Mr. Smith laughed outright this time. "But are you sure, my boy, that you ought to talk—just like this, about your aunt?"

Benny's eyes widened.

"Why, that's all right, Mr. Smith. Ev'rybody in town knows Aunt Jane. Why, Ma says folks say she'd save ter-day for ter-morrer, if she could. But she couldn't do that, could she? So that's just silly talk. But you wait till you see Aunt Jane."

"All right. I'll wait, Benny."

"Well, ye won't have ter wait long, Mr. Smith, 'cause here's her house. She lives over the groc'ry store, ter save rent, ye know. It's Uncle Frank's store. An' here we are," he finished, banging open a door and leading the way up a flight of ill-lighted stairs.

CHAPTER III
THE SMALL BOY AT THE KEYHOLE

At the top of the stairs Benny tried to open the door, but as it did not give at his pressure, he knocked lustily, and called "Aunt Jane, Aunt Jane!"

"Isn't this the bell?" hazarded Mr. Smith, his finger almost on a small push-button near him.

"Yep, but it don't go now. Uncle Frank wanted it fixed, but Aunt Jane said no; knockin' was just as good, an' 'twas lots cheaper, 'cause 'twould save mendin', and didn't use any 'lectricity. But Uncle Frank says—"

The door opened abruptly, and Benny interrupted himself to give eager greeting.

"Hullo, Aunt Jane! I've brought you somebody. He's Mr. Smith. An' you'll be glad. You see if yer ain't!"

In the dim hallway Mr. Smith saw a tall, angular woman with graying dark hair and high cheek bones. Her eyes were keen and just now somewhat sternly inquiring, as they were bent upon himself.

Perceiving that Benny considered his mission as master of ceremonies at an end, Mr. Smith hastened to explain.

"I came from your husband's brother, madam. He—er—sent me. He thought perhaps you had a room that I could have."

"A room?" Her eyes grew still more coldly disapproving.

"Yes, and board. He thought—that is, *they* thought that perhaps—you would be so kind."

"Oh, a boarder! You mean for pay, of course?"

"Most certainly!"

"Oh!" She softened visibly, and stepped back. "Well, I don't know. I never have—but that isn't saying I couldn't, of course. Come in. We can talk it over. *that* doesn't cost anything. Come in; this way, please." As she finished speaking she stepped to the low-burning gas jet and turned it carefully to give a little more light down the narrow hallway.

"Thank you," murmured Mr. Smith, stepping across the threshold.

Benny had already reached the door at the end of the hall. The woman began to tug at her apron strings.

"I hope you'll excuse my gingham apron, Mr.—er—Smith. Wasn't that the name?"

"Yes." The man bowed with a smile.

"I thought that was what Benny said. Well, as I was saying, I hope you'll excuse this apron." Her fingers were fumbling with the knot at the back. "I take it off, mostly, when the bell rings, evenings or afternoons; but I heard Benny, and I didn't suppose 'twas anybody but him. There, that's better!" With a jerk she switched off the dark blue apron, hung it over her arm, and smoothed down the spotless white apron which had been beneath the blue. The next instant she hurried after Benny with a warning cry. "Careful, child, careful! Oh, Benny, you're always in such a hurry!"

Benny, with a cheery "Come on!" had already banged open the door before him, and was reaching for the gas burner.

A moment later the feeble spark above had become a flaring sputter of flame.

"There, child, what did I tell you?" With a frown Mrs. Blaisdell reduced the flaring light to a moderate flame, and motioned Mr. Smith to a chair. Before she seated herself, however, she went back into the hall to lower the gas there.

During her momentary absence the man, Smith, looked about him, and as he looked he pulled at his collar. He felt suddenly a choking, suffocating sensation. He still had the curious feeling of trying to catch his breath when the woman came back and took the chair facing him. In a moment he knew why he felt so suffocated—it was because that nowhere could he see an object that was not wholly or partially covered with some other object, or that was not serving as a cover itself.

The floor bore innumerable small rugs, one before each chair, each door, and the fireplace. The chairs themselves, and the sofa, were covered with gray linen slips, which, in turn, were protected by numerous squares of lace and worsted of generous size. The green silk spread on the piano was nearly hidden beneath a linen cover, and the table showed a succession of layers of silk, worsted, and linen, topped by crocheted mats, on which rested several books with paper-enveloped covers. The chandelier, mirror, and picture frames gleamed dully from behind the mesh of pink mosquito netting. Even through the doorway into the hall might be seen the long, red-bordered white linen path that carried protection to the carpet beneath.

"I don't like gas myself." (With a start the man pulled himself together to listen to what the woman was saying.) "I think it's a foolish extravagance, when kerosene is so good and so cheap; but my husband will have it, and Mellicent, too, in spite of anything I say—Mellicent's my daughter. I tell 'em if we were rich, it would be different, of course. But this is neither here nor there, nor what you came to talk about! Now just what is it that you want, sir?"

"I want to board here, if I may."

"How long?"

"A year—two years, perhaps, if we are mutually satisfied."

"What do you do for a living?"

Smith coughed suddenly. Before he could catch his breath to answer Benny had jumped into the breach.

"He sounds something like a Congregationalist, only he ain't that, Aunt Jane, and he ain't after money for missionaries, either."

Jane Blaisdell smiled at Benny indulgently. Then she sighed and shook her head.

"You know, Benny, very well, that nothing would suit Aunt Jane better than to give money to all the missionaries in the world, if she only had it to give!" She sighed again as she turned to Mr. Smith. "You're working for some church, then, I take it."

Mr. Smith gave a quick gesture of dissent.

"I am a genealogist, madam, in a small way. I am collecting data for a book on the Blaisdell family."

"Oh!" Mrs. Blaisdell frowned slightly. The look of cold disapproval came back to her eyes. "But who pays you? *we* couldn't take the book, I'm sure. We couldn't afford it."

"That would not be necessary, madam, I assure you," murmured Mr. Smith gravely.

"But how do you get money to live on? I mean, how am I to know that I'll get my pay?" she persisted. "Excuse me, but that kind of business doesn't sound very good-paying; and, you see, I don't know you. And in these days—" An expressive pause finished her sentence.

Mr. Smith smiled.

"Quite right, madam. You are wise to be cautious. I had a letter of introduction to your brother from Mr. Robert Chalmers. I think he will vouch for me. Will that do?"

"Oh, that's all right, then. But that isn't saying how *much* you'll pay. Now, I think—"

There came a sharp knock at the outer door. The eager Benny jumped to his feet, but his aunt shook her head and went to the door herself. There was a murmur of voices, then a young man entered the hall and sat down in the chair near the hatrack. When Mrs. Blaisdell returned her eyes were very bright. Her cheeks showed two little red spots. She carried herself with manifest importance.

"If you'll just excuse me a minute," she apologized to Mr. Smith, as she swept by him and opened a door across the room, nearly closing it behind her.

Distinctly then, from beyond the imperfectly closed door, came to the ears of Benny and Mr. Smith these words, in Mrs. Blaisdell's most excited accents:—"Mellicent, it's Carl Pennock. He wants you to go auto-riding with him down to the Lake with Katie Moore and that crowd."

"Mother!" breathed an ecstatic voice.

What followed Mr. Smith did not hear, for a nearer, yet more excited, voice demanded attention.

"Gee! Carl Pennock!" whispered Benny hoarsely. "Whew! Won't my sister Bess be mad? She thinks Carl Pennock's the cutest thing going. All the girls do!"

With a warning "Sh-h!" and an expressive glance toward the hall, Mr. Smith tried to stop further revelations; but Benny was not to be silenced.

"They're rich—awful rich—the Pennocks are," he confided still more huskily. "An' there's a girl—Gussie. She's gone on Fred. He's my brother, ye know. He's seventeen; an' Bess is mad 'cause she isn't seventeen, too, so she can go an' play tennis same as Fred does. She'll be madder 'n ever now, if Mell goes auto-riding with Carl, an'—"

"Sh-h!" So imperative were Mr. Smith's voice and gesture this time that Benny fell back subdued.

At once then became distinctly audible again the voices from the other room. Mr. Smith, forced to hear in spite of himself, had the air of one who finds he has abandoned the frying pan for the fire.

"No, dear, it's quite out of the question," came from beyond the door, in Mrs. Blaisdell's voice. "I can't let you wear your pink. You will wear the blue or stay at home. Just as you choose."

"But, mother, dear, it's all out of date," wailed a young girl's voice.

"I can't help that. It's perfectly whole and neat, and you must save the pink for best."

"But I'm always saving things for best, mother, and I never wear my best. I never wear a thing when it's in style! By the time you let me wear the pink I shan't want to wear it. Sleeves'll be small then—you see if they aren't—I shall be wearing big ones. I want to wear big ones now, when other girls do. Please, mother!"

"Mellicent, why will you tease me like this, when you know it will do no good?—when you know I can't let you do it? Don't you think I want you to be as well-dressed as anybody, if we could afford it? Come, I'm waiting. You must wear the blue or stay at home. What shall I tell him?"

There was a pause, then there came an inarticulate word and a choking half-sob. The next moment the door opened and Mrs. Blaisdell appeared. The pink spots in her cheeks had deepened. She shut the door firmly, then hurried through the room to the hall beyond. Another minute and she was back in her chair.

"There," she smiled pleasantly. "I'm ready now to talk business, Mr. Smith."

And she talked business. She stated plainly what she expected to do for her boarder, and what she expected her boarder would do for her. She enlarged upon the advantages and minimized the discomforts, with the aid of a word now and then from the eager and interested Benny.

Mr. Smith, on his part, had little to say. That that little was most satisfactory, however, was very evident; for Mrs. Blaisdell was soon quite glowing with pride and pleasure. Mr. Smith was not glowing. He was plainly ill at ease, and, at times, slightly abstracted. His eyes frequently sought the door which Mrs. Blaisdell had closed so firmly a short time before. They were still turned in that direction when suddenly the door opened and a young girl appeared.

She was a slim little girl with long-lashed, starlike eyes and a wild-rose flush in her cheeks. Beneath her trim hat her light brown hair waved softly over her ears, glinting into gold where the light struck it. She looked excited and pleased, yet not quite happy. She wore a blue dress, plainly made.

"Don't stay late. Be in before ten, dear," cautioned Mrs. Blaisdell. "And Mellicent, just a minute, dear. This is Mr. Smith. You might as well meet him now. He's coming here to live—to board, you know. My daughter, Mr. Smith."

Mr. Smith, already on his feet, bowed and murmured a conventional something. From the starlike eyes he received a fleeting glance that made him suddenly conscious of his fifty years and the bald spot on the top of his head. Then the girl was gone, and her mother was speaking again.

"She's going auto-riding—Mellicent is—with a young man, Carl Pennock—one of the nicest in town. There are four others in the party. They're going down to the Lake for cake and ice cream, and they're all nice young people, else I shouldn't let her go, of course. She's eighteen, for all she's so small. She favors my mother in looks, but she's got the Blaisdell nose, though. Oh, and 'twas the Blaisdells you said you were writing a book about, wasn't it? You don't mean *our* Blaisdells, right here in Hillerton?"

"I mean all Blaisdells, wherever I find them," smiled Mr. Smith.

"Dear me! What, *us*? You mean *we'll* be in the book?" Now that the matter of board had been satisfactorily settled, Mrs. Blaisdell apparently dared to show some interest in the book.

"Certainly."

"You don't say! My, how pleased Hattie'll be—my sister-in-law, Jim's wife. She just loves to see her name in print—parties, and club banquets, and where she pours, you know. But maybe you don't take women, too."

"Oh, yes, if they are Blaisdells, or have married Blaisdells."

"Oh! That's where we'd come in, then, isn't it? Mellicent and I? And Frank, my husband, he'll like it, too,—if you tell about the grocery store. And of course you would, if you told about him. You'd have to—'cause that's all there is to tell. He thinks that's about all there is in the world, anyway,—that grocery store. And 'tis a good store, if I do say it. And there's his sister, Flora; and Maggie—But, there! Poor Maggie! She won't be in it, will she, after all? She isn't a Blaisdell, and she didn't marry one. Now that's too bad!"

"Ho! She won't mind." Benny spoke with conviction. "She'll just laugh and say it doesn't matter; and then Grandpa Duff'll ask for his drops or his glasses, or something, and she'll forget all about it. She won't care."

"Yes, I know; but—Poor Maggie! Always just her luck." Mrs. Blaisdell sighed and looked thoughtful. "But Maggie *knows* a lot about the Blaisdells," she added, brightening; "so she could tell you lots of things—about when they were little, and all that."

"Yes. But—that isn't—er—" Mr. Smith hesitated doubtfully, and Mrs. Blaisdell jumped into the pause.

"And, really, for that matter, she knows about us *now*, too, better than 'most anybody else. Hattie's always sending for her, and Flora, too, if they're sick, or anything. Poor Maggie! Sometimes I think they actually impose upon her. And she's such a good soul, too! I declare, I never see her but I wish I could do something for her. But, of course, with my means—But, there! Here I am, running on as usual. Frank says I never do know when to stop, when I get started on something; and of course you didn't come here to talk about poor Maggie. Now I'll go back to business. When is it you want to start in—to board, I mean?"

"To-morrow, if I may." With some alacrity Mr. Smith got to his feet. "And now we must be going—Benny and I. I'm at the Holland House. With your permission, then, Mrs. Blaisdell, I'll send up my trunks to-morrow morning. And now good-night—and thank you."

"Why—but, Mr. Smith!" The woman, too, came to her feet, but her face was surprised. "Why, you haven't even seen your room yet! How do you know you'll like it?"

"Eh? What? Oh!" Mr. Smith laughed. There was a quizzical lift to his eyebrows. "So I haven't, have I? And people usually do, don't they? Well—er—perhaps I will just take a look at—the room, though I'm not worrying any, I assure you. I've no doubt it will be quite right, quite right," he finished, as he followed Mrs. Blaisdell to a door halfway down the narrow hall.

Five minutes later, once more on the street, he was walking home with Benny. It was Benny who broke the long silence that had immediately fallen between them.

"Say, Mr. Smith, I'll bet ye *you*'ll never be rich!"

Mr. Smith turned with a visible start.

"Eh? What? I'll never be—What do you mean, boy?"

Benny giggled cheerfully.

"'Cause you paid Aunt Jane what she asked the very first time. Why, Aunt Jane never expects ter get what she asks, pa says. She sells him groceries in the store, sometimes, when Uncle Frank's away, ye know. Pa says what she asks first is for practice—just ter get her hand in; an' she expects ter get beat down. But you paid it, right off the bat. Didn't ye see how tickled Aunt Jane was, after she'd got over bein' surprised?"

"Why—er—really, Benny," murmured Mr. Smith.

But Benny had yet more to say.

"Oh, yes, sir, you could have saved a lot every week, if ye hadn't bit so quick. An' that's why I say you won't ever get rich. Savin' 's what does it, ye know—gets folks rich. Aunt Jane says so. She says a penny saved 's good as two earned, an' better than four spent."

"Well, really, indeed!" Mr. Smith laughed lightly. "That does look as if there wasn't much chance for me, doesn't it?"

"Yes, sir." Benny spoke soberly, and with evident sympathy. He spoke again, after a moment, but Mr. Smith did not seem to hear at once. Mr. Smith was, indeed, not a little abstracted all the way to Benny's home, though his good-night was very cheerful at parting. Benny would have been surprised, indeed, had he known that Mr. Smith was thinking, not about his foolishly extravagant agreement for board, but about a pair of starry eyes with wistful lights in them, and a blue dress, plainly made.

In the hotel that night, Mr. John Smith wrote the following letter to Edward D. Norton, Esq., Chicago:

> My Dear Ned,—Well, I'm here. I've been here exactly six hours, and already I'm in possession of not a little Blaisdell data for my—er—book. I've seen Mr. and Mrs. James, their daughter, Bessie, and their son, Benny. Benny, by the way, is a gushing geyser of current Blaisdell data which, I foresee, I shall find interesting, but embarrassing, perhaps, at times. I've also seen Miss Flora, and Mrs. Jane Blaisdell and her daughter, Mellicent.
>
> There's a "Poor Maggie" whom I haven't seen. But she isn't a Blaisdell. She's a Duff, daughter of the man who married Rufus Blaisdell's widow, some thirty years or more ago. As I said, I haven't seen her yet, but she, too, according to Mrs. Frank Blaisdell, must be a gushing geyser of Blaisdell data, so I probably soon shall see her. Why she's "poor" I don't know.
>
> As for the Blaisdell data already in my possession—I've no comment to make. Really, Ned, to tell the truth, I'm not sure I'm going to relish this job, after all. In spite of a perfectly clear conscience, and the virtuous realization that I'm here to bring nothing worse than a hundred thousand dollars apiece with the possible addition of a few millions on their devoted heads—in spite of all this, I yet have an uncomfortable feeling that I'm a small boy listening at the keyhole.
>
> However, I'm committed to the thing now, so I'll stuff it out, I suppose,—though I'm not sure, after all, that I wouldn't chuck the whole thing if it wasn't that I wanted to see how Mellicent will enjoy her pink dresses. How many pink dresses will a hundred thousand dollars buy, anyway,—I mean *pretty* pink dresses, all fixed up with frills and furbelows?
>
> As ever yours,
> Stan—er—John Smith.

CHAPTER IV
IN SEARCH OF SOME DATES

Very promptly the next morning Mr. John Smith and his two trunks appeared at the door of his new boarding-place. Mrs. Jane Blaisdell welcomed him cordially. She wore a high-necked, long-sleeved gingham apron this time, which she neither removed nor apologized for—unless her cheerful "You see, mornings you'll find me in working trim, Mr. Smith," might be taken as an apology.

Mellicent, her slender young self enveloped in a similar apron, was dusting his room as he entered it. She nodded absently, with a casual "Good-morning, Mr. Smith," as she continued at her work. Even the placing of the two big trunks, which the shuffling men brought in, won from her only a listless glance or two. Then, without speaking again, she left the room, as her mother entered it.

"There!" Mrs. Blaisdell looked about her complacently. "With this couch-bed with its red cover and cushions, and all the dressing things moved to the little room in there, it looks like a real sitting-room in here, doesn't it?"

"It certainly does, Mrs. Blaisdell."

"And you had 'em take the trunks in there, too. That's good," she nodded, crossing to the door of the small dressing-room beyond. "I thought you would. Well, I hope you'll be real happy with us, Mr. Smith, and I guess you will. And you needn't be a mite afraid of hurting anything. I've covered everything with mats and tidies and spreads."

"Yes, I see." A keen listener would have noticed an odd something in Mr. Smith's voice; but Mrs. Blaisdell apparently noticed nothing.

"Yes, I always do—to save wearing and soiling, you know. Of course, if we had money to buy new all the time, it would be different. But we haven't. And that's what I tell Mellicent when she complains of so many things to dust and brush. Now make yourself right at home, Mr. Smith. Dinner's at twelve o'clock, and supper is at six—except in the winter. We have it earlier then, so's we can go to bed earlier. Saves gas, you know. But it's at six now. I do like the long days, don't you? Well, I'll be off now, and let you unpack. As I said before, make yourself perfectly at home, perfectly at home."

Left alone, Mr. Smith drew a long breath and looked about him. It was a pleasant room, in spite of its cluttered appearance. There was an old-fashioned desk for his papers, and the chairs looked roomy and comfortable. The little dressing-room carried many conveniences, and the windows of both rooms looked out upon the green of the common.

"Oh, well, I don't know. This might be lots worse—in spite of the tidies!" chuckled Mr. John Smith, as he singled out the keys of his trunks.

At the noon dinner-table Mr. Smith met Mr. Frank Blaisdell. He was a portly man with rather thick gray hair and "mutton-chop" gray whiskers. He ate very fast, and a great deal, yet he still found time to talk interestedly with his new boarder.

He was plainly a man of decided opinions—opinions which he did not hesitate to express, and which he emphasized with resounding thumps of his fists on the table. The first time he did this, Mr. Smith, taken utterly by surprise, was guilty of a visible start. After that he learned to accept them with the serenity evinced by the rest of the family.

When the dinner was over, Mr. Smith knew (if he could remember them) the current market prices of beans, corn, potatoes, sugar, and flour; and he knew (again if he could remember) why some of these commodities were higher, and some lower, than they had been the week before. In a way, Mr. John Smith was interested. That stocks and bonds fluctuated, he was well aware. That "wheat" could be cornered, he realized. But of the ups and downs of corn and beans as seen by the retail grocer he knew very little. That is, he had known very little until after that dinner with Mr. Frank Blaisdell.

It was that afternoon that Mr. Smith began systematically to gather material for his Blaisdell book. He would first visit by turns all the Hillerton Blaisdells, he decided; then, when he had exhausted their resources, he would, of course, turn to the town records and cemeteries of Hillerton and the neighboring villages.

Armed with a pencil and a very businesslike looking notebook, therefore, he started at two o'clock for the home of James Blaisdell. Remembering Mr. Blaisdell's kind permission to come and ask all the questions he liked, he deemed it fitting to begin there.

He had no trouble in finding the house, but there was no one in sight this time, as he ascended the steps. The house, indeed, seemed strangely quiet. He was just about to ring the bell when around the corner of the veranda came a hurried step and a warning voice.

"Oh, please, don't ring the bell! What is it? Isn't it something that I can do for you?"

Mr. Smith turned sharply. He thought at first, from the trim, slender figure, and the waving hair above the gracefully poised head, that he was confronting a young woman. Then he saw the silver threads at the temples, and the fine lines about the eyes.

"I am looking for Mrs. Blaisdell—Mrs. James Blaisdell," he answered, lifting his hat.

"Oh, you're Mr. Smith. Aren't you Mr. Smith?" She smiled brightly, then went on before he could reply. "You see, Benny told me. He described you perfectly."

The man's eyebrows went up.

"Oh, did he? The young rascal! I fancy I should be edified to hear it—that description."

The other laughed. Then, a bit roguishly, she demanded:—"Should you like to hear it—really?"

"I certainly should. I've already collected a few samples of Benny's descriptive powers."

"Then you shall have this one. Sit down, Mr. Smith." She motioned him to a chair, and dropped easily into one herself. "Benny said you were tall and not fat; that you had a wreath of light hair 'round a bald spot, and whiskers that were clipped as even as Mr. Pennock's hedge; and that your lips, without speaking, said, 'Run away, little boy,' but that your eyes said, 'Come here.' Now I think Benny did pretty well." "So I judge, since you recognized me without any difficulty," rejoined Mr. Smith, a bit dryly. "But—YOU—? You see you have the advantage of me. Benny hasn't described you to me." He paused significantly.

"Oh, I'm just here to help out. Mrs. Blaisdell is ill upstairs—one of her headaches. That is why I asked you not to ring. She gets so nervous when the bell rings. She thinks it's callers, and that she won't be ready to receive them; and she hurries up and begins to dress. So I asked you not to ring."

"But she isn't seriously ill?"

"Oh, no, just a headache. She has them often. You wanted to see her?"

"Yes. But it's not important at all. Another time, just as well. Some questions—that is all."

"Oh, for the book, of course. Oh, yes, I have heard about that, too." She smiled again brightly. "But can't you wait? Mr. Blaisdell will soon be here. He's coming early so I can go home. I *have* to go home."

"And you are—"

"Miss Duff. My name is Duff."

"You don't mean—'Poor Maggie'!" (Not until the words were out did Mr. Smith realize quite how they would sound.) "Er—ah—that is—" He stumbled miserably, and she came to his rescue.

"Oh, yes, I'm—'Poor Maggie.'" There was an odd something in her expressive face that Mr. Smith could not fathom. He was groping for something—anything to say, when suddenly there was a sound behind them, and the little woman at his side sprang to her feet.

"Oh, Hattie, you came down!" she exclaimed as Mrs. James Blaisdell opened the screen door and stepped out on to the veranda. "Here's Mrs. Blaisdell now, Mr. Smith."

"Oh, it's only Mr. Smith!" With a look very like annoyance Mrs. Blaisdell advanced and held out her hand. She looked pale, and her hair hung a bit untidily about one ear below a somewhat twisted pyramid of puffs. Her dress, though manifestly an expensive one, showed haste in its fastenings. "Yes, I heard voices, and I thought some one had come—a caller. So I came down."

"I'm glad—if you're better," smiled Miss Maggie. "Then I'll go, if you don't mind. Mr. Smith has come to ask you some questions, Hattie. Good-bye!" With another cheery smile and a nod to Mr. Smith, she disappeared into the house. A minute later Mr. Smith saw her hurrying down a side path to the street.

"You called to ask some questions?" Mrs. Blaisdell sank languidly into a chair.

"About the Blaisdell family—yes. But perhaps another day, when you are feeling better, Mrs. Blaisdell."

"Oh, no." She smiled a little more cordially. "I can answer to-day as well as any time—though I'm not sure I can tell you very much, ever. I think it's fine you are making the book, though. Some way it gives a family such a standing, to be written up like that. Don't you think so? And the Blaisdells are really a very nice family—one of the oldest in Hillerton, though, of course, they haven't much money."

"I ought to find a good deal of material here, then, if they have lived here so long."

"Yes, I suppose so. Now, what can I tell you? Of course I can tell you about my own family. My husband is in the real estate business. You knew that, didn't you? Perhaps you see 'The Real Estate Journal.' His picture was in it a year ago last June. There was a write-up on Hillerton. I was in it, too, though there wasn't much about me. But I've got other clippings with more, if you'd like to see them—where I've poured, and been hostess, and all that, you know."

Mr. Smith took out his notebook and pencil.

"Let me see, Mrs. Blaisdell, your husband's father's name was Rufus, I believe. What was his mother's maiden name, please?"

"His mother's maiden name? Oh, 'Elizabeth.' Our little girl is named for her—Bessie, you know—you saw her last night. Jim wanted to, so I let him. It's a pretty name—Elizabeth—still, it sounds a little old-fashioned now, don't you think? Of course we are anxious to have everything just right for our daughter. A young lady soon coming out, so,—you can't be too particular. That's one reason why I wanted to get over here—on the West Side, I mean. Everybody who is anybody lives on the West Side in Hillerton. You'll soon find that out."

"No doubt, no doubt! And your mother Blaisdell's surname?" Mr. Smith's pencil was poised over the open notebook. "Surname? Mother Blaisdell's? Oh, before she was married. I see. But, dear me, I don't know. I suppose Jim will, or Flora, or maybe Frank—though I don't believe *he* will, unless her folks kept groceries. Did you ever see anybody that didn't know anything but groceries like Frank Blaisdell?" The lady sighed and shrugged her somewhat heavy shoulders with an expressive glance.

Mr. Smith smiled understandingly.

"Oh, well, it's good—to be interested in one's business, you know."

"But such a business!" murmured the lady, with another shrug.

"Then you can't tell me Mrs. Rufus Blaisdell's surname?"

"No. But Jim—Oh, I'll tell you who will know," she broke off interestedly; "and that's Maggie Duff. You saw her here a few minutes ago, you know. Father Duff's got all of Mother Blaisdell's papers and diaries. Oh, Maggie can tell you a lot of things. Poor Maggie! Benny says if we want *anything* we ask Aunt Maggie, and I don't know but he's right. And here I am, sending you to her, so soon!"

"Very well, then," smiled Mr. Smith. "I don't see but what I shall have to interview Miss Maggie, and Miss Flora. Is there nothing more, then, that you can tell me?"

"Well, there's Fred, my son. You haven't seen him yet. We're very proud of Fred. He's at the head of his class, and he's going to college and be a lawyer. And that's another reason why I wanted to come over to this side—on Fred's account. I want him to meet the right sort of people. You know it helps so much! We think we're going to have Fred a big man some day."

"And he was born, when?" Mr. Smith's pencil still poised above an almost entirely blank page.

"He's seventeen. He'll be eighteen the tenth of next month."

"And Miss Bessie, and Benny?"

"Oh, she's sixteen. She'll be seventeen next winter. She wants to come out then, but I think I shall wait—a little, she's so very young; though Gussie Pennock's out, and she's only seventeen, and the Pennocks are some of our very best people. They're the richest folks in town, you know."

"And Benny was born—when?"

"He's eight—or rather nine, next Tuesday. Dear me, Mr. Smith, don't you want *anything* but dates? They're tiresome things, I think,—make one feel so old, you know, and it shows up how many years you've been married. Don't you think so? But maybe you're a bachelor."

"Yes, I'm a bachelor."

"Are you, indeed? Well, you miss a lot, of course,—home and wife and children. Still, you gain some things. You aren't tied down, and you don't have so much to worry about. Is your mother living, or your father?"

"No. I have no—near relatives." Mr. Smith stirred a little uneasily, and adjusted his book. "Perhaps, now, Mrs. Blaisdell, you can give me your own maiden name."

"Oh, yes, I can give you that!" She laughed and bridled self-consciously. "But you needn't ask when I was born, for I shan't tell you, if you do. My name was Hattie Snow."

"'Harriet,' I presume." Mr. Smith's pencil was busily at work.

"Yes—Harriet Snow. And the Snows were just as good as the Blaisdells, if I do say it. There were a lot that wanted me—oh, I was pretty *then*, Mr. Smith." She laughed, and bridled again self-consciously. "But I took Jim. He was handsome then, very—big dark eyes and dark hair, and so dreamy and poetical-looking; and there wasn't a girl that hadn't set her cap for him. And he's been a good husband to me. To be sure, he isn't quite so ambitious as he might be, perhaps. _I_ always did believe in being somebody, and getting somewhere. Don't you? But Jim—he's always for hanging back and saying how much it'll cost. Ten to one he doesn't end up by saying we can't afford it. He's like Jane,—Frank's wife, where you board, you know,—only Jane's worse than Jim ever thought of being. She won't spend even what she's got. If she's got ten dollars, she won't spend but five cents, if she can help it. Now, I believe in taking some comfort as you go along. But Jane—greatest saver I ever did see. Better look out, Mr. Smith, that she doesn't try to save feeding you at all!" she finished merrily.

"I'm not worrying!" Mr. Smith smiled cheerily, snapped his book shut and got to his feet.

"Oh, won't you wait for Mr. Blaisdell? He can tell you more, I'm sure."

"Not to-day, thank you. At his office, some time, I'll see Mr. Blaisdell," murmured Mr. Smith, with an odd haste. "But I thank you very much, Mrs. Blaisdell," he bowed in farewell.

CHAPTER V
IN MISS FLORA'S ALBUM

It was the next afternoon that Mr. Smith inquired his way to the home of Miss Flora Blaisdell. He found it to be a shabby little cottage on a side street. Miss Flora herself answered his knock, peering at him anxiously with her near-sighted eyes.

Mr. Smith lifted his hat.

"Good-afternoon, Miss Blaisdell," he began with a deferential bow. "I am wondering if you could tell me something of your father's family." Miss Flora, plainly pleased, but flustered, stepped back for him to enter.

"Oh, Mr. Smith, come in, come in! I'm sure I'm glad to tell you anything I know," she beamed, ushering him into the unmistakably little-used "front room." "But you really ought to go to Maggie. I can tell you some things, but Maggie's got the Bible. Mother had it, you know, and it's all among her things. And of course we had to let it stay, as long as Father Duff lives. He doesn't want anything touched. Poor Maggie—she tried to get 'em for us; but, mercy! she never tried but once. But I've got some things. I've got pictures of a lot of them, and most of them I know quite a lot about."

As she spoke she nicked up from the table a big red plush photograph album. Seating herself at his side she opened it, and began to tell him of the pictures, one by one.

She did, indeed, know "quite a lot" of most of them. Tintypes, portraying stiffly held hands and staring eyes, ghostly reproductions of daguerreotypes of stern-lipped men and women, in old-time stock and kerchief; photographs of stilted family groups after the "he-is-mine-and-I-am-his" variety; snap-shots of adorable babies with blurred thumbs and noses—never had Mr. John Smith seen their like before.

Politely he listened. Busily, from time to time, he jotted down a name or date. Then, suddenly, as she turned a page, he gave an involuntary start. He was looking at a pictured face, evidently cut from a magazine.

"Why, what—who—" he stammered.

"That? Oh, that's Mr. Fulton, the millionaire, you know." Miss Flora's hands fluttered over the page a little importantly, adjusting a corner of the print. "You must have seen his picture. It's been everywhere. He's our cousin, too."

"Oh, is he?"

"Yes, 'way back somewhere. I can't tell you just how, only I know he is. His mother was a Blaisdell. That's why I've always been so interested in him, and read everything I could—in the papers and magazines, you know."

"Oh, I see." Mr. John Smith's voice had become a little uncertain.

"Yes. He ain't very handsome, is he?" Miss Flora's eyes were musingly fixed on the picture before her—which was well, perhaps: Mr. John Smith's face was a study just then.

"Er—n-no, he isn't."

"But he's turribly rich, I s'pose. I wonder how it feels to have so much money."

There being no reply to this, Miss Flora went on after a moment.

"It must be awful nice—to buy what you want, I mean, without fretting about how much it costs. I never did. But I'd like to."

"What would you do—if you could—if you had the money, I mean?" queried Mr. Smith, almost eagerly.

Miss Flora laughed.

"Well, there's three things I know I'd do. They're silly, of course, but they're what I *want*. It's a phonygraph, and to see Niagara Falls, and to go into Noell's restaurant and order what I want without even looking at the prices after 'em. Now you're laughing at me!"

"Laughing? Not a bit of it!" There was a curious elation in Mr. Smith's voice. "What's more, I hope you'll get them—some time."

Miss Flora sighed. Her face looked suddenly pinched and old.

"I shan't. I couldn't, you know. Why, if I had the money, I shouldn't spend it—not for them things. I'd be needing shoes or a new dress. And I *couldn't* be so rich I wouldn't notice what the prices was—of what I ate. But, then, I don't believe anybody's that, not even him." She pointed to the picture still open before them.

"No?" Mr. Smith, his eyes bent upon the picture, was looking thoughtful. He had the air of a man to whom has come a brand-new, somewhat disconcerting idea.

Miss Flora, glancing from the man to the picture, and back again, gave a sudden exclamation. "There, now I know who it is that you remind me of, Mr. Smith. It's him—Mr. Fulton, there."

"Eh? What?" Mr. Smith looked not a little startled.

"Something about the eyes and nose." Miss Flora was still interestedly comparing the man and the picture, "But, then, that ain't so strange. You're a Blaisdell yourself. Didn't you say you was a Blaisdell?"

"Er—y-yes, oh, yes. I'm a Blaisdell," nodded Mr. Smith hastily. "Very likely I've got the—er—Blaisdell nose. Eh?" Then he turned a leaf of the album abruptly, decidedly. "And who may this be?" he demanded, pointing to the tintype of a bright-faced young girl.

"That? Oh, that's my cousin Grace when she was sixteen. She died; but she was a wonderful girl. I'll tell you about her."

"Yes, do," urged Mr. Smith; and even the closest observer, watching his face, could not have said that he was not absorbedly interested in Miss Flora's story of "my cousin Grace."

It was not until the last leaf of the album was reached that they came upon the picture of a small girl, with big, hungry eyes looking out from beneath long lashes.

"That's Mellicent—where you're boarding, you know—when she was little." Miss Flora frowned disapprovingly. "But it's horrid, poor child!"

"But she looks so—so sad," murmured Mr. Smith.

"Yes, I know. She always did." Miss Flora sighed and frowned again. She hesitated, then burst out, as if irresistibly impelled from within. "It's only just another case of never having what you want *when* you want it, Mr. Smith. And it ain't 'cause they're poor, either. They *ain't* poor—not like me, I mean. Frank's always done well, and he's been a good provider; but it's my sister-in-law—her way, I mean. Not that I'm saying anything against Jane. I ain't. She's a good woman, and she's very kind to me. She's always saying what she'd do for me if she only had the money. She's a good housekeeper, too, and her house is as neat as wax. But it's just that she never thinks she can *use* anything she's got till it's so out of date she don't want it. I dressmake for her, you see, so I know—about her sleeves and skirts, you know. And if she ever does wear a decent thing she's so afraid it will rain she never takes any comfort in it!"

"Well, that is—unfortunate."

"Yes, ain't it? And she's brought up that poor child the same way. Why, from babyhood, Mellicent never had her rattles till she wanted blocks, nor her blocks till she wanted dolls, nor her dolls till she was big enough for beaus! And that's what made the poor child always look so wall-eyed and hungry. She was hungry—even if she did get enough to eat."

"Mrs. Blaisdell probably believed in—er—economy," hazarded Mr. Smith.

"Economy! My stars, I should think she did! But, there, I ought not to have said anything, of course. It's a good trait. I only wish some other folks I could mention had more of it. There's Jim's wife, for instance. Now, if she's got ten cents, she'll spend fifteen—and five more to show *how* she spent it. She and Jane ought to be shaken up in a bag together. Why, Mr. Smith, Jane doesn't let herself enjoy anything. She's always keeping it for a better time. Though sometimes I think she *does* enjoy just seeing how far she can make a dollar go. But Mellicent don't, nor Frank; and it's hard on them."

"I should say it might be." Mr. Smith was looking at the wistful eyes under the long lashes.

"'Tis; and 'tain't right, I believe. There *is* such a thing as being too economical. I tell Jane she'll be like a story I read once about a man who pinched and saved all his life, not even buying peanuts, though he just doted on 'em. And when he did get rich, so he could buy the peanuts, he bought a big bag the first thing. But he didn't eat 'em. He hadn't got any teeth left to chew 'em with."

"Well, that was a catastrophe!" laughed Mr. Smith, as he pocketed his notebook and rose to his feet. "And now I thank you very much, Miss Blaisdell, for the help you've been to me."

"Oh, you're quite welcome, indeed you are, Mr. Smith," beamed Miss Blaisdell. "It's done me good, just to talk to you about all these folks and pictures. I we enjoyed it. I do get lonesome sometimes, all alone, so! and I ain't so busy as I wish I was, always. But I'm afraid I haven't helped you much—just this."

"Oh, yes, you have—perhaps more than you think," smiled the man, with an odd look in his eyes.

"Have I? Well, I'm glad, I'm sure. And don't forget to go to Maggie's, now. She'll have a lot to tell you. Poor Maggie! And she'll be so glad to show you!"

"All right, thank you; I'll surely interview—Miss Maggie," smiled the man in good-bye.

He had almost said "poor" Maggie himself, though why she should be *poor* Maggie had come to be an all-absorbing question with him. He had been tempted once to ask Miss Flora, but something had held him back. That evening at the supper-table, however, in talking with Mrs. Jane Blaisdell, the question came again to his lips; and this time it found utterance.

Mrs. Jane herself had introduced Miss Maggie's name, and had said an inconsequential something about her when Mr. Smith asked:—

"Mrs. Blaisdell, please,—may I ask? I must confess to a great curiosity as to why Miss Duff is always 'poor Maggie.'"

Mrs. Blaisdell laughed pleasantly.

"Why, really, I don't know," she answered, "only it just comes natural, that's all. Poor Maggie's been so unfortunate. There! I did it again, didn't I? That only goes to show how we all do it, unconsciously."

Frank Blaisdell, across the table, gave a sudden emphatic sniff.

"Humph! Well, I guess if you had to live with Father Duff, Jane, it would be 'poor Jane' with you, all right!"

"Yes, I know." His wife sighed complacently.

"Father Duff's a trial, and no mistake. But Maggie doesn't seem to mind."

"Mind! Aunt Maggie's a saint—that's what she is!" It was Mellicent who spoke, her young voice vibrant with suppressed feeling. "She's the dearest thing ever! There *couldn't* be anybody better than Aunt Maggie!"

Nothing more was said just then, but in the evening, later, after Mellicent had gone to walk with young Pennock, and her father had gone back down to the store, Mrs. Blaisdell took up the matter of "Poor Maggie" again.

"I've been thinking what you said," she began, "about our calling her 'poor Maggie,' and I've made up my mind it's because we're all so sorry for her. You see, she's been so unfortunate, as I said. Poor Maggie! I've so often wished there was something I could do for her. Of course, if we only had money—but we haven't; so I can't. And even money wouldn't take away her father, either. Oh, mercy! I didn't mean that, really,—not the way it sounded," broke off Mrs. Blaisdell, in shocked apology. "I only meant that she'd have her father to care for, just the same."

"He's something of a trial, I take it, eh?" smiled Mr. Smith.

"Trial! I should say he was. Poor Maggie! How ever she endures it, I can't imagine. Of course, we call him Father Duff, but he's really not any relation to us—I mean to Frank and the rest. But their mother married him when they were children, and they never knew their own father much, so he's the only father they know. When their mother died, Maggie had just entered college. She was eighteen, and such a pretty girl! I knew the family even then. Frank was just beginning to court me.

"Well, of course Maggie had to come home right away. None of the rest wanted to take care of him and Maggie had to. There was another Duff sister then—a married sister (she's died since), but *she* wouldn't take him, so Maggie had to. Of course, none of the Blaisdells wanted the care of him — and he wasn't their father, anyway. Frank was wanting to marry me, and Jim and Flora were in school and wanted to stay there, of course. So Maggie came. Poor girl! It was real hard for her. She was so ambitious, and so fond of books. But she came, and went right into the home and kept it so Frank and Jim and Flora could live there just the same as when their mother was alive. And she had to do all the work, too. They were too poor to keep a girl. Kind of hard, wasn't it?—and Maggie only eighteen!"

"It was, indeed!" Mr. Smith's lips came together a bit grimly.

"Well, after a time Frank and Jim married, and there was only Flora and Father Duff at home. Poor Maggie tried then to go to college again. She was over twenty-one, and supposed to be her own mistress, of course. She found a place where she could work and pay her way through college, and Flora said she'd keep the house and take care of Father Duff. But, dear me; it wasn't a month before that ended, and Maggie had to come home again. Flora wasn't strong, and the work fretted her. Besides, she never could get along with Father Duff, and she was trying to learn dressmaking, too. She stuck it out till she got sick, though, then of course Maggie had to come back."

"Well, by Jove!" ejaculated Mr. Smith.

"Yes, wasn't it too bad? Poor Maggie, she tried it twice again. She persuaded her father to get a girl. But that didn't work, either. The first girl and her father fought like cats and dogs, and the last time she got one her father was taken sick, and again she had to come home. Some way, it's always been that way with poor Maggie. No sooner does she reach out to take something than it's snatched away, just as she thinks she's got it. Why, there was her father's cousin George—he was going to help her once. But a streak of bad luck hit him at just that minute, and he gave out."

"And he never tried—again?"

"No. He went to Alaska then. Hasn't ever been back since. He's done well, too, they say, and I always thought he'd send back something; but he never has. There was some trouble, I believe, between him and Father Duff at the time he went to Alaska, so that explains it, probably. Anyway, he's never done anything for them. Well, when he gave out, Maggie just gave up college then, and settled down to take care of her father, though I guess she's always studied some at home; and I know that for years she didn't give up hope but that she could go some time. But I guess she has now. Poor Maggie!"

"How old is she?"

"Why, let me see—forty-three, forty-four—yes, she's forty-five. She had her forty-third birthday here—I remember I gave her a handkerchief for a birthday present—when she was helping me take care of Mellicent through the pneumonia; and that was two years ago. She used to come here and to Jim's and Flora's days at a time; but she isn't quite so free as she was— Father Duff's worse now, and she don't like to leave him nights, much, so she can't come to us so often. See?"

"Yes, I—see." There was a queer something in Mr. Smith's voice. "And just what is the matter with Mr. Duff?"

"Matter!" Mrs. Jane Blaisdell gave a short laugh and shrugged her shoulders. "Everything's the matter—with Father Duff! Oh, it's nerves, mostly, the doctor says, and there are some other things—long names that I can't remember. But, as I said, everything's the matter with Father Duff. He's one of those men where there isn't anything quite right. Frank says he's got so he just objects to everything—on general principles. If it's blue, he says it ought to be black, you know. And, really, I don't know but Frank's right. How Maggie stands him I don't see; but she's devotion itself. Why, she even gave up her lover years ago, for him. She wouldn't leave her father, and, of course, nobody would think of taking *him* into the family, when he wasn't *born* into it, so the affair was broken off. I don't know, really, as Maggie cared much. Still, you can't tell. She never was one to carry her heart on her sleeve. Poor Maggie! I've always so wished I could do something for her!

"There, how I have run on! But, then, you asked, and you're interested, I know, and that's what you're here for—to find out about the Blaisdells."

"To—to—f-find out—" stammered Mr. Smith, grown suddenly very red.

"Yes, for your book, I mean."

"Oh, yes—of course; for my book," agreed Mr. Smith, a bit hastily. He had the guilty air of a small boy who has almost been caught in a raid on the cooky jar.

"And although poor Maggie isn't really a Blaisdell herself, she's nearly one; and they've got lots of Blaisdell records down there—among Mother Blaisdell's things, you know. You'll want to see those."

"Yes; yes, indeed. I'll want to see those, of course," declared Mr. Smith, rising to his feet, preparatory to going to his own room.

CHAPTER VI
POOR MAGGIE

It was some days later that Mr. Smith asked Benny one afternoon to show him the way to Miss Maggie Duff's home.

"Sure I will," agreed Benny with alacrity. "You don't ever have ter do any teasin' ter get me ter go ter Aunt Maggie's."

"You're fond of Aunt Maggie, then, I take it."

Benny's eyes widened a little.

"Why, of course! Everybody's fond of Aunt Maggie. Why, I don't know anybody that don't like Aunt Maggie."

"I'm sure that speaks well—for Aunt Maggie," smiled Mr. Smith.

"Yep! A feller can take some comfort at Aunt Maggie's," continued Benny, trudging along at Mr. Smith's side. "She don't have anythin' just for show, that you can't touch, like 'tis at my house, and there ain't anythin' but what you can use without gettin' snarled up in a mess of covers an' tidies, like 'tis at Aunt Jane's. But Aunt Maggie don't save anythin', Aunt Jane says, an' she'll die some day in the poor-house, bein' so extravagant. But I don't believe she will. Do you, Mr. Smith?"

"Well, really, Benny, I—er—" hesitated the man.

"Well, I don't believe she will," repeated Benny. "I hope she won't, anyhow. Poorhouses ain't very nice, are they?"

"I—I don't think I know very much about them, Benny."

"Well, I don't believe they are, from what Aunt Jane says. And if they ain't, I don't want Aunt Maggie ter go. She hadn't ought ter have anythin'— but Heaven—after Grandpa Duff. Do you know Grandpa Duff?"

"No, my b-boy." Mr. Smith was choking over a cough.

"He's sick. He's got a chronic grouch, ma says. Do you know what that is?"

"I—I have heard of them."

"What are they? Anything like chronic rheumatism? I know what chronic means. It means it keeps goin' without stoppin'—the rheumatism, I mean, not the folks that's got it. *they* don't go at all, sometimes. Old Dr. Cole don't, and that's what he's got. But when I asked ma what a grouch was, she said little boys should be seen and not heard. Ma always says that when she don't want to answer my questions. Do you? Have you got any little boys, Mr. Smith?"

"No, Benny. I'm a poor old bachelor."

"Oh, are you *poor*, too? That's too bad."

"Well, that is, I—I—"

"Ma was wonderin' yesterday what you lived on. Haven't you got any money, Mr. Smith?"

"Oh, yes, Benny, I've got money enough—to live on." Mr. Smith spoke promptly, and with confidence this time.

"Oh, that's nice. You're glad, then, ain't you? Ma says we haven't—got enough ter live on, I mean; but pa says we have, if we didn't try ter live like everybody else lives what's got more."

Mr. Smith bit his lip, and looked down a little apprehensively at the small boy at his side.

"I—I'm not sure, Benny, but _I_ shall have to say little boys should be seen and not—" He stopped abruptly. Benny, with a stentorian shout, had run ahead to a gate before a small white cottage. On the cozy, vine-shaded porch sat a white-haired old man leaning forward on his cane.

"Hi, there, Grandpa Duff, I've brought somebody ter see ye!" The gate was open now, and Benny was halfway up the short walk. "It's Mr. Smith. Come in, Mr. Smith. Here's grandpa right here."

With a pleasant smile Mr. Smith doffed his hat and came forward.

"Thank you, Benny. How do you do, Mr. Duff?"

The man on the porch looked up sharply from beneath heavy brows.

"Humph! Your name's Smith, is it?"

"That's what they call me." The corners of Mr. Smith's mouth twitched a little.

"Humph! Yes, I've heard of you."

"You flatter me!" Mr. Smith, on the topmost step, hesitated. "Is your—er—daughter in, Mr. Duff?" He was still smiling cheerfully.

Mr. Duff was not smiling. His somewhat unfriendly gaze was still bent upon the newcomer.

"Just what do you want of my daughter?"

"Why, I—I—" Plainly nonplused, the man paused uncertainly. Then, with a resumption of his jaunty cheerfulness, he smiled straight into the unfriendly eyes. "I'm after some records, Mr. Duff,—records of the Blaisdell family. I'm compiling a book on—

"Humph! I thought as much," interrupted Mr. Duff curtly, settling back in his chair. "As I said, I've heard of you. But you needn't come here asking your silly questions. I shan't tell you a thing, anyway, if you do. It's none of your business who lived and died and what they did before you were born. If the Lord had wanted you to know he'd 'a' put you here then instead of now!"

Looking very much as if he had received a blow in the face, Mr. Smith fell back.

"Aw, grandpa"—began Benny, in grieved expostulation. But a cheery voice interrupted, and Mr. Smith turned to see Miss Maggie Duff emerging from the doorway.

"Oh, Mr. Smith, how do you do?" she greeted him, extending a cordial hand. "Come up and sit down."

For only the briefest of minutes he hesitated. Had she heard? Could she have heard, and yet speak so unconcernedly? It seemed impossible. And yet—He took the chair she offered—but with a furtive glance toward the old man. He had only a moment to wait.

Sharply Mr. Duff turned to his daughter.

"This Mr. Smith tells me he has come to see those records. Now, I'm—"

"Oh, father, dear, you couldn't!" interrupted his daughter with admonishing earnestness. "You mustn't go and get all those down!" (Mr. Smith almost gasped aloud in his amazement, but Miss Maggie did not seem to notice him at all.) "Why, father, you couldn't—they're too heavy for you! There are the Bible, and all those papers. They're too heavy father. I couldn't let you. Besides, I shouldn't think you'd want to get them!" If Mr. Smith, hearing this, almost gasped aloud in his amazement, he quite did so at what happened next. His mouth actually fell open as he saw the old man rise to his feet with stern dignity.

"That will do, Maggie. I'm not quite in my dotage yet. I guess I'm still able to fetch downstairs a book and a bundle of papers." With his thumping cane a resolute emphasis to every other step, the old man hobbled into the house.

"There, grandpa, that's the talk!" crowed Benny. "But you said—"

"Er—Benny, dear," interposed Miss Maggie, in a haste so precipitate that it looked almost like alarm, "run into the pantry and see what you can find in the cooky jar." The last of her sentence was addressed to Benny's flying heels as they disappeared through the doorway.

Left together, Mr. Smith searched the woman's face for some hint, some sign that this extraordinary shift-about was recognized and understood; but Miss Maggie, with a countenance serenely expressing only cheerful interest, was over by the little stand, rearranging the pile of books and newspapers on it.

"I think, after all," she began thoughtfully, pausing in her work, "that it will be better indoors. It blows so out here that you'll be bothered in your copying, I am afraid."

She was still standing at the table, chatting about the papers, however, when at the door, a few minutes later, appeared her father, in his arms a big Bible, and a sizable pasteboard box.

"Right here, father, please," she said then, to Mr. Smith's dumfounded amazement. "Just set them down right here."

The old man frowned and cast disapproving eyes on his daughter and the table.

"There isn't room. I don't want them there," he observed coldly. "I shall put them in here." With the words he turned back into the house.

Once again Mr. Smith's bewildered eyes searched Miss Maggie's face and once again they found nothing but serene unconcern. She was already at the door.

"This way, please," she directed cheerily. And, still marveling, he followed her into the house.

Mr. Smith thought he had never seen so charming a living-room. A comfortable chair invited him, and he sat down. He felt suddenly rested and at home, and at peace with the world. Realizing that, in some way, the room had produced this effect, he looked curiously about him, trying to solve the secret of it.

Reluctantly to himself he confessed that it was a very ordinary room. The carpet was poor, and was badly worn. The chairs, while comfortable looking, were manifestly not expensive, and had seen long service. Simple curtains were at the windows, and a few fair prints were on the walls. Two or three vases, of good lines but cheap materials, held flowers, and there was a plain but roomy set of shelves filled with books—not immaculate, leather-backed, gilt-lettered "sets" but rows of dingy, worn volumes, whose very shabbiness was at once an invitation and a promise. Nowhere, however, could Mr. Smith see protecting cover mat, or tidy. He decided then that this must be why he felt suddenly so rested and at peace with all mankind. Even as the conviction came to him, however he was suddenly aware that everything was not, after all, peaceful or harmonious.

At the table Mr. Duff and his daughter were arranging the Bible and the papers. Miss Maggie suggested piles in a certain order: her father promptly objected, and arranged them otherwise. Miss Maggie placed the papers first for perusal: her father said "Absurd!" and substituted the Bible. Miss Maggie started to draw up a chair to the table: her father derisively asked her if she expected a man to sit in that—and drew up a different one. Yet Mr. Smith, when he was finally invited to take a seat at the table, found everything quite the most convenient and comfortable possible.

Once more into Miss Maggie's face he sent a sharply inquiring glance, and once more he encountered nothing but unruffled cheerfulness.

With a really genuine interest in the records before him, Mr. Smith fell to work then. The Bible had been in the Blaisdell family for generations, and it was full of valuable names and dates. He began at once to copy them.

Mr. Duff, on the other side of the table, was arranging into piles the papers before him. He complained of the draft, and Miss Maggie shut the window. He said then that he didn't mean he wanted to suffocate, and she opened the one on the other side. The clock had hardly struck three when he accused her of having forgotten his medicine. Yet when she brought it he refused to take it. She had not brought the right kind of spoon, he said, and she knew perfectly well he never took it out of that narrow-bowl kind. He complained of the light, and she lowered the curtain; but he told her that he didn't mean he didn't want to see at all, so she put it up halfway. He said his coat was too warm, and she brought another one. He put it on grudgingly, but he declared that it was as much too thin as the other was too thick.

Mr. Smith, in spite of his efforts to be politely deaf and blind, found himself unable to confine his attention to birth, death, and marriage notices.

Once he almost uttered an explosive "Good Heavens, how do you stand it?" to his hostess. But he stopped himself just in time, and fiercely wrote with a very black mark that Submit Blaisdell was born in eighteen hundred and one. A little later he became aware that Mr. Duff's attention was frowningly turned across the table toward himself.

"If you will spend your time over such silly stuff, why don't you use a bigger book?" demanded the old man at last.

"Because it wouldn't fit my pocket," smiled Mr. Smith.

"Just what business of yours is it, anyhow, when these people lived and died?"

"None, perhaps," still smiled Mr. Smith good-humoredly.

"Why don't you let them alone, then? What do you expect to find?"

"Why, I—I—" Mr. Smith was plainly nonplused.

"Well, I can tell you it's a silly business, whatever you find. If you find your grandfather's a bigger man than you are, you'll be proud of it, but you ought to be ashamed of it—'cause you aren't bigger yourself! On the other hand, if you find he *isn't* as big as you are, you'll be ashamed of that, when you ought to be proud of it—'cause you've gone him one better. But you won't. I know your kind. I've seen you before. But can't you do any work, real work?"

"He is doing work, real work, now, father," interposed Miss Maggie quickly. "He's having a woeful time, too. If you'd only help him, now, and show him those papers."

A real terror came into Mr. Smith's eyes, but Mr. Duff was already on his feet.

"Well, I shan't," he observed tartly. "I'M not a fool, if he is. I'm going out to the porch where I can get some air."

"There, work as long as you like, Mr. Smith. I knew you'd rather work by yourself," nodded Miss Maggie, moving the piles of papers nearer him.

"But, good Heavens, how do you stand—" exploded Mr. Smith before he realized that this time he had really said the words aloud. He blushed a painful red.

Miss Maggie, too, colored. Then, abruptly, she laughed. "After all, it doesn't matter. Why shouldn't I be frank with you? You couldn't help seeing—how things were, of course, and I forgot, for a moment, that you were a stranger. Everybody in Hillerton understands. You see, father is nervous, and not at all well. We have to humor him."

"But do you mean that you always have to tell him to do what you don't want, in order to—well—that is—" Mr. Smith, finding himself in very deep water, blushed again painfully.

Miss Maggie met his dismayed gaze with cheerful candor.

"Tell him to do what I *don't* want in order to get him to do what I do want him to? Yes, oh, yes. But I don't mind; really I don't. I'm used to it now. And when you know how, what does it matter? After all, where is the difference? To most of the world we say, 'Please do,' when we want a thing, while to him we have to say, 'Please don't.' That's all. You see, it's really very simple—when you know how."

"Simple! Great Scott!" muttered Mr. Smith. He wanted to say more; but Miss Maggie, with a smiling nod, turned away, so he went back to his work.

Benny, wandering in from the kitchen, with both hands full of cookies, plumped himself down on the cushioned window-seat, and drew a sigh of content.

"Say, Aunt Maggie."

"Yes, dear."

"Can I come ter live with you?"

"Certainly not!" The blithe voice and pleasant smile took all the sting from the prompt refusal.

"What would father and mother do?"

"Oh, they wouldn't mind."

"Benny!"

"They wouldn't. Maybe pa would—a little; but Bess and ma wouldn't. And I'D like it."

"Nonsense, Benny!" Miss Maggie crossed to a little stand and picked up a small box. "Here's a new picture puzzle. See if you can do it."

Benny shifted his now depleted stock of cookies to one hand, dropped to his knees on the floor, and dumped the contents of the box upon the seat before him.

"They won't let me eat cookies any more at home—in the house, I mean. Too many crumbs."

"But you know you have to pick up your crumbs here, dear."

"Yep. But I don't mind—after I've had the fun of eatin' first. But they won't let me drop 'em ter begin with, there, nor take any of the boys inter the house. Honest, Aunt Maggie, there ain't anything a feller can do, 'seems so, if ye live on the West Side," he persisted soberly.

Mr. Smith, copying dates at the table, was conscious of a slightly apprehensive glance in his direction from Miss Maggie's eyes, as she murmured:—

"But you're forgetting your puzzle, Benny. You've put only five pieces together."

"I can't do puzzles there, either." Benny's voice was still mournful.

"All the more reason, then, why you should like to do them here. See, where does this dog's head go?"

Listlessly Benny took the bit of pictured wood in his fingers and began to fit it into the pattern before him.

"I used ter do 'em an' leave 'em 'round, but ma says I can't now. Callers might come and find 'em, an' what would they say—on the West Side! An' that's the way 'tis with everything. Ma an' Bess are always doin' things, or not doin' 'em, for those callers. An' I don't see why. They never come—not new ones."

"Yes, yes, dear, but they will, when they get acquainted. You haven't found where the dog's head goes yet."

"Pa says he don't want ter get acquainted. He'd rather have the old friends, what don't mind baked beans, an' shirt-sleeves, an' doin' yer own work, an' what thinks more of yer heart than they do of yer pocketbook. But ma wants a hired girl. An' say, we have ter wash our hands every meal now—on the table, I mean—in those little glass wash-dishes. Ma went down an' bought some, an' she's usin' 'em every day, so's ter get used to 'em. She says everybody that is anybody has 'em nowadays. Bess thinks they're great, but I don't. I don't like 'em a mite."

"Oh, come, come, Benny! It doesn't matter—it doesn't really matter, does it, if you do have to use the little dishes? Come, you're not half doing the puzzle."

"I know it." Benny shifted his position, and picked up a three-cornered bit of wood carrying the picture of a dog's paw. "But I was just thinkin'. You see, things are so different—on the West Side. Why even pa—he's different. He isn't there hardly any now. He's got a new job."

"What?" Miss Maggie turned from the puzzle with a start.

"Oh, just for evenin's. It's keepin' books for a man. It brings in quite a lot extry, ma says; but she wouldn't let me have some new roller skates when mine broke. She's savin' up for a chafin' dish. What's a chafin' dish? Do you know? You eat out of it, some way—I mean, it cooks things ter eat; an' Bess wants one. Gussie Pennock's got one. *all* our eatin's different, 'seems so, on the West Side. Ma has dinners nights now, instead of noons. She says the Pennocks do, an' everybody does who is anybody. But I don't like it. Pa don't, either, an' half the time he can't get home in time for it, anyhow, on account of gettin' back to his new job, ye know, an' —"

"Oh, I've found where the dog's head goes," cried Miss Maggie, There was a hint of desperation in her voice. "I shall have your puzzle all done for you myself, if you don't look out, Benny. I don't believe you can do it, anyhow."

"I can, too. You just see if I can't!" retorted Benny, with sudden spirit, falling to work in earnest. "I never saw a puzzle yet I couldn't do!"

Mr. Smith, bending assiduously over his work at the table, heard Miss Maggie's sigh of relief—and echoed it, from sympathy.

CHAPTER VII
POOR MAGGIE AND SOME OTHERS

It was half an hour later, when Mr. Smith and Benny were walking across the common together, that Benny asked an abrupt question.

"Is Aunt Maggie goin' ter be put in your book, Mr. Smith?"

"Why—er—yes; her name will be entered as the daughter of the man who married the Widow Blaisdell, probably. Why?"

"Nothin'. I was only thinkin'. I hoped she was. Aunt Maggie don't have nothin' much, yer know, except her father an' housework—housework either for him or some of us. An' I guess she's had quite a lot of things ter bother her, an' make her feel bad, so I hoped she'd be in the book. Though if she wasn't, she'd just laugh an' say it doesn't matter, of course. That's what she always says."

"Always says?" Mr. Smith's voice was mildly puzzled. "Yes, when things plague, an' somethin' don't go right. She says it helps a lot ter just remember that it doesn't matter. See?"

"Well, no,—I don't think I do see," frowned Mr. Smith.

"Oh, yes," plunged in Benny; "'cause, you see, if yer stop ter think about it—this thing that's plaguin' ye—you'll see how really small an' no-account it is, an' how, when you put it beside really big things it doesn't matter at all—it doesn't *really* matter, ye know. Aunt Maggie says she's done it years an' years, ever since she was just a girl, an' somethin' bothered her; an' it's helped a lot."

"But there are lots of things that *do* matter," persisted Mr. Smith, still frowning.

"Oh, yes!" Benny swelled a bit importantly, "I know what you mean. Aunt Maggie says that, too; an' she says we must be very careful an' not get it wrong. It's only the little things that bother us, an' that we wish were different, that we must say 'It doesn't matter' about. It *does* matter whether we're good an' kind an' tell the truth an' shame the devil; but it *doesn't* matter whether we have ter live on the West Side an' eat dinner nights instead of noons, an' not eat cookies any of the time in the house,—see?"

"Good for you, Benny,—and good for Aunt Maggie!" laughed Mr. Smith suddenly.

"Aunt Maggie? Oh, you don't know Aunt Maggie, yet. She's always tryin' ter make people think things don't matter. You'll see!" crowed Benny.

A moment later he had turned down his own street, and Mr. Smith was left to go on alone.

Very often, in the days that followed, Mr. Smith thought of this speech of Benny's. He had opportunity to verify it, for he was seeing a good deal of Miss Maggie, and it seemed, indeed, to him that half the town was coming to her to learn that something "didn't matter"—though very seldom, except to Benny, did he hear her say the words themselves. It was merely that to her would come men, women, and children, each with a sorry tale of discontent or disappointment. And it was always as if they left with her their burden, for when they turned away, head and shoulders were erect once more, eyes were bright, and the step was alert and eager.

He used to wonder how she did it. For that matter, he wondered how she did—a great many things.

Mr. Smith was, indeed, seeing a good deal of Miss Maggie these days. He told himself that it was the records that attracted him. But he did not always copy records. Sometimes he just sat in one of the comfortable chairs and watched Miss Maggie, content if she gave him a word now and then.

He liked the way she carried her head, and the way her hair waved away from her shapely forehead. He liked the quiet strength of the way her capable hands lay motionless in her lap when their services were not required. He liked to watch for the twinkle in her eye, and for the dimple in her cheek that told a smile was coming. He liked to hear her talk to Benny. He even liked to hear her talk to her father—when he could control his temper sufficiently. Best of all he liked his own comfortable feeling of being quite at home, and at peace with all the world—the feeling that always came to him now whenever he entered the house, in spite of the fact that the welcome accorded him by Mr. Duff was hardly more friendly than at the first.

To Mr. Smith it was a matter of small moment whether Mr. Duff welcomed him cordially or not. He even indulged now and then in a bout of his own with the gentleman, chuckling inordinately when results showed that he had pitched his remark at just the right note of contrariety to get what he wanted.

For the most part, however, Mr. Smith, at least nominally, spent his time at his legitimate task of studying and copying the Blaisdell family records, of which he was finding a great number. Rufus Blaisdell apparently had done no little "digging" himself in his own day, and Mr. Smith told Miss Maggie that it was all a great "find" for him.

Miss Maggie seemed pleased. She said that she was glad if she could be of any help to him, and she told him to come whenever he liked. She arranged the Bible and the big box of papers on a little table in the corner, and told him to make himself quite at home; and she showed so plainly that she regarded him as quite one of the family, that Mr. Smith might be pardoned for soon considering himself so.

It was while at work in this corner that he came to learn so much of Miss Maggie's daily life, and of her visitors.

Although many of these visitors were strangers to him, some of them he knew.

One day it was Mrs. Hattie Blaisdell, with a countenance even more florid than usual. She was breathless and excited, and her eyes were worried. She was going to give a luncheon, she said. She wanted Miss Maggie's silver spoons, and her forks, and her hand painted sugar-and-creamer, and Mother Blaisdell's cut-glass dish.

Mr. Smith, supposing that Miss Maggie herself was to be at the luncheon, was just rejoicing within him that she was to have this pleasant little outing, when he heard Mrs. Blaisdell telling her to be sure to come at eleven to be in the kitchen, and asking where could she get a maid to serve in the dining-room, and what should she do with Benny. He'd have to be put somewhere, or else he'd be sure to upset everything.

Mr. Smith did not hear Miss Maggie's answer to all this, for she hurried her visitor to the kitchen at once to look up the spoons, she said. But indirectly he obtained a very conclusive reply; for he found Miss Maggie gone one day when he came; and Benny, who was in her place, told him all about it, even to the dandy frosted cake Aunt Maggie had made for the company to eat.

Another day it was Mrs. Jane Blaisdell who came. Mrs. Jane had a tired frown between her brows and a despairing droop to her lips. She carried a large bundle which she dropped unceremoniously into Miss Maggie's lap.

"There, I'm dead beat out, and I've brought it to you. You've just got to help me," she finished, sinking into a chair.

"Why, of course, if I can. But what is it?" Miss Maggie's deft fingers were already untying the knot.

"It's my old black silk. I'm making it over."

"*Again?* But I thought the last time it couldn't ever be done again."

"Yes, I know; but there's lots of good in it yet," interposed Mrs. Jane decidedly; "and I've bought new velvet and new lace, and some buttons and a new lining. I *thought* I could do it alone, but I've reached a point where I just have got to have help. So I came right over."

"Yes, of course, but" — Miss Maggie was lifting a half-finished sleeve doubtfully — "why didn't you go to Flora? She'd know exactly — "

Mrs. Jane stiffened.

"Because I can't afford to go to Flora," she interrupted coldly. "I have to pay Flora, and you know it. If I had the money I should be glad to do it, of course. But I haven't, and charity begins at home I think. Besides, I do go to her for *new* dresses. But this old thing—! Of course, if you don't *want* to help me — "

"Oh, but I do," plunged in Miss Maggie hurriedly. "Come out into the kitchen where we'll have more room," she exclaimed, gathering the bundle into her arms and springing to her feet.

"I've got some other lace at home — yards and yards. I got a lot, it was so cheap," recounted Mrs. Jane, rising with alacrity. "But I'm afraid it won't do for this, and I don't know as it will do for anything, it's so — "

The kitchen door slammed sharply, and Mr. Smith heard no more. Half an hour later, however, he saw Mrs. Jane go down the walk. The frown was gone from her face and the droop from the corners of her mouth. Her step was alert and confident. She carried no bundle.

The next day it was Miss Flora. Miss Flora's thin little face looked more pinched than ever, and her eyes more anxious, Mr. Smith thought. Even her smile, as she acknowledged Mr. Smith's greeting, was so wan he wished she had not tried to give it.

She sat down then, by the window, and began to chat with Miss Maggie; and very soon Mr. Smith heard her say this: —

"No, Maggie, I don't know, really, what I am going to do — truly I don't. Business is so turrible dull! Why, I don't earn enough to pay my rent, hardly, now, ter say nothin' of my feed."

Miss Maggie frowned.

"But I thought that Hattie — ISN'T Hattie having some new dresses — and Bessie, too?"

A sigh passed Miss Flora's lips.

"Yes, oh, yes; they are having three or four. But they don't come to *me* any more. They've gone to that French woman that makes the Pennocks' things, you know, with the queer name. And of course it's all right, and you can't blame 'em, livin' on the West Side, as they do now. And, of course, I ain't so up ter date as she is. And just her name counts."

"Nonsense! Up to date, indeed!" (Miss Maggie laughed merrily, but Mr. Smith, copying dates at the table, detected a note in the laugh that was not merriment.) "You're up to date enough for me. I've got just the job for you, too. Come out into the kitchen." She was already almost at the door. "Why, Maggie, you haven't, either!" (In spite of the incredulity of voice and manner, Miss Flora sprang joyfully to her feet.) "You never had me make you a—" Again the kitchen door slammed shut, and Mr. Smith was left to finish the sentence for himself.

But Mr. Smith was not finishing sentences. Neither was his face expressing just then the sympathy which might be supposed to be showing, after so sorry a tale as Miss 'Flora had been telling. On the contrary, Mr. Smith, with an actual elation of countenance, was scribbling on the edge of his notebook words that certainly he had never found in the Blaisdell records before him: "Two months more, then—a hundred thousand dollars. And may I be there to see it!"

Half an hour later, as on the previous day, Mr. Smith saw a metamorphosed woman hurrying down the little path to the street. But the woman to-day was carrying a bundle—and it was the same bundle that the woman the day before had brought.

But not always, as Mr. Smith soon learned, were Miss Maggie's visitors women. Besides Benny, with his grievances, young Fred Blaisdell came sometimes, and poured into Miss Maggie's sympathetic ears the story of Gussie Pennock's really remarkable personality, or of what he was going to do when he went to college—and afterwards.

Mr. Jim Blaisdell drifted in quite frequently Sunday afternoons, though apparently all he came for was to smoke and read in one of the big comfortable chairs. Mr. Smith himself had fallen into the way of strolling down to Miss Maggie's almost every Sunday after dinner.

One Saturday afternoon Mr. Frank Blaisdell rattled up to the door in his grocery wagon. His face was very red, and his mutton-chop whiskers were standing straight out at each side.

Jane had collapsed, he said, utterly collapsed. All the week she had been house-cleaning and doing up curtains; and now this morning, expressly against his wishes, to save hiring a man, she had put down the parlor carpet herself. Now she was flat on her back, and supper to be got for the boarder, and the Saturday baking yet to be done. And could Maggie come and help them out?

Before Miss Maggie could answer, Mr. Smith hurried out from his corner and insisted that "the boarder" did not want any supper anyway—and could they not live on crackers and milk for the coming few days?

But Miss Maggie laughed and said, "Nonsense!" And in an incredibly short time she was ready to drive back in the grocery wagon. Later, when he went home, Mr. Smith found her there, presiding over one of the best suppers he had eaten since his arrival in Hillerton. She came every day after that, for a week, for Mrs. Jane remained "flat on her back" seven days, with a doctor in daily attendance, supplemented by a trained nurse peremptorily ordered by that same doctor from the nearest city.

Miss Maggie, with the assistance of Mellicent, attended to the housework. But in spite of the excellence of the cuisine, meal time was a most unhappy period to everybody concerned, owing to the sarcastic comments of Mr. Frank Blaisdell as to how much his wife had "saved" by not having a man to put down that carpet.

Mellicent had little time now to go walking or auto-riding with Carl Pennock. Her daily life was, indeed, more pleasure-starved than ever—all of which was not lost on Mr. Smith. Mr. Smith and Mellicent were fast friends now. Given a man with a sympathetic understanding on one side, and a girl hungry for that same sympathy and understanding, and it could hardly be otherwise. From Mellicent's own lips Mr. Smith knew now just how hungry a young girl can be for fun and furbelows.

"Of course I've got my board and clothes, and I ought to be thankful for them," she stormed hotly to him one day. "And I *am* thankful for them. But sometimes it seems as if I'd actually be willing to go hungry for meat and potato, if for once—just once—I could buy a five-pound box of candy, and eat it up all at once, if I wanted to! But now, why now I can't even treat a friend to an ice-cream soda without seeing mother's shocked, reproachful eyes over the rim of the glass!"

It was not easy then (nor many times subsequently) for Mr. Smith to keep from asking Mellicent the utterly absurd question of how many five-pound boxes of candy she supposed one hundred thousand dollars would buy. But he did keep from it—by heroic self-sacrifice and the comforting recollection that she would know some day, if she cared to take the trouble to reckon it up.

In Mellicent's love affair with young Pennock Mr. Smith was enormously interested. Not that he regarded it as really serious, but because it appeared to bring into Mellicent's life something of the youth and gayety to which he thought she was entitled. He was almost as concerned as was Miss Maggie, therefore, when one afternoon, soon after Mrs. Jane Blaisdell's complete recovery from her "carpet tax" (as Frank Blaisdell termed his wife's recent illness), Mellicent rushed into the Duff living-room with rose-red cheeks and blazing eyes, and an explosive:—"Aunt Maggie, Aunt Maggie, can't you get mother to let me go away somewhere—anywhere, right off?"

"Why, Mellicent! Away? And just to-morrow the Pennocks' dance?"

"But that's it—that's why I want to go," flashed Mellicent. "I don't want to be at the dance—and I don't want to be in town, and *not* at the dance."

Mr. Smith, at his table in the corner, glanced nervously toward the door, then bent assiduously over his work, as being less conspicuous than the flight he had been tempted for a moment to essay. But even this was not to be, for the next moment, to his surprise, the girl appealed directly to him.

"Mr. Smith, please, won't *you* take me somewhere to-morrow?"

"Mellicent!" Even Miss Maggie was shocked now, and showed it.

"I can't help it, Aunt Maggie. I've just got to be away!" Mellicent's voice was tragic.

"But, my dear, to *ask* a gentleman—" reproved Miss Maggie. She came to an indeterminate pause. Mr. Smith had crossed the room and dropped into a chair near them.

"See here, little girl, suppose you tell us just what is behind—all this," he began gently.

Mellicent shook her head stubbornly.

"I can't. It's too—silly. Please let it go that I want to be away. That's all."

"Mellicent, we can't do that." Miss Maggie's voice was quietly firm. "We can't do—anything, until you tell us what it is."

There was a brief pause. Mellicent's eyes, still mutinous, sought first the kindly questioning face of the man, then the no less kindly but rather grave face of the woman. Then in a little breathless burst it came.

"It's just something they're all saying Mrs. Pennock said—about me."

"What was it?" Two little red spots had come into Miss Maggie's cheeks.

"Yes, what was it?" Mr. Smith was looking actually belligerent.

"It was just that—that they weren't going to let Carl Pennock go with me any more—anywhere, or come to see me, because I—I didn't belong to their set."

"Their set!" exploded Mr. Smith.

Miss Maggie said nothing, but the red spots deepened.

"Yes. It's just—that we aren't rich like them. I haven't got—money enough."

"That you haven't got—got—Oh, ye gods!" For no apparent reason whatever Mr. Smith threw back his head suddenly and laughed. Almost instantly, however, he sobered: he had caught the expression of the two faces opposite.

"I beg your pardon," he apologized promptly. "It was only that to me—there was something very funny about that."

"But, Mellicent, are you sure? I don't believe she ever said it," doubted Miss Maggie.

"He hasn't been near me—for a week. Not that I care!" Mellicent turned with flashing eyes. "I don't care a bit—not a bit—about *that*!"

"Of course you don't! It's not worth even thinking of either. What does it matter if she did say it, dear? Forget it!"

"But I can't bear to have them all talk—and notice," choked Mellicent. "And we were together such a lot before; and now—I tell you I *can't* go to that dance to-morrow night!"

"And you shan't, if you don't want to," Mr. Smith assured her. "Right here and now I invite you and your Aunt Maggie to drive with me to-morrow to Hubbardville. There are some records there that I want to look up. We'll get dinner at the hotel. It will take all day, and we shan't be home till late in the evening. You'll go?"

"Oh, Mr. Smith, you—you *dear*! Of course we'll go! I'll go straight now and telephone to somebody—everybody—that I shan't be there; that I'm going to be *out of town*!" She sprang joyously to her feet—but Miss Maggie held out a restraining hand.

"Just a minute, dear. You don't care—you *said* you didn't care—that Carl Pennock doesn't come to see you any more?"

"Indeed I don't!"

"Then you wouldn't want others to think you did, would you?"

"Of course not!" The red dyed Mellicent's forehead.

"You have said that you'd go to this party, haven't you? That is, you accepted the invitation, didn't you, and people know that you did, don't they?"

"Why, yes, of course! But that was before—Mrs. Pennock said what she did."

"Of course. But—just what do you think these people are going to say to-morrow night, when you aren't there?"

"Why, that I—I—" The color drained from her face and left it white. "They wouldn't *expect* me to go after that—insult."

"Then they'll understand that you—*care*, won't they?"

"Why, I—I—They—I *can't*—" She turned sharply and walked to the window. For a long minute she stood, her back toward the two watching her. Then, with equal abruptness, she turned and came back. Her cheeks were very pink now, her eyes very bright. She carried her head with a proud little lift.

"I think, Mr. Smith, that I won't go with you to-morrow, after all," she said steadily. "I've decided to go—to that dance."

The next moment the door shut crisply behind her.

CHAPTER VIII
A SANTA CLAUS HELD UP

It was about five months after the multi-millionaire, Mr. Stanley G. Fulton, had started for South America, that Edward D. Norton, Esq., received the following letter:—

Dear Ned:—I'm glad there's only one more month to wait. I feel like Santa Claus with a box of toys, held up by a snowdrift, and I just can't wait to see the children dance—when they get them.

And let me say right here and now how glad I am that I did this thing. Oh, yes, I'll admit I still feel like the small boy at the keyhole, at times, perhaps; but I'll forget that—when the children begin to dance.

And, really, never have I seen a bunch of people whom I thought a little money would do more good to than the Blaisdells here in Hillerton. My only regret is that I didn't know about Miss Maggie Duff, so that she could have had some, too. (Oh, yes, I've found out all about "Poor Maggie" now, and she's a dear—the typical self-sacrificing, self-effacing bearer of everybody's burdens, including a huge share of her own!) However, she isn't a Blaisdell, of course, so I couldn't have worked her into my scheme very well, I suppose, even if I had known about her. They are all fond of her—though they impose on her time and her sympathies abominably. But I reckon she'll get some of the benefits of the others' thousands. Mrs. Jane, in particular, is always wishing she could do something for "Poor Maggie," so I dare say she'll be looked out for all right.

As to who will prove to be the wisest handler of the hundred thousand, and thus my eventual heir, I haven't the least idea. As I said before, they all need money, and need it badly—need it to be comfortable and happy, I mean. They aren't really poor, any of them, except, perhaps, Miss Flora. She is a little hard up, poor soul. Bless her heart! I wonder what she'll get first, Niagara, the phonograph, or something to eat without looking at the price. Did I ever write you about those "three wishes" of hers?

I can't see that any of the family are really extravagant unless, perhaps, it's Mrs. James—"Hattie." She *is* ambitious, and is inclined to live on a scale a little beyond her means, I judge. But that will be all right, of course, when she has the money to gratify her tastes. Jim—poor fellow, I shall be glad to see him take it easy, for once. He reminds me of the old horse I saw the other day running one of those infernal treadmill threshing machines—always going, but never getting there. He works, and works hard, and then he gets a job nights and works harder; but he never quite catches up with his bills, I fancy. What a world of solid comfort he'll take with that hundred thousand! I can hear him draw the long breath now—for once every bill paid!

Of course, the Frank Blaisdells are the most thrifty of the bunch—at least, Mrs. Frank, "Jane," is—and I dare say they would be the most conservative handlers of my millions. But time will tell. Anyhow, I shall be glad to see them enjoy themselves meanwhile with the hundred thousand. Maybe Mrs. Jane will be constrained to clear my room of a few of the mats and covers and tidies! I have hopes. At least, I shall surely have a vacation from her everlasting "We can't afford it," and her equally everlasting "Of course, if I had the money I'd do it." Praise be for that!—and it'll be worth a hundred thousand to me, believe me, Ned.

As for her husband—I'm not sure how he will take it. It isn't corn or peas or flour or sugar, you see, and I'm not posted as to his opinion of much of anything else. He'll spend some of it, though,—I'm sure of that. I don't think he always thoroughly appreciates his wife's thrifty ideas of economy. I haven't forgotten the night I came home to find Mrs. Jane out calling, and Mr. Frank rampaging around the house with every gas jet at full blast. It seems he was packing his bag to go on a hurried business trip. He laughed a little sheepishly—I suppose he saw my blinking amazement at the illumination—and said something about being tired of always feeling his way through pitch-dark rooms. So, as I say, I'm not quite sure of Mr. Frank when he comes into possession of the hundred thousand. He's been cooped up in the dark so long he may want to blow in the whole hundred thousand in one grand blare of light. However, I reckon I needn't worry—he'll still have Mrs. Jane—to turn some of the gas jets down!

As for the younger generation—they're fine, every one of them; and just think what this money will mean to them in education and advantages! Jim's son, Fred, eighteen, is a fine, manly boy. He's got his mother's ambitions, and he's keen for college—even talks of working his way (much to his mother's horror) if his father can't find the money to send him. Of course, that part will be all right now—in a month.

The daughter, Bessie (almost seventeen), is an exceedingly pretty girl. She, too, is ambitious—almost too much so, perhaps, for her happiness, in the present state of their pocketbook. But of course that, too, will be all right, after next month. Benny, the nine-year-old, will be concerned as little as any one over that hundred thousand dollars, I imagine. The real value of the gift he will not appreciate, of course; in fact, I doubt if he even approves of it—lest his privileges as to meals and manners be still further curtailed. Poor Benny! Now, Mellicent—

Perhaps in no one do I expect to so thoroughly rejoice as I do in poor little pleasure-starved Mellicent. I realize, of course, that it will mean to her the solid advantages of college, music-culture, and travel; but I must confess that in my dearest vision, the child is reveling in one grand whirl of pink dresses and chocolate bonbons. Bless her dear heart! I *gave* her one five-pound box of candy, but I never repeated the mistake. Besides enduring the manifestly suspicious disapproval of her mother because I had made the gift, I have had the added torment of seeing that box of chocolates doled out to that poor child at the rate of two pieces a day. They aren't gone yet, but I'll warrant they're as hard as bullets—those wretched bonbons. I picked the box up yesterday. You should have heard it rattle!

But there is yet another phase of the money business in connection with Mellicent that pleases me mightily. A certain youth by the name of Carl Pennock has been beauing her around a good deal, since I came. The Pennocks have some money—fifty thousand, or so, I believe—and it is reported that Mrs. Pennock has put her foot down on the budding romance—because the Blaisdells *have not got money enough!* (Begin to see where my chuckles come in?) However true this report may be, the fact remains that the youth has not been near the house for a month past, nor taken Mellicent anywhere. Of course, it shows him and his family up—for just what they are; but it has been mortifying for poor Mellicent. She's showing her pluck like a little trump, however, and goes serenely on her way with her head just enough in the air—but not too much.

I don't think Mellicent's real heart is affected in the least—she's only eighteen, remember—but her pride *is*. And her mother—! Mrs. Jane is thoroughly angry as well as mortified. She says Mellicent is every whit as good as those Pennocks, and that the woman who would let a paltry thing like money stand in the way of her son's affections is a pretty small specimen. For her part, she never did have any use for rich folks, anyway, and she is proud and glad that she's poor! I'm afraid Mrs. Jane was very angry when she said that. However, so much for her—and she may change her opinion one of these days.

My private suspicion is that young Pennock is already repentant, and is pulling hard at his mother's leading-strings; for I was with Mellicent the other day when we met the lad face to face on the street. Mellicent smiled and nodded casually, but Pennock—he turned all colors of the rainbow with terror, pleading, apology, and assumed indifference all racing each other across his face. Dear, dear, but he was a sight!

There is, too, another feature in the case. It seems that a new family by the name of Gaylord have come to town and opened up the old Gaylord mansion. Gaylord is a son of old Peter Gaylord, and is a millionaire. They are making quite a splurge in the way of balls and liveried servants, and motor cars, and the town is agog with it all. There are young people in the family, and especially there is a girl, Miss Pearl, whom, report says, the Pennocks have selected as being a suitable mate for Carl. At all events the Pennocks and the Gaylords have struck up a furious friendship, and the young people of both families are in the forefront of innumerable social affairs—in most of which Mellicent is left out.

So now you have it—the whole story. And next month comes to Mellicent's father one hundred thousand dollars. Do you wonder I say the plot thickens?

As for myself—you should see me! I eat whatever I like. (The man who says health biscuit to me now gets knocked down— and I've got the strength to do it, too!) I can walk miles and not know it. I've gained twenty pounds, and I'm having the time of my life. I'm even enjoying being a genealogist—a little. I've about exhausted the resources of Hillerton, and have begun to make trips to the neighboring towns. I can even spend an afternoon in an old cemetery copying dates from moss-grown gravestones, and not entirely lose my appetite for dinner—I mean, supper. I was even congratulating myself that I was really quite a genealogist when, the other day, I met the *real thing*. Heavens, Ned, that man had fourteen thousand four hundred and seventy-two dates at his tongue's end, and he said them all over to me. He knows the name of every Blake (he was a Blake) back to the year one, how many children they had (and they had some families then, let me tell you!), and when they all died, and why. I met him one morning in a cemetery. I was hunting for a certain stone and I asked him a question. Heavens! It was like setting a match to one of those Fourth-of-July flower-pot sky-rocket affairs. That question was the match that set him going, and thereafter he was a gushing geyser of names and dates. I never heard anything like it.

He began at the Blaisdells, but skipped almost at once to the Blakes—there were a lot of them near us. In five minutes he had me dumb from sheer stupefaction. In ten minutes he had made a century run, and by noon he had got to the Crusades. We went through the Dark Ages very appropriately, waiting in an open tomb for a thunderstorm to pass. We had got to the year one when I had to leave to drive back to Hillerton. I've invited him to come to see Father Duff. I thought I'd like to have them meet. He knows a lot about the Duffs—a Blake married one, 'way back somewhere. I'd like to hear him and

Father Duff talk—or, rather, I'd like to hear him *try* to talk to Father Duff. Did I ever write you Father Duff's opinion of genealogists? I believe I did.

I'm not seeing so much of Father Duff these days. Now that it's grown a little cooler he spends most of his time in his favorite chair before the cook stove in the kitchen.

Jove, what a letter this is! It should be shipped by freight and read in sections. But I wanted you to know how things are here. You can appreciate it the more—when you come.

You're not forgetting, of course, that it's on the first day of November that Mr. Stanley G. Fulton's envelope of instructions is to be opened.

As ever yours,
John Smith.

CHAPTER IX
"DEAR COUSIN STANLEY"

It was very early in November that Mr. Smith, coming home one afternoon, became instantly aware that something very extraordinary had happened.

In the living-room were gathered Mr. Frank Blaisdell, his wife, Jane, and their daughter, Mellicent. Mellicent's cheeks were pink, and her eyes more starlike than ever. Mrs. Jane's cheeks, too, were pink. Her eyes were excited, but incredulous. Mr. Frank was still in his white work-coat, which he wore behind the counter, but which he never wore upstairs in his home. He held an open letter in his hand.

It was an ecstatic cry from Mellicent that came first to Mr. Smith's ears.

"Oh, Mr. Smith, Mr. Smith, you can't guess what's happened! You couldn't guess in a million years!"

"No? Something nice, I hope." Mr. Smith was looking almost as happily excited as Mellicent herself.

"Nice—NICE!" Mellicent clasped her hands before her. "Why, Mr. Smith, we are going to have a hundred thousand—"

"Mellicent, I wouldn't talk of it—yet," interfered her mother sharply.

"But, mother, it's no secret. It can't be kept secret!"

"Of course not—if it's true. But it isn't true," retorted the woman, with excited emphasis. "No man in his senses would do such a thing."

"Er—ah—w-what?" stammered Mr. Smith, looking suddenly a little less happy.

"Leave a hundred thousand dollars apiece to three distant relations he never saw."

"But he was our cousin—you said he was our cousin," interposed Mellicent, "and when he died—"

"The letter did not say he had died," corrected her mother. "He just hasn't been heard from. But he will be heard from—and then where will our hundred thousand dollars be?"

"But the lawyer's coming to give it to us," maintained Mr. Frank stoutly. Then abruptly he turned to Mr. Smith. "Here, read this, please, and tell us if we have lost our senses—or if somebody else has."

Mr. Smith took the letter. A close observer might have noticed that his hand shook a little. The letterhead carried the name of a Chicago law firm, but Mr. Smith did not glance at that. He plunged at once into the text of the letter.

"Aloud, please, Mr. Smith. I want to hear it again," pleaded Mellicent.

Dear Sir (read Mr. Smith then, after clearing his throat),—I understand that you are a distant kinsman of Mr. Stanley G. Fulton, the Chicago millionaire.

Some six months ago Mr. Fulton left this city on what was reported to be a somewhat extended exploring tour of South America. Before his departure he transferred to me, as trustee, certain securities worth about $300,000. He left with me a sealed envelope, entitled "Terms of Trust," and instructed me to open such envelope in six months from the date written thereon—if he had not returned—and thereupon to dispose of the securities according to the terms of the trust. I will add that he also left with me a second sealed envelope entitled "Last Will and Testament," but instructed me not to open such envelope until two years from the date written thereon.

The period of six months has now expired. I have opened the envelope entitled "Terms of Trust," and find that I am directed to convert the securities into cash with all convenient speed, and forthwith to pay over one third of the net proceeds to his kinsman, Frank G. Blaisdell; one third to his kinsman, James A. Blaisdell; and one third to his kinswoman, Flora B. Blaisdell, all of Hillerton.

I shall, of course, discharge my duty as trustee under this instrument with all possible promptness. Some of the securities have already been converted into cash, and within a few days I shall come to Hillerton to pay over the cash in the form of certified checks; and I shall ask you at that time to be so good as to sign a receipt for your share. Meanwhile this letter is to apprise you of your good fortune and to offer you my congratulations.

Very truly yours,
Edward D. Norton.

"Oh-h!" breathed Mellicent.

"Well, what do you think of it?" demanded Mr. Frank Blaisdell, his arms akimbo.

"Why, it's fine, of course. I congratulate you," cried Mr. Smith, handing back the letter.

"Then it's all straight, you think?"

"Most assuredly!"

"Je-hos-a-phat!" exploded the man.

"But he'll come back—you see if he don't!" Mrs. Jane's voice was still positive.

"What if he does? You'll still have your hundred thousand," smiled Mr. Smith.

"He won't take it back?"

"Of course not! I doubt if he could, if he wanted to."

"And we're really going to have a whole hundred thousand dollars?" breathed Mellicent.

"I reckon you are—less the inheritance tax, perhaps."

"What's that? What do you mean?" demanded Mrs. Jane. "Do you mean we've got to *pay* because we've got that money?"

"Why, y-yes, I suppose so. Isn't there an inheritance tax in this State?"

"How much does it cost?" Mrs. Jane's lips were at their most economical pucker. "Do we have to pay a *great* deal? Isn't there any way to save doing that?"

"No, there isn't," cut in her husband crisply. "And I guess we can pay the inheritance tax—with a hundred thousand to pay it out of. We're going to *spend* some of this money, Jane."

The telephone bell in the hall jangled its peremptory summons, and Mr. Frank answered it. In a minute he returned, a new excitement on his face.

"It's Hattie. She's crazy, of course. They're coming right over."

"Oh, yes! And they've got it, too, haven't they?" remembered Mellicent. "And Aunt Flora, and—" She stopped suddenly, a growing dismay in her eyes. "Why, he didn't—he didn't leave a cent to *Aunt Maggie!*" she cried.

"Gosh! that's so. Say, now, that's too bad!" There was genuine concern in Frank Blaisdell's voice.

"But why?" almost wept Mellicent.

Her mother sighed sympathetically.

"Poor Maggie! How she is left out—always!"

"But we can give her some of ours, mother,—we can give her some of ours," urged the girl.

"It isn't ours to give—yet," remarked her mother, a bit coldly.

"But, mother, you *will* do it," importuned Mellicent. "You've always said you would, if you had it to give."

"And I say it again, Mellicent. I shall never see her suffer, you may be sure,—if I have the money to relieve her. But—" She stopped abruptly at the sound of an excited voice down the hall. Miss Flora, evidently coming in through the kitchen, was hurrying toward them.

"Jane—Mellicent—where are you? Isn't anybody here? Mercy me!" she panted, as she reached the room and sank into a chair. "Did you ever hear anything like it in all your life? You had one, too, didn't you?" she cried, her eyes falling on the letter in her brother's hand. "But 'tain't true, of course!"

Miss Flora wore no head-covering. She wore one glove (wrong side out), and was carrying the other one. Her dress, evidently donned hastily for the street, was unevenly fastened, showing the topmost button without a buttonhole.

"Mr. Smith says it's true," triumphed Mellicent.

"How does he know? Who told him 'twas true?" demanded Miss Flora.

So almost accusing was the look in her eyes that Mr. Smith actually blinked a little. He grew visibly confused.

"Why—er—ah—the letter speaks for itself Miss Flora," he stammered.

"But it *can't* be true," reiterated Miss Flora. "The idea of a man I never saw giving me a hundred thousand dollars like that!—and Frank and Jim, too!"

"But he's your cousin—you said he was your cousin," Mr. Smith reminded her. "And you have his picture in your album. You showed it to me."

"I know it. But, my sakes! I didn't know *he* knew I was his cousin. I don't s'pose he's got *my* picture in *his* album! But how did he know about us? It's some other Flora Blaisdell, I tell you."

"There, I never thought of that," cried Jane. "It probably is some other Blaisdells. Well, anyhow, if it is, we won't have to pay that inheritance tax. We can save that much."

"Save! Well, what do we lose?" demanded her husband apoplectically.

At this moment the rattling of the front-door knob and an imperative knocking brought Mrs. Jane to her feet.

"There's Hattie, now, and that door's locked," she cried, hurrying into the hall.

When she returned a moment later Harriet Blaisdell and Bessie were with her.

There was about Mrs. Harriet Blaisdell a new, indescribable air of commanding importance. To Mr. Smith she appeared to have grown inches taller.

"Well, I do hope, Jane, *now* you'll live in a decent place," she was saying, as they entered the room, "and not oblige your friends to climb up over a grocery store."

"Well, I guess you can stand the grocery store a few more days, Hattie," observed Frank Blaisdell dryly. "How long do you s'pose we'd live—any of us—if 'twa'n't for the grocery stores to feed us? Where's Jim?"

"Isn't he here? I told him I was coming here, and to come right over himself at once; that the very first thing we must have was a family conclave, just ourselves, you know, so as to plan what to give out to the public."

"Er—ah—" Mr. Smith was on his feet, looking somewhat embarrassed; "perhaps, then, you would rather I were not present at the—er—family conclave."

"Nonsense!" shouted Frank Blaisdell.

"Why, you *are* one of the family, 'seems so," cried Mellicent.

"No, indeed, Mr. Smith, don't go," smiled Mrs. Hattie pleasantly. "Besides, you are interested in what concerns us, I know—for the book; so, of course, you'll be interested in this legacy of dear Cousin Stanley's."

Mr. Smith collapsed suddenly behind his handkerchief, with one of the choking coughs to which he appeared to be somewhat addicted.

"Ain't you getting a little familiar with 'dear Cousin Stanley,' Hattie?" drawled Frank Blaisdell.

Miss Flora leaned forward earnestly.

"But, Hattie, we were just sayin', 'fore you came, that it couldn't be true; that it must mean some other Blaisdells somewhere."

"Absurd!" scoffed Harriet. "There couldn't be any other Frank and Jim and Flora Blaisdell, in a Hillerton, too. Besides, Jim said over the telephone that that was one of the best law firms in Chicago. Don't you suppose they know what they're talking about? I'm sure, I think it's quite the expected thing that he should leave his money to his own people. Come, don't let's waste any more time over that. What we've got to decide is what to *do*. First, of course, we must order expensive mourning all around."

"Mourning!" ejaculated an amazed chorus.

"Oh, great Scott!" spluttered Mr. Smith, growing suddenly very red. "I never thought—" He stopped abruptly, his face almost purple.

But nobody was noticing Mr. Smith. Bessie Blaisdell had the floor.

"Why, mother, I look perfectly horrid in black, you know I do," she was wailing. "And there's the Gaylords' dance just next week; and if I'm in mourning I can't go there, nor anywhere. What's the use in having all that money if we've got to shut ourselves up like that, and wear horrid stuffy black, and everything?"

"For shame, Bessie!" spoke up Miss Flora, with unusual sharpness for her. "I think your mother is just right. I'm sure the least we can do in return for this wonderful gift is to show our respect and appreciation by going into the very deepest black we can. I'm sure I'd be glad to."

"Wait!" Mrs. Harriet had drawn her brows together in deep thought. "I'm not sure, after all, that it would be best. The letter did not say that dear Cousin Stanley had died—he just hadn't been heard from. In that case, I don't think we ought to do it. And it would be too bad—that Gaylord dance is going to be the biggest thing of the season, and of course if we *were* in black—No; on the whole, I think we won't, Bessie. Of course, in two years from now, when we get the rest, it will be different."

"When you—what?" It was a rather startled question from Mr. Smith.

"Oh, didn't you know? There's another letter to be opened in two years from now, disposing of the rest of the property. And he was worth millions, you know, millions!"

"But maybe he—er—Did it say you were to—to get those millions then?"

"Oh, no, it didn't *say* it, Mr. Smith." Mrs. Harriet Blaisdell's smile was a bit condescending. "But of course we will. We are his kinsmen. He said we were. He just didn't give it all now because he wanted to give himself two more years to come back in, I suppose. You know he's gone exploring. And, of course, if he hadn't come back by then, he would be dead. Then we'd get it all. Oh, yes, we shall get it, I'm sure."

"Oh-h!" Mr. Smith settled back in his chair. He looked somewhat nonplused.

"Humph! Well, I wouldn't spend them millions—till I'd got 'em, Hattie," advised her brother-in-law dryly.

"I wasn't intending to, Frank," she retorted with some dignity. "But that's neither here nor there. What we're concerned with now is what to do with what we have got. Even this will make a tremendous sensation in Hillerton. It ought to be written up, of course, for the papers, and by some one who knows. We want it done just right. Why, Frank, do you realize? We shall be rich—RICH—and all in a flash like this! I wonder what the Pennocks will say *now* about Mellicent's not having money enough for that precious son of theirs! Oh, I can hardly believe it yet. And it'll mean—everything to us. Think what we can do for the children. Think—"

"Aunt Jane, Aunt Jane, is ma here?" Wide open banged the front door as Benny bounded down the hall. "Oh, here you are! Say, is it true? Tommy Hooker says our great-grandfather in Africa has died an' left us a million dollars, an' that we're richer'n Mr. Pennock or even the Gaylords, or anybody! Is it true? Is it?"

His mother laughed indulgently.

"Not quite, Benny, though we have been left a nice little fortune by your cousin, Stanley G. Fulton—remember the name, dear, your cousin, Stanley G. Fulton. And it wasn't Africa, it was South America."

"And did you all get some, too?" panted Benny, looking eagerly about him.

"We sure did," nodded his Uncle Frank, "all but poor Mr. Smith here. I guess Mr. Stanley G. Fulton didn't know he was a cousin, too," he joked, with a wink in Mr. Smith's direction.

"But where's Aunt Maggie? Why ain't she here? She got some, too, didn't she?" Benny began to look anxious.

His mother lifted her eyebrows.

"No. You forget, my dear. Your Aunt Maggie is not a Blaisdell at all. She's a Duff—a very different family."

"I don't care, she's just as good as a Blaisdell," cut in Mellicent; "and she seems like one of us, anyway."

"And she didn't get anything?" bemoaned Benny. "Say," he turned valiantly to Mr. Smith, "shouldn't you think he might have given Aunt Maggie a little of that money?"

"I should, indeed!" Mr. Smith spoke with peculiar emphasis.

"I guess he would if he'd known her!"

"I'm sure he would!" Once more the peculiar earnestness vibrated through Mr. Smith's voice.

"But now he's dead, an' he can't. I guess if he could see Aunt Maggie he'd wish he hadn't died 'fore he could fix her up just as good as the rest."

"I'm *very* sure he would!" Mr. Smith was laughing now, but his voice was just as emphatic, and there was a sudden flame of color in his face.

"Your Cousin Stanley isn't dead, my dear,—that is, we are not sure he is dead," spoke up Benny's mother quickly. "He just has not been heard from for six months."

"But he must be dead, or he'd have come back," reasoned Miss Flora, with worried eyes; "and I, for my part, think we *ought* to go into mourning, too."

"Of course he'd have come back," declared Mrs. Jane, "and kept the money himself. Don't you suppose he knew what he'd written in that letter, and don't you suppose he'd have saved those three hundred thousand dollars if he could? Well, I guess he would! The man is dead. That's certain enough."

"Well, anyhow, we're not going into mourning till we have to." Mrs. Harriet's lips snapped together with firm decision.

"Of course not. I'm sure I don't see any use in having the money if we've got to wear black and not go anywhere," pouted Bessie.

"Are we rich, then, really, ma?" demanded Benny.

"We certainly are, Benny."

"Richer 'n the Pennocks?"

"Very much."

"An' the Gaylords?"

"Well—hardly that"—her face clouded perceptibly—"that is, not until we get the rest—in two years." She brightened again.

"Then, if we're rich we can have everything we want, can't we?" Benny's eyes were beginning to sparkle.

"Well—" hesitated his mother.

"I guess there'll be enough to satisfy your wants, Benny," laughed his Uncle Frank.

Benny gave a whoop of delight.

"Then we can go back to the East Side and live just as we've a mind to, without carin' what other folks do, can't we?" he crowed. "Cause if we *are* rich we won't have ter keep tryin' ter make folks *think* we are. They'll know it without our tryin'."

"Benny!" The rest were laughing; but Benny's mother had raised shocked hands of protest. "You are incorrigible, child. The East Side, indeed! We shall live in a house of our own, now, of course—but it won't be on the East Side."

"And Fred'll go to college," put in Miss Flora eagerly.

"Yes; and I shall send Bessie to a fashionable finishing school," bowed Mrs. Harriet, with a shade of importance.

"Hey, Bess, you've got ter be finished," chuckled Benny.

"What's Mell going to do?" pouted Bessie, looking not altogether pleased. "Hasn't she got to be finished, too?"

"Mellicent hasn't got the money to be finished—yet," observed Mrs. Jane tersely.

"Oh, I don't know what I'm going to do," breathed Mellicent, drawing an ecstatic sigh. "But I hope I'm going to do—just what I want to, for once!"

"And I'll make you some pretty dresses that you can wear right off, while they're in style," beamed Miss Flora.

Frank Blaisdell gave a sudden laugh.

"But what are *you* going to do, Flo? Here you've been telling what everybody else is going to do with the money."

A blissful sigh, very like Mellicent's own, passed Miss Flora's lips.

"Oh, I don't know," she breathed in an awe-struck voice. "It don't seem yet—that it's really mine."

"Well, 'tisn't," declared Mrs. Jane tartly, getting to her feet. "And I, for one, am going back to work—in the kitchen, where I belong. And—Well, if here ain't Jim at last," she broke off, as her younger brother-in-law appeared in the doorway.

"You're too late, pa, you're too late! It's all done," clamored Benny. "They've got everything all settled."

The man in the doorway smiled.

"I knew they would have, Benny; and I haven't been needed, I'm sure,—your mother's here."

Mrs. Harriet bridled, but did not look unpleased.

"But, say, Jim," breathed Miss Flora, "ain't it wonderful—ain't it perfectly wonderful?"

"It is, indeed,—very wonderful," replied Mr. Jim

A Babel of eager voices arose then, but Mr. Smith was not listening now. He was watching Mr. Jim's face, and trying to fathom its expression.

A little later, when the women had gone into the kitchen and Mr. Frank had clattered back to his work downstairs, Mr. Smith thought he had the explanation of that look on Mr. Jim's face. Mr. Jim and Benny were standing over by the fireplace together. "Pa, ain't you glad—about the money?" asked Benny.

"I should be, shouldn't I, my son?"

"But you look—so funny, and you didn't say anything, hardly."

There was a moment's pause. The man, with his eyes fixed on the glowing coals in the grate, appeared not to have heard. But in a moment he said:—

"Benny, if a poor old horse had been climbing a long, long hill all day with the hot sun on his back, and a load that dragged and dragged at his heels, and if he couldn't see a thing but the dust of the road that blinded and choked him, and if he just felt that he couldn't go another step, in spite of the whip that snapped 'Get there—get there!' all day in his ears—how do you suppose that poor old horse would feel if suddenly the load, and the whip, and the hill, and the dust disappeared, and he found himself in a green pasture with the cool gurgle of water under green trees in his ears—how do you suppose that poor old horse would feel?"

"Say, he'd like it great, wouldn't he? But, pa, you didn't tell me yet if you liked the money."

The man stirred, as if waking from a trance. He threw his arm around Benny's shoulders.

"Like it? Why, of course, I like it, Benny, my boy! Why, I'm going to have time now—to get acquainted with my children!"

Across the room Mr. Smith, with a sudden tightening of his throat, slipped softly into the hall and thence to his own room. Mr. Smith, just then, did not wish to be seen.

CHAPTER X
WHAT DOES IT MATTER?

The days immediately following the receipt of three remarkable letters by the Blaisdell family were nerve-racking for all concerned. Held by Mrs. Jane's insistence that they weren't sure yet that the thing was true, the family steadfastly refused to give out any definite information. Even the eager Harriet yielded to Jane on this point, acknowledging that it *would* be mortifying, of course, if they *should* talk, and nothing came of it.

Their enigmatic answers to questions, and their expressive shrugs and smiles, however, were almost as exciting as the rumors themselves; and the Blaisdells became at once a veritable storm center of surmises and gossip—a state of affairs not at all unpleasing to some of them, Mrs. Harriet in particular.

Miss Maggie Duff, however, was not so well pleased. To Mr. Smith, one day, she freed her mind—and Miss Maggie so seldom freed her mind that Mr. Smith was not a little surprised.

"I wish," she began, "I do wish that if that Chicago lawyer is coming, he'd come, and get done with it! Certainly the present state of affairs is almost unbearable."

"It does make it all the harder for you, to have it drag along like this, doesn't it?" murmured Mr. Smith uneasily.

"For—ME?"

"That you are not included in the bequest, I mean."

She gave an impatient gesture.

"I didn't mean that. I wasn't thinking of myself. Besides, as I've told you before, there is no earthly reason why I should have been included. It's the delay, I mean, for the Blaisdells—for the whole town, for that matter. This eternal 'Did you know?' and 'They say' is getting on my nerves!"

"Why, Miss Maggie, I didn't suppose you *had* any nerves," bantered the man.

She threw him an expressive glance.

"Haven't I!" she retorted. Then again she gave the impatient gesture. "But even the gossip and the questioning aren't the worst. It's the family themselves. Between Hattie's pulling one way and Jane the other, I feel like a bone between two quarrelsome puppies. Hattie is already house-hunting, on the sly, and she's bought Bessie an expensive watch and a string of gold beads. Jane, on the other hand, insists that Mr. Fulton will come back and claim the money, so she's running her house now on the principle that she's *lost* a hundred thousand dollars, and so must economize in every possible way. You can imagine it!"

"I don't have to—imagine it," murmured the man.

Miss Maggie laughed.

"I forgot. Of course you don't. You do live there, don't you? But that isn't all. Flora, poor soul, went into a restaurant the other day and ordered roast turkey, and now she's worrying for fear the money won't come and justify her extravagance. Mellicent, with implicit faith that the hundred thousand is coming wants to wear her best frocks every day. And, as if she were not already quite excited enough, young Pennock has very obviously begun to sit up and take notice."

"You don't mean he is trying to come back—so soon!" disbelieved Mr. Smith.

"Well, he's evidently caught the glitter of the gold from afar," smiled Miss Maggie. "At all events, he's taking notice."

"And—Miss Mellicent?" There was a note of anxiety in Mr. Smith's voice.

"Doesn't see him, *apparently*. But she comes and tells me his every last move (and he's making quite a number of them just now!), so I think she does see—a little."

"The young rascal! But she doesn't—care?"

"I think not—really. She's just excited now, as any young girl would be; and I'm afraid she's taking a little wicked pleasure in—not seeing him."

"Humph! I can imagine it," chuckled Mr. Smith.

"But it's all bad—this delay," chafed Miss Maggie again. "Don't you see? It's neither one thing nor another. That's why I do wish that lawyer would come, if he's coming."

"I reckon he'll be here before long," murmured Mr. Smith, with an elaborately casual air. "But—I wish you were coming in on the deal." His kindly eyes were gazing straight into her face now.

She shook her head.

"I'm a Duff, not a Blaisdell—except when they want—" She bit her lip. A confused red suffused her face. "I mean, I'm not a Blaisdell at all," she finished hastily.

"Humph! That's exactly it!" Mr. Smith was sitting energetically erect. "You're not a Blaisdell—except when they want something of you!"

"Oh *please*, I didn't mean to say—I *didn't* say—*that*," cried Miss Maggie, in very genuine distress.

"No, I know you didn't, but I did," flared the man. "Miss Maggie, it's a downright shame—the way they impose on you sometimes."

"Nonsense! I like to have them—I mean, I like to do what I can for them," she corrected hastily, laughing in spite of herself.

"You like to get all tired out, I suppose."

"I get rested—afterward."

"And it doesn't matter, anyway, of course," he gibed.

"Not a bit," she smiled.

"Yes, I suspected that." Mr. Smith was still sitting erect, still speaking with grim terseness. "But let me tell you right here and now that I don't approve of that doctrine of yours."

"'Doctrine'?"

"That 'It-doesn't-matter' doctrine of yours. I tell you it's very pernicious—very! I don't approve of it at all."

There was a moment's silence.

"No?" Miss Maggie said then, demurely. "Oh, well—it doesn't matter—if you don't."

He caught the twinkle in her eyes and threw up his hands despairingly.

"You are incorrigible!"

With a sudden businesslike air of determination Miss Maggie faced him.

"Just what is the matter with that doctrine, please, and what do you mean?" she smiled.

"I mean that things *do* matter, and that we merely shut our eyes to the real facts in the case when we say that they don't. War, death, sin, evil—the world is full of them, and they do matter."

"They do matter, indeed." Miss Maggie was speaking very gravely now. "They matter—woefully. I never say 'It doesn't matter' to war, or death, or sin, or evil. But there are other things—"

"But the other things matter, too," interrupted the man irritably. "Right here and now it matters that you don't share in the money; it matters that you slave half your time for a father who doesn't anywhere near appreciate you; it matters that you slave the rest of the time for every Tom and Dick and Harry and Jane and Mehitable in Hillerton that has run a sliver under a thumb, either literally or metaphorically. It matters that—"

But Miss Maggie was laughing merrily. "Oh, Mr. Smith, Mr. Smith, you don't know what you are saying!"

"I do, too. It's *you* who don't know what you are saying!"

"But, pray, what would you have me say?" she smiled.

"I'd have you say it *does* matter, and I'd have you insist on having your rights, every time."

"And what if I had?" she retaliated sharply. "My rights, indeed!"

The man fell back, so sudden and so astounding was the change that had come to the woman opposite him. She was leaning forward in her chair, her lips trembling, her eyes a smouldering flame.

"What if I had insisted on my rights, all the way up?" she quivered. "Would I have come home that first time from college? Would I have stepped into Mother Blaisdell's shoes and kept the house? Would I have swept and baked and washed and ironed, day in and day out, to make a home for father and for Jim and Frank and Flora? Would I have come back again and again, when my beloved books were calling, calling, always calling? Would I have seen other girls love and marry and go to homes of their own, while I—Oh, what am I saying, what am I saying?" she choked, covering her eyes with the back of her hand, and turning her face away. "Please, if you can, forget what I said. Indeed, I *never*—broke out like that—before. I am so—ashamed!"

"Ashamed! Well, you needn't be." Mr. Smith, on his feet, was trying to work off his agitation by tramping up and down the small room.

"But I am ashamed," moaned Miss Maggie, her face still averted. "And I can't think why I should have been so—so wild. It was just something that you said—about my rights, I think. You see—all my life I've just *had* to learn to say 'It doesn't matter,' when there were so many things I wanted to do, and couldn't. And—don't you see?—I found out, after a while, that it didn't really matter, half so much—college and my own little wants and wishes as that I should do—what I had to do, willingly and pleasantly at home."

"But, good Heavens, how could you keep from tearing 'round and throwing things?"

"I couldn't—all the time. I—I smashed a bowl once, and two cups." She laughed shamefacedly, and met his eyes now. "But I soon found—that it didn't make me or anybody else—any happier, and that it didn't help things at all. So I tried—to do the other way. And now, please, *please* say you'll forget all this—what I've been saying. Indeed, Mr. Smith I am very much ashamed."

"Forget it!" Mr. Smith turned on his heel and marched up and down the room again. "Confound that man!"

"What man?"

"Mr. Stanley G. Fulton, if you must know, for not giving you any of that money."

"Money, money, money!" Miss Maggie threw out both her hands with a gesture of repulsion. "If I've heard that word once, I've heard it a hundred times in the last week. Sometimes I wish I might never hear it again."

"You don't want to be deaf, do you? Well, you'd have to be, to escape hearing that word."

"I suppose so. But—" again she threw out her hands.

"You don't mean—" Mr. Smith was regarding her with curious interest. "Don't you *want*—money, really?"

She hesitated; then she sighed.

"Oh, yes, of course. We all want money. We have to have money, too; but I don't think it's—everything in the world, by any means."

"You don't think it brings happiness, then?"

"Sometimes. Sometimes not."

"Most of—er—us would be willing to take the risk."

"Most of us would."

"Now, in the case of the Blaisdells here—don't you think this money is going to bring happiness to them?"

There was no answer. Miss Maggie seemed to be thinking.

"Miss Maggie," exclaimed Mr. Smith, with a concern all out of proportion to his supposed interest in the matter, "you don't mean to say you *don't* think this money is going to bring them happiness!"

Miss Maggie laughed a little.

"Oh, no! This money'll bring them happiness all right, of course,— particularly to some of them. But I was just wondering; if you don't know how to spend five dollars so as to get the most out of it, how will you spend five hundred, or five hundred thousand—and get the most out of that?"

"What do you mean?"

But Miss Maggie shook her head.

"Nothing. I was just thinking," she said.

CHAPTER XI
SANTA CLAUS ARRIVES

It was not long after this that Mr. Smith found a tall, gray-haired man, with keen gray eyes, talking with Mrs. Jane Blaisdell and Mellicent in the front room over the grocery store.

"Well—" began Mr. Smith, a joyful light of recognition in his eyes. Then suddenly he stooped and picked up something from the floor. When he came upright his face was very red. He did not look at the tall, gray-haired man again as he advanced into the room.

Mellicent turned to him eagerly.

"Oh, Mr. Smith, it's the lawyer—he's come. And it's true. It *is* true!"

"This is Mr. Smith, Mr. Norton," murmured Mrs. Jane Blaisdell to the keen-eyed man, who, also, for no apparent reason, had grown very red. "Mr. Smith's a Blaisdell, too,—distant, you know. He's doing a Blaisdell book."

"Indeed! How interesting! How are you, Mr.—Smith?" The lawyer smiled and held out his hand, but there was an odd constraint in his manner. "So you're a Blaisdell, too, are you?"

"Er—yes," said Mr. Smith, smiling straight into the lawyer's eyes.

"But not near enough to come in on the money, of course," explained Mrs. Jane. "He isn't a Hiller-Blaisdell. He's just boarding here, while he writes his book."

"Oh I see. So he isn't near enough to come in—on the money." This time it was the lawyer who was smiling straight into Mr. Smith's eyes.

But he did not smile for long. A sudden question from Mellicent seemed to freeze the smile on his lips.

"Mr. Norton, please, what was Mr. Stanley G. Fulton like?" she begged.

"Why—er—you must have seen his pictures in the papers," stammered the lawyer.

"Yes, what was he like? Do tell us," urged Mr. Smith with a bland smile, as he seated himself.

"Why—er—" The lawyer came to a still more unhappy pause.

"Of course, we've seen his pictures," broke in Mellicent, "but those don't tell us anything. And *you knew him*. So won't you tell us what he was like, please, while we're waiting for father to come up? Was he nice and jolly, or was he stiff and haughty? What was he like?"

"Yes, what was he like?" coaxed Mr. Smith again. Mr. Smith, for some reason, seemed to be highly amused.

The lawyer lifted his head suddenly. An odd flash came to his eyes.

"Like? Oh, just an ordinary man, you know,—somewhat conceited, of course." (A queer little half-gasp came from Mr. Smith, but the lawyer was not looking at Mr. Smith.) "Eccentric—you've heard that, probably. And he *has* done crazy things, and no mistake. Of course, with his money and position, we won't exactly say he had bats in his belfry—isn't that what they call it?—but—"

Mr. Smith gave a real gasp this time, and Mrs. Jane Blaisdell ejaculated:—

"There, I told you so! I knew something was wrong. And now he'll come back and claim the money. You see if he don't! And if we've gone and spent any of it—" A gesture of despair finished her sentence.

"Give yourself no uneasiness on that score, madam," the lawyer assured her gravely. "I think I can safely guarantee he will not do that."

"Then you think he's—dead?"

"I did not say that, madam. I said I was very sure he would not come back and claim this money that is to be paid over to your husband and his brother and sister. Dead or alive, he has no further power over that money now."

"Oh-h!" breathed Mellicent. "Then it *is*—ours!"

"It is yours," bowed the lawyer.

"But Mr. Smith says we've probably got to pay a tax on it," thrust in Mrs. Jane, in a worried voice. "Do you know how much we'll *have* to pay? And isn't there any way we can save doing that?" Before Mr. Norton could answer, a heavy step down the hall heralded Mr. Frank Blaisdell's advance, and in the ensuing confusion of his arrival, Mr. Smith slipped away. As he passed the lawyer, however, Mellicent thought she heard him mutter, "You rascal!" But afterwards she concluded she must have been mistaken, for the two men appeared to become at once the best of friends. Mr. Norton remained in town several days, and frequently she saw him and Mr. Smith chatting pleasantly together, or starting off apparently for a walk. Mellicent was very sure, therefore, that she must have been mistaken in thinking she had heard Mr. Smith utter so remarkable an exclamation as he left the room that first day.

During the stay of Mr. Norton in Hillerton, and for some days afterward, the Blaisdells were too absorbed in the mere details of acquiring and temporarily investing their wealth to pay attention to anything else. Under the guidance of Mr. Norton, Mr. Robert Chalmers, and the heads of two other Hillerton banks, the three legatees set themselves to the task of "finding a place to put it," as Miss Flora breathlessly termed it.

Mrs. Hattie said that, for her part, she should like to leave their share all in the bank: then she'd have it to spend whenever she wanted it. She yielded to the shocked protestations of the others, however, and finally consented that her husband should invest a large part of it in the bonds he so wanted, leaving a generous sum in the bank in her own name. She was assured that the bonds were just as good as money, anyway, as they were the kind that were readily convertible into cash.

Mrs. Jane, when she understood the matter, was for investing every cent of theirs where it would draw the largest interest possible. Mrs. Jane had never before known very much about interest, and she was fascinated with its delightful possibilities. She spent whole days joyfully figuring percentages, and was awakened from her happy absorption only by the unpleasant realization that her husband was not in sympathy with her ideas at all. He said that the money was his, not hers, and that, for once in his life, he was going to have his way. "His way" in this case proved to be the prompt buying-out of the competing grocery on the other corner, and the establishing of good-sized bank account. The rest of the money he said Jane might invest for a hundred per cent, if she wanted to.

Jane was pleased to this extent, and asked if it were possible that she could get such a splendid rate as one hundred per cent. She had not figured on that! She was not so pleased later, when Mr. Norton and the bankers told her what she *could* get—with safety; and she was very angry because they finally appealed to her husband and she was obliged to content herself with a paltry five or six per cent, when there were such lovely mining stocks and oil wells everywhere that would pay so much more.

She told Flora that she ought to thank her stars that *she* had the money herself in her own name, to do just as she pleased with, without any old-fogy men bossing her.

But Flora only shivered and said "Mercy me!" and that, for her part, she wished she didn't have to say what to do with it. She was scared of her life of it, anyway, and she was just sure she should lose it, whatever she did with it; and she 'most wished she didn't have it, only it would be nice, of course, to buy things with it—and she supposed she would buy things with it, after a while, when she got used to it, and was not afraid to spend it.

Miss Flora was, indeed, quite breathless most of the time, these days. She tried very hard to give the kind gentlemen who were helping her no trouble, and she showed herself eager always to take their advice. But she wished they would not ask her opinion; she was always afraid to give it, and she didn't have one, anyway; only she did worry, of course, and she had to ask them sometimes if they were real sure the places they had put her money were perfectly safe, and just couldn't blow up. It was so comforting always to see them smile, and hear them say: "Perfectly, my dear Miss Flora, perfectly! Give yourself no uneasiness." To be sure, one day, the big fat man, not Mr. Chalmers, did snap out: "No, madam; only the Lord Almighty can guarantee a government bond—the whole country may be blown to atoms by a volcano to-morrow morning!"

She was startled, terribly startled; but she saw at once, of course, that it must be just his way of joking, for of course there wasn't any volcano big enough to blow up the whole United States; and, anyway, she did not think it was nice of him, and it was almost like swearing, to say "the Lord Almighty" in that tone of voice. She never liked that fat man again. After that she always talked to Mr. Chalmers, or to the other man with a wart on his nose.

Miss Flora had never had a check-book before, but she tried very hard to learn how to use it, and to show herself not too stupid. She was glad there were such a lot of checks in the book, but she didn't believe she'd ever spend them all—such a lot of money! She had had a savings-bank book, to be sure, but she not been able to put anything in the bank for a long time, and she had been worrying a good deal lately for fear she would have to draw some out, business had been so dull. But she would not have to do that now, of course, with all this money that had come to her.

They told her that she could have all the money she wanted by just filling out one of the little slips in her check-book the way they had told her to do it and taking it to Mr. Chalmers's bank—that there were a good many thousand dollars there waiting for her to spend, just as she liked; and that, when they were gone, Mr. Chalmers would tell her how to sell some of her bonds and get more. It seemed very wonderful!

There were other things, too, that they had told her—too many for her to remember—something about interest, and things called coupons that must be cut off the bonds at certain times. She tried to remember it all; but Mr. Chalmers had been very kind and had told her not to fret. He would help her when the time came. Meanwhile, he had rented her a nice tin box (that pulled out like a drawer) in the safety-deposit vault under the bank, where she could keep her bonds and all the other papers—such a lot of them!—that Mr. Chalmers told her she must keep very carefully.

But it was all so new and complicated, and everybody was always talking at once, so!

No wonder, indeed, that Miss Flora was quite breathless with it all.

By the time the Blaisdells found themselves able to pay attention to Hillerton, or to anything outside their own astounding personal affairs, they became suddenly aware of the attention Hillerton was paying to *them*.

The whole town was agog. The grocery store, the residence of Frank Blaisdell, and Miss Flora's humble cottage might be found at nearly any daylight hour with from one to a dozen curious-eyed gazers on the sidewalk before them. The town paper had contained an elaborate account of the bequest and the remarkable circumstances attending it; and Hillerton became the Mecca of wandering automobiles for miles around. Big metropolitan dailies got wind of the affair, recognized the magic name of Stanley G. Fulton, and sent reporters post-haste to Hillerton.

Speculation as to whether the multi-millionaire was really dead was prevalent everywhere, and a search for some clue to his reported South American exploring expedition was undertaken in several quarters. Various rumors concerning the expedition appeared immediately, but none of them seemed to have any really solid foundation. Interviews with the great law firm having the handling of Mr. Fulton's affairs were printed, but even here little could be learned save the mere fact of the letter of instructions, upon which they had acted according to directions, and the other fact that there still remained one more packet—understood to be the last will and testament—to be opened in two years' time if Mr. Fulton remained unheard from. The lawyers were bland and courteous, but they really had nothing to say, they declared, beyond the already published facts.

In Hillerton the Blaisdells accepted this notoriety with characteristic variation. Miss Flora, after cordially welcoming one "nice young man," and telling him all about how strange and wonderful it was, and how frightened she felt, was so shocked and distressed to find all that she said (and a great deal that she did not say!) staring at her from the first page of a big newspaper, that she forthwith barred her doors, and refused to open them till she satisfied herself, by surreptitious peeps through the blinds, that it was only a neighbor who was knocking for admittance. An offer of marriage from a Western ranchman and another from a Vermont farmer (both entire strangers) did not tend to lessen her perturbation of mind.

Frank, at the grocery store, rather welcomed questioners—so long as there was a hope of turning them into customers; but his wife and Mellicent showed almost as much terror of them as did Miss Flora herself.

James Blaisdell and Fred stoically endured such as refused to be silenced by their brusque non-committalism. Benny, at first welcoming everything with the enthusiasm he would accord to a circus, soon sniffed his disdain, as at a show that had gone stale.

Of them all, perhaps Mrs. Hattie was the only one that found in it any real joy and comfort. Even Bessie, excited and interested as she was, failed to respond with quite the enthusiasm that her mother showed. Mrs. Hattie saw every reporter, talked freely of "dear Cousin Stanley" and his wonderful generosity, and explained that she would go into mourning, of course, if she knew he was really dead. She sat for two new portraits for newspaper use, besides graciously posing for staff photographers whenever requested to do so; and she treasured carefully every scrap of the printed interviews or references to the affair that she could find. She talked with the townspeople, also, and told Al Smith how fine it was that he could have something really worth while for his book.

Mr. Smith, these days, was keeping rather closely to his work, especially when reporters were in evidence. He had been heard to remark, indeed, that he had no use for reporters. Certainly he fought shy of those investigating the Fulton-Blaisdell legacy. He read the newspaper accounts, though, most attentively, particularly the ones from Chicago that Mr. Norton kindly sent him sometimes. It was in one of these papers that he found this paragraph:—

There seems to be really nothing more that can be learned about the extraordinary Stanley G. Fulton-Blaisdell affair. The bequests have been paid, the Blaisdells are reveling in their new wealth, and Mr. Fulton is still unheard from. There is nothing now to do but to await the opening of the second mysterious packet two years hence. This, it is understood, is the final disposition of his estate; and if he is really dead, such will doubtless prove to be the case. There are those, however, who, remembering the multi-millionaire's well-known eccentricities, are suspecting him of living in quiet retirement somewhere, laughing in his sleeve at the tempest in the teapot that he has created; and that long before the two years are up, he will be back on Chicago's streets, debonair and smiling as ever. The fact that so little can be found in regard to the South American exploring expedition might give color to this suspicion; but where on this terrestrial ball could Mr. Stanley G. Fulton find a place to live in *unreported* retirement?

Mr. Smith did not show this paragraph to the Blaisdells. He destroyed the paper containing it, indeed, promptly and effectually—with a furtive glance over his shoulder as he did so. It was at about this time, too, that Mr. Smith began to complain of his eyes and to wear smoked glasses. He said he found the new snow glaring.

"But you look so funny, Mr. Smith," said Benny, the first time he saw him. "Why, I didn't hardly know you!"

"Didn't you, Benny?" asked Mr. Smith, with suddenly a beaming countenance. "Oh, well, that doesn't matter, does it?" And Mr. Smith gave an odd little chuckle as he turned away.

CHAPTER XII
THE TOYS RATTLE OUT

Early in December Mrs. Hattie, after an extended search, found a satisfactory home. It was a somewhat pretentious house, not far from the Gaylord place. Mrs. Hattie had it repapered and repainted throughout and two new bathrooms put in. (She said that everybody who was anybody always had lots of bathrooms.) Then she set herself to furnishing it. She said that, of course, very little of their old furniture would do at all. She was talking to Maggie Duff about it one day when Mr. Smith chanced to come in. She was radiant that afternoon in a handsome silk dress and a new fur coat.

"You're looking very well—and happy, Mrs. Blaisdell," smiled Mr. Smith as he greeted her.

"I am well, and I'm perfectly happy, Mr. Smith," she beamed. "How could I help it? You know about the new home, of course. Well, it's all ready, and I'm ordering the furnishings. Oh, you don't know what it means to me to be able at last to surround myself with all the beautiful things I've so longed for all my life!"

"I'm very glad, I'm sure." Mr. Smith said the words as if he meant them.

"Yes, of course; and poor Maggie here, she says she's glad, too,—though I don't see how she can be, when she never got a cent, do you, Mr. Smith? But, poor Maggie, she's got so used to being left out—"

"Hush, hush!" begged Miss Maggie.

"You'll find money isn't everything in this world, Hattie Blaisdell," growled Mr. Duff, who, to-day, for some unknown reason, had deserted the kitchen cookstove for the living-room base-burner. "And when I see what a little money does for some folks I'm glad I'm poor. I wouldn't be rich if I could. Furthermore, I'll thank you to keep your sympathy at home. It ain't needed nor wanted—here."

"Why, Father Duff," bridled Mrs. Hattie indignantly, "you know how poor Maggie has had to—"

"Er—but tell us about the new home," interrupted Mr. Smith quickly, "and the fine new furnishings."

"Why, there isn't much to tell yet—about the furnishings, I mean. I haven't got them yet. But I can tell you what I'm *going* to have." Mrs. Hattie settled herself more comfortably, and began to look happy again. "As I was saying to Maggie, when you came in, I shall get almost everything new—for the rooms that show, I mean,—for, of course, my old things won't do at all. And I'm thinking of the pictures. I want oil paintings, of course, in gilt frames." She glanced a little disdainfully at the oak-framed prints on Miss Maggie's walls.

"Going in for old masters, maybe," suggested Mr. Duff, with a sarcasm that fell pointless at Mrs. Hattie's feet.

"Old masters?"

"Yes—oil paintings."

"Certainly not." Her chin came up a little. "I'm not going to have anything old in my house—where it can be seen—For once I'm going to have *new* things—all new things. You have to make a show or you won't be recognized by the best people."

"But, Hattie, my dear," began Miss Maggie, flushing a little, and carefully avoiding Mr. Smith's eyes, "old masters are—are very valuable, and—"

"I don't care if they are," retorted Mrs. Hattie, with decision. "If they're old, I don't want them, and that settles it. I'm going to have velvet carpets and the handsomest lace curtains that I can find; and I'm going to have some of those gold chairs, like the Pennocks have, only nicer. Theirs are awfully dull, some of them. And I'm going to buy—"

"Humph! Pity you can't buy a little common sense—somewhere!" snarled old man Duff, getting stiffly to his feet. "You'll need it, to swing all that style."

"Oh, father!" murmured Miss Maggie.

"Oh, I don't mind what Father Duff says," laughed Mrs. Hattie. But there was a haughty tilt to her chin and an angry sparkle in her eyes as she, too, arose. "I'm just going, anyway, so you don't need to disturb yourself, Father Duff."

But Father Duff, with another "Humph!" and a muttered something about having all he wanted already of "silly chatter," stamped out into the kitchen, with the usual emphasis of his cane at every other step.

It was just as well, perhaps, that he went, for Mrs. Hattie Blaisdell had been gone barely five minutes when her sister-in-law, Mrs. Jane, came in.

"I've come to see you about a very important matter, Maggie," she announced, as she threw off her furs—not new ones—and unbuttoned her coat—which also was not new.

"Then certainly I will take myself out of the way," said Mr. Smith, with a smile, making a move to go.

"No, please don't." Mrs. Jane held up a detaining hand. "Part of it concerns you, and I'm glad you're here, anyway. I should like your advice."

"Concerns me?" puzzled the man.

"Yes. I'm afraid I shall have to give up boarding you, and one thing I came to-day for was to ask Maggie if she'd take you. I wanted to give poor Maggie the first chance at you, of course."

"*Chance* at me!" Mr. Smith laughed,—but unmistakably he blushed. "The first—But, my dear woman, it is just possible that Miss Maggie may wish to—er—decline this great honor which is being conferred upon her, and she may hesitate, for the sake of my feelings, to do it before me. *now* I'm very sure I ought to have left at once."

"Nonsense!" (Was Miss Maggie blushing the least bit, too?) "I shall be very glad to take Mr. Smith as a boarder if he wants to come—but *he's* got something to say about it, remember. But tell me, why are you letting him go, Jane?" "Now this surely *will* be embarrassing," laughed Mr. Smith again nervously. "Do I eat too much, or am I merely noisy, and a nuisance generally?"

But Mrs. Jane did not appear to have heard him. She was looking at Miss Maggie, her eyes somber, intent.

"Well, I'll tell you. It's Hattie." "Hattie!" exclaimed two amazed voices.

"Yes. She says it's perfectly absurd for me to take boarders, with all our money; and she's making a terrible fuss about where we live. She says she's ashamed—positively ashamed of us—that we haven't moved into a decent place yet."

Miss Maggie's lips puckered a little.

"Do you want to go?"

"Y-yes, only it will cost so much. I've always wanted a house—with a yard, I mean; and 'twould be nice for Mellicent, of course."

"Well, why don't you go? You have the money."

"Y-yes, I know I have; but it'll cost so much, Maggie. Don't you see? It costs not only the money itself, but all the interest that the money could be earning. Why, Maggie, I never saw anything like it." Her face grew suddenly alert and happy. "I never knew before how much money, just *money*, could earn, while you didn't have to do a thing but sit back and watch it do it. It's the most fascinating thing I ever saw. I counted up the other day how much we'd have if we didn't spend a cent of it for ten years—the legacy, I mean."

"But, great Scott, madam!" expostulated Mr. Smith. "Aren't you going to spend any of that money before ten years' time?"

Mrs. Jane fell back in her chair. The anxious frown came again to her face.

"Oh, yes, of course. We have spent a lot of it, already. Frank has bought out that horrid grocery across the street, and he's put a lot in the bank, and he spends from that every day, I know. And I'm *willing* to spend some, of course. But we had to pay so much inheritance tax and all that it would be my way not to spend much till the interest had sort of made that up, you know; but Frank and Mellicent—they won't hear to it a minute. They want to move, too, and they're teasing me all the time to get new clothes, both for me and for her. But Hattie's the worst. I can't do a thing with Hattie. Now what shall I do?"

"I should move. You say yourself you'd like to," answered Miss Maggie promptly.

"What do you say, Mr. Smith?"

Mr. Smith leaped to his feet and thrust his hands into his pockets as he took a nervous turn about the room, before he spoke.

"Good Heavens, woman, that money was given you to—that is, it was probably given you to use. Now, why don't you use it?"

"But I am using it," argued Mrs. Jane earnestly. "I think I'm making the very best possible use of it when I put it where it will earn more. Don't you see? Besides, what does the Bible say about that man with one talent that didn't make it earn more?"

With a jerk Mr. Smith turned on his heel and renewed his march.

"I think the only thing money is good for is to exchange it for something you want," observed Miss Maggie sententiously.

"There, that's it!" triumphed Mr. Smith, wheeling about. "That's exactly it!"

Mrs. Jane sighed and shook her head. She gazed at Miss Maggie with fondly reproving eyes.

"Yes, we all know your ideas of money, Maggie. You're very sweet and dear, and we love you; but you *are* extravagant."

"Extravagant!" demurred Miss Maggie.

"Yes. You use everything you have every day; and you never protect a thing. Actually, I don't believe there's a tidy or a linen slip in this house." (DID Mr. Smith breathe a fervent "Thank the Lord!" Miss Maggie wondered.) "And that brings me right up to something else I was going to say. I want you to know that I'm going to help you."

Miss Maggie looked distressed and raised a protesting hand; but Mrs. Jane smilingly shook her head and went on.

"Yes, I am. I always said I should, if I had money, and I shall—though I must confess that I'd have a good deal more heart to do it if you weren't quite so extravagant. I've already given you Mr. Smith to board."

"Oh, I say!" spluttered Mr. Smith.

But again she only smilingly shook her head and continued speaking.

"And if we move, I'm going to give you the parlor carpet, and some rugs to protect it."

"Thank you; but, really, I don't want the parlor carpet," refused Miss Maggie, a tiny smouldering fire in her eyes.

"And I shall give you some money, too," smiled Mrs. Jane, very graciously,—"when the interest begins to come in, you know. I shall give you some of that. It's too bad you should have nothing while I have so much."

"Jane, *please!*" The smouldering fire in Miss Maggie's eyes had become a flame now.

"Nonsense, Maggie, you mustn't be so proud. It's no shame to be poor. Wasn't I poor just the other day? However, since it distresses you so, we won't say any more about it now. I'll go back to my own problems. Then, you advise me—you both advise me—to move, do you?"

"I do, most certainly," bowed Miss Maggie, still with a trace of constraint.

"And you, Mr. Smith?"

Mr. Smith turned and threw up both his hands.

"For Heaven's sake, lady, go home, and spend—some of that money!"

Mrs. Jane laughed a bit ruefully.

"Well, I don't see but what I shall have to, with everybody against me like this," she sighed, getting slowly to her feet. "But if you knew—if either of you knew—how really valuable money is, and how much it would earn for you, if you'd only let it, I don't believe you'd be quite so fast to tell me to go and spend it."

"Perhaps not; but then, you see, we don't know," smiled Miss Maggie, once again her cheery self.

Mr. Smith said nothing. Mr. Smith had turned his back just then.

When Mrs. Jane was gone, Mr. Smith faced Miss Maggie with a quizzical smile.

"Well?" he hazarded.

"You mean—"

"I'm awaiting orders—as your new boarder."

"Oh! They'll not be alarming, I assure you. Do you really want to come?"

"Indeed I do! And I think it's mighty good of you to take me. But— *should* you, do you think? Haven't you got enough, with your father to care for? Won't it be too hard for you?"

She shook her head.

"I think not. Besides, I'm going to have help. Annabelle and Florence Martin, a farmer's daughters are very anxious to be in town to attend school this winter, and I have said that I would take them. They will work for their board."

The man gave a disdainful sniff.

"I can imagine how much work you'll let them do! It strikes me the 'help' is on the other foot. However, we'll let that pass. I shall be glad enough to come, and I'll stay—unless I find you're doing too much and going beyond your strength. But, how about—your father?"

"Oh, he won't mind. I'll arrange that he proposes the idea himself. Besides,"—she twinkled merrily—"you really get along wonderfully with father, you know. And, as for the work—I shall have more time now: Hattie will have some one else to care for her headaches, and Jane won't put down any more carpets, I fancy, for a while."

"Well, I should hope!" he shrugged. "Honestly, Miss Maggie, one of the best things about this Blaisdell money, in my eyes, is that it may give you a little rest from being chief cook and bottle washer and head nurse combined, on tap for any minute. But, say, that woman *will* spend some of that money, won't she?"

Miss Maggie smiled significantly.

"I think she will. I saw Frank last evening—though I didn't think it necessary to say so to her. He came to see me. I think you'll find that they move very soon, and that the ladies of the family have some new clothes."

"Well, I hope so."

"You seem concerned."

"Concerned? Er—ah—well, I am," he asserted stoutly. "Such a windfall of wealth ought to bring happiness, I think; and it seemed to, to Mrs. Hattie, though, of course, she'll learn better, as time goes on how to spend her money. But Mrs. Jane—And, by the way, how is Miss Flora bearing up—under the burden?"

Miss Maggie laughed.

"Poor Flora!"

"'Poor Flora'! And do I hear 'Poor Maggie' say 'Poor Flora'?"

"Oh, she won't be 'poor' long," smiled Miss Maggie. "She'll get used to it—this stupendous sum of money—one of these days. But just now she's nearly frightened to death."

"Frightened!"

"Yes-both because she's got it, and because she's afraid she'll lose it. That doesn't sound logical, I know, but Flora isn't being logical just now. To begin with, she hasn't the least idea how to spend money. Under my careful guidance, however, she has bought her a few new dresses—though they're dead black—"

"Black!" interrupted the man.

"Yes, she's put on mourning," smiled Miss Maggie, as he came to a dismayed stop. "She would do it. She declared she wouldn't feel half decent unless she did, with that poor man dead, and giving her all that money."

"But he isn't dead—that is, they aren't sure he's dead," amended Mr. Smith hastily.

"But Flora thinks he is. She says he must be, or he would have appeared in time to save all that money. She's very much shocked, especially at Hattie, that there is so little respect being shown his memory. So she is all the more determined to do the best she can on her part."

"But she—she didn't know him, so she can't—er—really *mourn* for him," stammered the man. There was a most curious helplessness on Mr. Smith's face.

"No, she says she can't really mourn," smiled Miss Maggie again, "and that's what worries her the most of anything—because she *can't* mourn, and when he's been so good to her—and he with neither wife nor chick nor child *to* mourn for him, she says. But she's determined to go through the outward form of it, at least. So she's made herself some new black dresses, and she's bought a veil. She's taken Mr. Fulton's picture (she had one cut from a magazine, I believe), and has had it framed and, hung on her wall. On the mantel beneath it she keeps fresh flowers always. She says it's the nearest she can come to putting flowers on his grave, poor man!"

"Good Heavens!" breathed Mr. Smith, falling limply into a chair.

"And she doesn't go anywhere, except to church, and for necessary errands."

"That explains why I haven't seen her. I had wondered where she was."

"Yes. She's very conscientious. But she *is* going later to Niagara. I've persuaded her to do that. She'll go with a party, of course,—one of those 'personally conducted' affairs, you know. Poor dear! she's so excited! All her life she's wanted to see Niagara. Now she's going, and she can hardly believe it's true. She wants a phonograph, too, but she's decided not to get that until after six months' mourning is up—it's too frivolous and jolly for a house of mourning."

"Oh, good Heavens!" breathed Mr. Smith again.

"It is funny, isn't it, that she takes it quite so seriously? Bessie suggested (I'm afraid Bessie was a little naughty!) that she get the phonograph, but not allow it to play anything but dirges and hymn tunes."

"But isn't the woman going to take *any* comfort with that money?" demanded Mr. Smith.

"Indeed, she is! She's taking comfort now. You have no idea, Mr. Smith, what it means to her, to feel that she need never want again, and that she can buy whatever she pleases, without thinking of the cost. That's why she's frightened—because she *is* so happy. She thinks it can't be right to be so happy. It's too pleasant—to be right. When she isn't being frightened about that, she's being frightened for fear she'll lose it, and thus not have it any more. I don't think she quite realizes yet what a big sum of money it is, and that she'd have to lose a great deal before she lost it all."

"Oh, well, she'll get used to that, in time. They'll all get used to it— in time," declared Mr. Smith, his face clearing a little. "Then they'll begin to live sanely and sensibly, and spend the money as it should be spent. Of course, you couldn't expect them to know what to do, at the very first, with a sum like that dropped into their laps. What would you do yourself? Yes, what would you do?" repeated Mr. Smith, his face suddenly alert and interested again. "What would you do if you should fall heir to a hundred thousand dollars—to-morrow?"

"What would I do? What wouldn't I do?" laughed Miss Maggie. Then abruptly her face changed. Her eyes became luminous, unfathomable. "There is so much that a hundred thousand dollars could do—so much! Why, I would—" Her face changed again abruptly. She sniffed as at an odor from somewhere. Then lightly she sprang to her feet and crossed to the stove. "What would I do with a hundred thousand dollars?" she demanded, whisking open a damper in the pipe. "I'd buy a new base-burner that didn't leak gas! That's what I'd do with a hundred thousand dollars. Are you going to give it to me?"

"Eh? Ah-what?" Mr. Smith was visibly startled.

Miss Maggie laughed merrily.

"Don't worry. I wasn't thinking of charging quite that for your board. But you seemed so interested, I didn't know but what you were going to hand over the hundred thousand, just to see what I would do with it," she challenged mischievously. "However, I'll stop talking nonsense, and come down to business. If you'll walk this way, Mr. New Boarder, I'll let you choose which of two rooms you'd like."

And Mr. Smith went. But, as had occurred once or twice before, Mr. Smith's face, as he followed her, was a study.

CHAPTER XIII
THE DANCING BEGINS

Christmas saw many changes in the Blaisdell families.

The James Blaisdells had moved into the big house near the Gaylord place. Mrs. Hattie had installed two maids in the kitchen, bought a handsome touring car, and engaged an imposing-looking chauffeur. Fred had entered college, and Bessie had been sent to a fashionable school on the Hudson. Benny, to his disgust, had also been sent away to an expensive school. Christmas, however, found them all at home for the holidays, and for the big housewarming that their parents were planning to give on Christmas night.

The Frank Blaisdells had also moved. They were occupying a new house not too far from the grocery store. They had not bought it yet. Mrs. Jane said that she wished to live in it awhile, so as to be sure she would really like it. Besides, it would save the interest on the money for that much time, anyway. True, she had been a little disturbed when her husband reminded her that they would be paying rent meanwhile. But she said that didn't matter; she was not going to put all that money into a house just yet, anyway,—not till she was sure it was the best they could do for the price.

They, too, were planning a housewarming. Theirs was to come the night after Christmas. Mrs. Jane told her husband that they should not want theirs the same night, of course, as Hattie's, and that if she had hers right away the next night, she could eat up any of the cakes or ice cream that was left from Hattie's party, and thus save buying so much new for herself. But her husband was so indignant over the idea of eating "Hattie's leavings" that she had to give up this part of her plan, though she still arranged to have her housewarming on the day following her sister-in-law's.

Mellicent, like Bessie, was home from school, though not from the same school. Mrs. Jane had found another one that was just as good as Bessie's, she said, and which did not cost near so much money. Mr. Smith was not living with them now, of course. He was boarding at Miss Maggie Duff's.

Miss Flora was living in the same little rented cottage she had occupied for many years. She said that she should move, of course, when she got through her mourning, but, until then she thought it more suitable for her to stay where she was. She had what she wanted to eat, now, however, and she did not do dressmaking any longer. She still did her own housework, in spite of Harriet Blaisdell's insistence that she get a maid. She said that there was plenty of time for all those things when she had finished her mourning. She went out very little, though she did go to the housewarming at her brother James's—"being a relative, so," she decided that no criticism could be made.

It seemed as if all Hillerton went to that housewarming. Those who were not especially invited to attend went as far as the street or the gate, and looked on enviously. Mrs. Hattie had been very generous with her invitations, however. She said that she had asked everybody who ever pretended to go anywhere. She told Maggie Duff that, of course, after this, she should be more exclusive—very exclusive, in fact; but that this time Jim wanted to ask everybody, and she didn't mind so much—she was really rather glad to have all these people see the house, and all—they certainly never would have the chance again.

Mr. Smith attended with Miss Maggie. Mrs. Hattie had very kindly included him in the invitation. She had asked Father Duff, too, especially, though she said she knew, of course, that he would not go—he never went anywhere. Father Duff bristled up at this, and declared that he guessed he would go, after all, just to show them that he could, if he wanted to. Mrs. Hattie grew actually pale, but Miss Maggie exclaimed joyfully that, of course, he would go—he ought to go, to show proper respect! Father Duff said no then, very decidedly; that nothing could hire him to go, and that he had no respect to show. He declared that he had no use for gossip and gabble and unwholesome eating; and he said that he should not think Maggie would care to go, either,—unless she could be in the kitchen, where it would seem natural to her!

Mrs. Hattie, however, smiled kindly, and said, of course, now she could afford to hire better help than Maggie (caterers from the city and all that), so Maggie would not have to be in the kitchen, and that with practice she would soon learn not to mind at all being 'round among folks in the parlor.

Father Duff had become so apoplectically angry at this that Mr. Smith, who chanced to be present, and who also was very angry, was forced to forget his own wrath in his desire to make the situation easier for Miss Maggie.

He had not supposed that Miss Maggie would go at all, after that. He had even determined not to go himself. But Miss Maggie, after a day's thought, had laughed and had said, with her eyes twinkling: "Oh, well, it doesn't matter, you know,—it doesn't *really* matter, does it?" And they had gone.

It was a wonderful party. Mr. Smith enjoyed it hugely. He saw almost everybody he knew in Hillerton, and many that he did not know. He heard the Blaisdells and their new wealth discussed from all viewpoints, and he heard some things about the missing millionaire benefactor that were particularly interesting—to him. The general opinion seemed to be that the man was dead; though a few admitted that there was a possibility, of course, that he was merely lost somewhere in darkest South America and would eventually get back to civilization, certainly long before the time came to open the second letter of instructions. Many professed to know the man well, through magazine and newspaper accounts (there were times when Mr. Smith adjusted more carefully the smoked glasses which he was still wearing); and some had much to say of the millionaire's characteristics, habits, and eccentricities; all of which Mr. Smith enjoyed greatly.

Then, too, there were the Blaisdells themselves. They were all there, even to Miss Flora, who was in dead black; and Mr. Smith talked with them all.

Miss Flora told him that she was so happy she could not sleep nights, but that she was rather glad she couldn't sleep, after all, for she spent the time mourning for poor Mr. Fulton, and thinking how good he had been to her. And *that* made it seem as if she was doing *something* for him. She said, Yes, oh, yes, she was going to stop black mourning in six months, and go into grays and lavenders; and she was glad Mr. Smith thought that was long enough, quite long enough for the black, but she could not think for a moment of putting on colors now, as he suggested. She said, too, that she had decided not to go to Niagara for the present. And when he demurred at this, she told him that really she would rather not. It would be warmer in the spring, and she would much rather wait till she could enjoy every minute without feeling that—well, that she was almost dancing over the poor man's grave, as it were.

Mr. Smith did not urge her after that. He turned away, indeed, rather precipitately—so precipitately that Miss Flora wondered if she could have said anything to offend him.

Mr. Smith talked next with Mrs. Jane Blaisdell. Mrs. Jane was looking particularly well that evening. Her dress was new, and in good style, yet she in some way looked odd to Mr. Smith. In a moment he knew the reason: she wore no apron. Mr. Smith had never seen her without an apron before. Even on the street she wore a black silk one. He complimented her gallantly on her fine appearance. But Mrs. Jane did not smile. She frowned.

"Yes, I know. Thank you, of course," she answered worriedly. "But it cost an awful lot—this dress did; but Frank and Mellicent would have it. That child!—have you seen her to-night?"

"Miss Mellicent? Yes, in the distance. She, too is looking most charming, Mrs. Blaisdell."

The woman tapped her foot impatiently.

"Yes, I know she is—and some other folks so, too, I notice. Was she with that Pennock boy?"

"Not when I saw her."

"Well, she will be, if she isn't now. He follows her everywhere."

"But I thought—that was broken up." Mr. Smith now was frowning.

"It was. *you* know what that woman said—the insult! But now, since this money came—" She let an expressive gesture complete the sentence.

Mr. Smith laughed.

"I wouldn't worry, Mrs. Blaisdell. I don't think he'll make much headway—now."

"Indeed, he won't—if I can help myself!" flashed the woman indignantly.

"I reckon he won't stand much show with Miss Mellicent—after what's happened."

"I guess he won't," snapped the woman. "He isn't worth half what *she* is now. As if I'd let her look at *him*!"

"But I meant—" Mr. Smith stopped abruptly. There was an odd expression on his face.

Mrs. Blaisdell filled the pause.

"But, really, Mr. Smith, I don't know what I am going to do—with Mellicent," she sighed.

"Do with her?"

"Yes. She's as wild as a hawk and as—as flighty as a humming-bird, since this money came. She's so crazy with joy and excited."

"What if she is?" challenged Mr. Smith, looking suddenly very happy himself. "Youth is the time for joy and laughter; and I'm sure I'm glad she is taking a little pleasure in life."

Mrs. Blaisdell frowned again.

"But, Mr. Smith, you know as well as I do that life isn't all pink dresses and sugar-plums. It is a serious business, and I have tried to bring her up to understand it. I have taught her to be thrifty and economical, and to realize the value of a dollar. But now—she doesn't *see* a dollar but what she wants to spend it. What can I do?"

"You aren't sorry—the money came?" Mr. Smith was eyeing her with a quizzical smile.

"Oh, no, no, indeed!" Mrs. Blaisdell's answer was promptly emphatic. "And I hope I shall be found worthy of the gift, and able to handle it wisely."

"Er-ah—you mean—" Mr. Smith was looking slightly taken aback.

"I mean that I regard wealth as one of the greatest of trusts, to be wisely administered, Mr. Smith," she amplified a bit importantly.

"Oh-h!" subsided the man.

"That is why it distresses me so to see my daughter so carried away with the mere idea of spending. I thought I'd taught her differently," sighed the woman.

"Perhaps you taught her—too well. But I wouldn't worry," smiled Mr. Smith, as he turned away.

Deliberately then Mr. Smith went in search of Mellicent. He found her in the music-room, which had been cleared for dancing. She was surrounded by four young men. One held her fan, one carried her white scarf on his arm, a third was handing her a glass of water. The fourth was apparently writing his name on her dance card. The one with the scarf Mr. Smith recognized as Carl Pennock. The one writing on the dance programme he knew was young Hibbard Gaylord.

Mr. Smith did not approach at once. Leaning against a window-casing near by, he watched the kaleidoscopic throng, bestowing a not too conspicuous attention upon the group about Miss Mellicent Blaisdell.

Mellicent was the picture of radiant loveliness. The rose in her cheeks matched the rose of her gown, and her eyes sparkled with happiness. So far as Mr. Smith could see, she dispensed her favors with rare impartiality; though, as he came toward them finally, he realized at once that there was a merry wrangle of some sort afoot. He had not quite reached them when, to his surprise, Mellicent turned to him in very evident relief.

"There, here's Mr. Smith," she cried gayly. "I'm going to sit it out with him. I shan't dance it with either of you."

"Oh, Miss Blaisdell!" protested young Gaylord and Carl Pennock abjectly.

But Mellicent shook her head.

"No. If you *will* both write your names down for the same dance, it is nothing more than you ought to expect."

"But divide it, then. Please divide it," they begged. "We'll be satisfied."

"_I_ shan't be!" Mellicent shook her head again merrily.

"I shan't be satisfied with anything—but to sit it out with Mr. Smith. Thank you, Mr. Smith," she bowed, as she took his promptly offered arm.

And Mr. Smith bore her away followed by the despairing groans of the two disappointed youths and the taunting gibes of their companions.

"There! Oh, I'm so glad you came," sighed Mellicent. "You didn't mind?"

"Mind? I'm in the seventh heaven!" avowed Mr. Smith with exaggerated gallantry. "And it looked like a real rescue, too."

Mellicent laughed. Her color deepened.

"Those boys—they're so silly!" she pouted.

"Wasn't one of them young Pennock?"

"Yes, the tall, dark one."

"He's come back, I see."

She flashed an understanding look into his eyes.

"Oh, yes, he's come back. I wonder if he thinks I don't know—_why!_"

"And—you?" Mr. Smith was smiling quizzically.

She shrugged her shoulders with a demure dropping of her eyes.

"Oh, I let him come back—to a certain extent. I shouldn't want him to think I cared or noticed enough to keep him from coming back—some."

"But there's a line beyond which he may not pass, eh?"

"There certainly is!—but let's not talk of him. Oh, Mr. Smith, I'm so happy!" she breathed ecstatically.

"I'm very glad."

In a secluded corner they sat down on a gilt settee.

"And it's all so wonderful, this—all this! Why Mr. Smith, I'm so happy I—I want to cry all the time. And that's so silly—to want to cry! But I do. So long—all my life—I've had to _wait_ for things so. It was always by and by, in the future, that I was going to have—anything that I wanted. And now to have them like this, all at once, everything I want—why, Mr. Smith, it doesn't seem as if it could be true. It just can't be true!"

"But it is true, dear child; and I'm so glad—you've got your five-pound box of candy all at once at last. And I _hope_ you can treat your friends to unlimited soda waters."

"Oh, I can! But that isn't all. Listen!" A new eagerness came to her eyes. "I'm going to give mother a present—a frivolous, foolish present, such as I've always wanted to. I'm going to give her a gold breast-pin with an amethyst in it. She's always wanted one. And I'm going to take my own money for it, too,—not the new money that father gives me, but some money I've been saving up for years—dimes and quarters and half-dollars in my baby-bank. Mother always made me save 'most every cent I got, you see. And I'm going to take it now for this pin. She won't mind if I do spend it foolishly now— with all the rest we have. And she'll be so pleased with the pin!"

"And she's always wanted one?"

"Yes, always; but she never thought she could afford it. But now—! I'm going to open the bank to-morrow and count it; and I'm so excited over it!" She laughed shamefacedly. "I don't believe Mr. Fulton himself ever took more joy counting his millions than I shall take in counting those quarters and half-dollars to-morrow."

"I don't believe he ever did." Mr. Smith spoke with confident emphasis, yet in a voice that was not quite steady. "I'm sure he never did."

"What a comfort you are, Mr. Smith," smiled Mellicent, a bit mistily. "You always *understand* so! And we miss you terribly—honestly we do!— since you went away. But I'm glad Aunt Maggie's got you. Poor Aunt Maggie! That's the only thing that makes me feel bad,—about the money, I mean,—and that is that she didn't have some, too. But mother's going to give her some. She *says* she is, and—"

But Mellicent did not finish her sentence. A short, sandy-haired youth came up and pointed an accusing finger at her dance card; and Mellicent said yes, the next dance was his. But she smiled brightly at Mr. Smith as she floated away, and Mr. Smith, well content, turned and walked into the adjoining room.

He came face to face then with Mrs. Hattie and her daughter. These two ladies, also, were pictures of radiant loveliness—especially were they radiant, for every beam of light found an answering flash in the shimmering iridescence of their beads and jewels and opalescent sequins.

"Well, Mr. Smith, what do you think of my party?"

As she asked the question Mrs. Hattie tapped his shoulder with her fan.

"I think a great deal—of your party," smiled the man. "And you?" He turned to Miss Bessie.

"Oh, it'll do—for Hillerton." Miss Bessie smiled mischievously into her mother's eyes, shrugged her shoulders, and passed on into the music-room.

"As if it wasn't quite the finest thing Hillerton ever had—except the Gaylord parties, of course," bridled Mrs. Hattie, turning to Mr. Smith. "That's just daughter's way of teasing me—and, of course, now she *is* where she sees the real thing in entertaining—she goes home with those rich girls in her school, you know. But this is a nice party, isn't it Mr. Smith?"

"It certainly is."

"Daughter says we should have wine; that everybody who is anybody has wine now—champagne, and cigarettes for the ladies. Think of it—in Hillerton! Still, I've heard the Gaylords do. I've never been there yet, though, of course, we shall be invited now. I'm crazy to see the inside of their house; but I don't believe it's *much* handsomer than this. Do you? But there! You don't know, of course. You've never been there, any more than I have, and you're a man of simple tastes, I judge, Mr. Smith." She smiled graciously. "Benny says that Aunt Maggie's got the nicest house he ever saw, and that Mr. Smith says so, too. So, you see, I have grounds for my opinion."

Mr. Smith laughed.

"Well, I'm not sure I ever said just that to Benny, but I'll not dispute it. Miss Maggie's house is indeed wonderfully delightful—to live in."

"I've no doubt of it," conceded Mrs. Hattie complacently. "Poor Maggie! She always did contrive to make the most of everything she had. But she's never been ambitious for really nice things, I imagine. At least, she always seems contented enough with her shabby chairs and carpets. While I—" She paused, looked about her, then drew a blissful sigh. "Oh, Mr. Smith, you don't know—you *can't* know what it is to me to just look around and realize that they are all mine—these beautiful things!"

"Then you're very happy, Mrs. Blaisdell?"

"Oh, yes. Why, Mr. Smith, there isn't a piece of furniture in this room that didn't cost more than the Pennocks'—I know, because I've been there. And my curtains are nicer, too, and my pictures, they're so much brighter— some of her oil paintings are terribly dull-looking. And my Bessie—did you notice her dress to-night? But, there! You didn't, of course. And if you had, you wouldn't have realized how expensive it was. What do you know about the cost of women's dresses?" she laughed archly. "But I don't mind telling you. It was one hundred and fifty dollars, a *hundred and fifty dollars*, and it came from New York. I don't believe that white muslin thing of Gussie Pennock's cost fifty! You know Gussie?"

"I've seen her."

"Yes, of course you have—with Fred. He used to go with her a lot. He goes with Pearl Gaylord more now. There, you can see them this minute, dancing together—the one in the low-cut, blue dress. Pretty, too, isn't she? Her father's worth a million, I suppose. I wonder how 'twould feel to be worth—a million." She spoke musingly, her eyes following the low-cut blue dress. "But, then, maybe I shall know, some time,—from Cousin Stanley, I mean," she explained smilingly, in answer to the question she thought she saw behind Mr. Smith's smoked glasses. "Oh, of course, there's nothing sure about it. But he gave us *some*, and if he's dead, of course, that other letter'll be opened in two years; and I don't see why he wouldn't give us the rest, as long as he'd shown he remembered he'd got us. Do you?"

"Well—er—as to that—" Mr. Smith hesitated. He had grown strangely red.

"Well, there aren't any other relations so near, anyway, so I can't help thinking about it, and wondering," she interposed. "And 'twould be *millions*, not just one million. He's worth ten or twenty, they say. But, then, we shall know in time."

"Oh, yes, you'll know—in time," agreed Mr. Smith with a smile, turning away as another guest came up to his hostess.

Mr. Smith's smile had been rather forced, and his face was still somewhat red as he picked his way through the crowded rooms to the place where he could see Frank Blaisdell standing alone, surveying the scene, his hands in his pockets.

"Well, Mr. Smith, this is some show, ain't it?" greeted the grocer, as Mr. Smith approached. "It certainly is."

"Gee! I should say so—though I can't say I'm stuck on the brand, myself. But, as for this money business, do you know? I'm as bad as Flo. I can't sense it yet—that it's true. Gosh! Look at Hattie, now. Ain't she swingin' the style to-night?"

"She certainly is looking handsome and very happy."

"Well, she ought to. I believe in lookin' happy. I believe in takin' some comfort as you go along—not that I've taken much, in times past. But I'm goin' to now."

"Good! I'm glad to hear it."

"Well, I *am*. Why, man, I'm just like a potato-top grown in a cellar, and I'm comin' out and get some sunshine. And Mellicent is, too. Poor child! *she's* been a potato-top in a cellar all right. But now—Have you seen her to-night?"

"I have—and a very charming sight she was," smiled Mr. Smith.

"Ain't she, now?" The father beamed proudly. "Well, she's goin' to be that right along now. She's *goin'* where she wants to go, and *do* what she wants to do; and she's goin' to have all the fancy fluma-diddles to wear she wants."

"Good! I'm glad to hear that, too," laughed Mr. Smith.

"Well, she is. This savin' an' savin' is all very well, of course, when you have to. But I've saved all my life and, by jingo, I'm goin' to spend now! You see if I don't."

"I hope you will."

"Thank you. I'm glad to have one on my side, anyhow. I only wish— You couldn't talk my wife 'round to your way of thinkin', could you?" he shrugged, with a whimsical smile. "My wife's eaten sour cream to save the sweet all her life, an' she hain't learned yet that if she'd eat the sweet to begin with she wouldn't have no sour cream—'twouldn't have time to get sour. An' there's apples, too. She eats the specked ones always; so she don't never eat anything but the worst there is. An' she says they're the meanest apples she ever saw. Now I tell her if she'll only pick out the best there is every time, as I do she'll not only enjoy every apple she eats, but she'll think they're the nicest apples that ever grew. Funny, ain't it? Here I am havin' to urge my wife to spend money, while my sister-in-law here—Talk about ducks takin' to the water! That ain't no name for the way she sails into Jim's little pile."

Mr. Smith laughed.

"By the way, where is Mr. Jim?" he asked.

The other shook his head.

"Hain't seen him—but I can guess where he is, pretty well. You go down that hall and turn to your left. In a little room at the end you'll find him. That's his den. He told Hattie 'twas the only room in the house he'd ask for, but he wanted to fix it up himself. Hattie, she wanted to buy all sorts of truck and fix it up with cushions and curtains and Japanese gimcracks like she see a den in a book, and make a showplace of it. But Jim held out and had his way. There ain't nothin' in it but books and chairs and a couch and a big table; and they're all old—except the books—so Hattie don't show it much, when she's showin' off the house. You'll find him there all right. You see if you don't. Jim always would rather read than eat, and he hates shindigs of this sort a little worse 'n I do." "All right. I'll look him up," nodded Mr. Smith, as he turned away.

Deliberately, but with apparent carelessness, strolled Mr. Smith through the big drawing-rooms, and down the hall. Then to the left—the directions were not hard to follow, and the door of the room at the end was halfway open, giving a glimpse of James Blaisdell and Benny before the big fireplace.

With a gentle tap and a cheerful "Do you allow intruders?" Mr. Smith pushed open the door.

James Blaisdell sprang to his feet.

"Er—I—oh, Mr. Smith, come in, come right in!" The frown on his face gave way to a smile. "I thought—Well, never mind what I thought. Sit down, won't you?"

"Thank you, if you don't mind."

Mr. Smith dropped into a chair and looked about him.

"Ain't it great?" beamed Benny. "It's 'most as nice as Aunt Maggie's, ain't it? And I can eat all the cookies here I want to, and come in even if my shoes are muddy, and bring the boys in, too."

"It certainly is—great," agreed Mr. Smith, his admiring eyes sweeping the room again.

To Mr. Smith it was like coming into another world. The deep, comfortable chairs, the shaded lights, the leaping fire on the hearth, the book-lined walls—even the rhythmic voices of the distant violins seemed to sing of peace and quietness and rest.

"Dad's been showin' me the books he used ter like when he was a little boy like me," announced Benny. "Hain't he got a lot of 'em?—books, I mean."

"He certainly has."

Mr. James Blaisdell stirred a little in his chair.

"I suppose I have—crowded them a little," he admitted. "But, you see, there were so many I'd always wanted, and when the chance came—well, I just bought them; that's all."

"And you have the time now to read them."

"I have, thank—Well, I suppose I should say thanks to Mr. Stanley G. Fulton," he laughed, with some embarrassment. "I wish Mr. Fulton could know—how much I do thank him," he finished soberly, his eyes caressing the rows of volumes on the shelves. "You see, when you've wanted something all your life—" He stopped with an expressive gesture.

"You don't care much for—that, then, I take it," inferred Mr. Smith, with a wave of his hand toward the distant violins.

"Dad says there's only one thing worse than a party, and that's two parties," piped up Benny from his seat on the rug.

Mr. Smith laughed heartily, but the other looked still more discomfited.

"I'm afraid Benny is—is telling tales out of school," he murmured.

"Well, 'tis out of school, ain't it?" maintained Benny. "Say, Mr. Smith, did you have ter go ter a private school when you were a little boy? Ma says everybody does who is anybody. But if it's Cousin Stanley's money that's made us somebody, I wished he'd kept it at home—'fore I had ter go ter that old school."

"Oh, come, come, my boy," remonstrated the father, drawing his son into the circle of his arm. "That's neither kind nor grateful; besides, you don't know what you're talking about. Come, suppose we show Mr. Smith some of the new books."

From case to case, then, they went, the host eagerly displaying and explaining, the guest almost as eagerly watching and listening. And in the kindling eye and reverent fingers of the man handling the volumes, Mr. Smith caught some inkling of what those books meant to Jim Blaisdell.

"You must be fond of—books, Mr. Blaisdell," he said somewhat awkwardly, after a time.

"Ma says dad'd rather read than eat," giggled Benny; "but pa says readin' is eatin'. But I'd rather have a cookie, wouldn't you, Mr. Smith?"

"You wait till you find what there is in these books, my son," smiled his father. "You'll love them as well as I do, some day. And your brother—" He paused, a swift shadow on his face. He turned to Mr. Smith. "My boy, Fred, loves books, too. He helped me a lot in my buying. He was in here—a little while ago. But he couldn't stay, of course. He said he had to go and dance with the girls—his mother expected it."

"Ho! Mother! Just as if he didn't want ter go himself!" grinned Benny derisively. "You couldn't hire him ter stay away—'specially if Pearl Gaylord's 'round."

"Oh, well, he's young, and young feet always dance When Pan pipes," explained the father, with a smile that was a bit forced. "But Pan doesn't always pipe, and he's ambitious—Fred is." The man turned eagerly to Mr. Smith again. "He's going to be a lawyer—you see, he's got a chance now. He's a fine student. He led his class in high school, and he'll make good in college, I'm sure. He can have the best there is now, too, without killing himself with work to get it. He's got a fine mind, and—" The man stopped abruptly, with a shamed laugh. "But—enough of this. You'll forgive 'the

fond father,' I know. I always forget myself when I'm talking of that boy—
or, rather perhaps it's that I'm *remembering* myself. You see, I want him to do
all that I wanted to do—and couldn't. And—"

"Jim, *jim!*" It was Mrs. Hattie in the doorway. "There, I might have
known where I'd find you. Come, the guests are going, and are looking for
you to say good-night. Jim, you'll have to come! Why, what'll people say?
They'll think we don't know anything—how to behave, and all that. Mr.
Smith, you'll excuse him, I know."

"Most certainly," declared Mr. Smith. "I must be going myself, for that
matter," he finished, as he followed his hostess through the doorway.

Five minutes later he had found Miss Maggie, and was making his
adieus.

Miss Maggie, on the way home, was strangely silent.

"Well, that was some party," began Mr. Smith after waiting for her to
speak.

"It was, indeed."

"Quite a house!" "Yes."

"How pretty Miss Mellicent looked!"

"Very pretty."

"I'm glad at last to see that poor child enjoying herself."

"Yes."

Mr. Smith frowned and stole a sidewise glance at his companion. Was
it possible? Could Miss Maggie be showing at last a tinge of envy and
jealousy? It was so unlike her! And yet—

"Even Miss Flora seemed to be having a good time, in spite of that
funereal black," he hazarded again.

"Yes."

"And I'm sure Mrs. James Blaisdell and Miss Bessie were very radiant
and shining."

"Oh, yes, they—shone."

Mr. Smith bit his lip, and stole another sidewise glance.

"Er—how did you enjoy it? Did you have a good time?"

"Oh, yes, very."

There was a brief silence. Mr. Smith drew a long breath and began again.

"I had no idea Mr. James Blaisdell was so fond of—er—books. I had quite a chat with him in his den."

No answer.

"He says Fred—"

"Did you see that Gaylord girl?" Miss Maggie was galvanized into sudden life. "He's perfectly bewitched with her. And she—that ridiculous dress—and for a young girl! Oh, I wish Hattie would let those people alone!"

"Oh, well, he'll be off to college next week," soothed Mr. Smith.

"Yes, but whom with? Her brother!—and he's worse than she is, if anything. Why, he was drunk to-night, actually drunk, when he came! I don't want Fred with him. I don't want Fred with any of them."

"No, I don't like their looks myself very well, but—I fancy young Blaisdell has a pretty level head on him. His father says—"

"His father worships him," interrupted Miss Maggie. "He worships all those children. But into Fred—into Fred he's pouring his whole lost youth. You don't know. You don't understand, of course, Mr. Smith. You haven't known him all the way, as I have." Miss Maggie's voice shook with suppressed feeling. "Jim was always the dreamer. He fairly lived in his books. They were food and drink to him. He planned for college, of course. From boyhood he was going to write—great plays, great poems, great novels. He was always scribbling—something. I think he even tried to sell his things, in his 'teens; but of course nothing came of that—but rejection slips.

"At nineteen he entered college. He was going to work his way. Of course, we couldn't send him. But he was too frail. He couldn't stand the double task, and he broke down completely. We sent him into the country to recuperate, and there he met Hattie Snow, fell head over heels in love with her blue eyes and golden hair, and married her on the spot. Of course, there was nothing to do then but to go to work, and Mr. Hammond took him into his real estate and insurance office. He's been there ever since, plodding, plodding, plodding."

"By George!" murmured Mr. Smith sympathetically.

"You can imagine there wasn't much time left for books. I think, when he first went there, he thought he was still going to write the great poem, the great play, the great novel, that was to bring him fame and money. But he soon learned better. Hattie had little patience with his scribbling, and had less with the constant necessity of scrimping and economizing. She was always ambitious to get ahead and be somebody, and, of course, as the babies came and the expenses increased, the demand for more money became more and more insistent. But Jim, poor Jim! He never was a money-maker. He worked, and worked hard, and then he got a job for evenings and worked harder. But I don't believe he ever quite caught up. That's why I was so glad when this money came—for Jim. And now, don't you see? he's thrown his whole lost youth into Fred. And Fred—"

"Fred is going to make good. You see if he doesn't!"

"I hope he will. But—I wish those Gaylords had been at the bottom of the Red Sea before they ever came to Hillerton," she fumed with sudden vehemence as she entered her own gate.

CHAPTER XIV
FROM ME TO YOU WITH LOVE

It was certainly a gay one—that holiday week. Beginning with the James Blaisdells' housewarming it was one continuous round of dances, dinners, sleigh-rides and skating parties for Hillerton's young people, particularly for the Blaisdells, the Pennocks, and the Gaylords.

Mr. Smith, at Miss Maggie's, saw comparatively little of it all, though he had almost daily reports from Benny, Mellicent, or Miss Flora, who came often to Miss Maggie's for a little chat. It was from Miss Flora that he learned the outcome of Mellicent's present to her mother. The week was past, and Miss Flora had come down to Miss Maggie's for a little visit.

Mr. Smith still worked at the table in the corner of the living-room, though the Duff-Blaisdell records were all long ago copied. He was at work now sorting and tabulating other Blaisdell records. Mr. Smith seemed to find no end to the work that had to be done on his Blaisdell book.

As Miss Flora entered the room she greeted Mr. Smith cordially, and dropped into a chair.

"Well, they've gone at last," she panted, handing her furs to Miss Maggie; "so I thought I'd come down and talk things over. No, don't go, Mr. Smith," she begged, as he made a move toward departure. "I hain't come; to say nothin' private; besides, you're one of the family, anyhow. Keep right on with your work; please."

Thus entreated, Mr. Smith went back to his table, and Miss Flora settled herself more comfortably in Miss Maggie's easiest chair.

"So they're all gone," said Miss Maggie cheerily.

"Yes; an' it's time they did, to my way of thinkin'. Mercy me, what a week it has been! They hain't been still a minute, not one of 'em, except for a few hours' sleep—toward mornin'."

"But what a good time they've had!" exulted Miss Maggie.

"Yes. And didn't it do your soul good to see Mellicent? But Jane—Jane nearly had a fit. She told Mellicent that all this gayety was nothing but froth and flimsiness and vexation of spirit. That she knew it because she'd been all through it when she was young, and she knew the vanity of it. And Mellicent—what do you suppose that child said?"

"I can't imagine," smiled Miss Maggie.

"She said *she* wanted to see the vanity of it, too. Pretty cute of her, too, wasn't it? Still it's just as well she's gone back to school, I think myself. She's been repressed and held back so long, that when she did let loose, it was just like cutting the puckering string of a bunched-up ruffle—she flew in all directions, and there was no holding her back anywhere; and I suppose she has been a bit foolish and extravagant in the things she's asked for. Poor dear, though, she did get one setback."

"What do you mean?"

"Did she tell you about the present for her mother?"

"That she was going to get it—yes."

Across the room Mr. Smith looked up suddenly.

"Well, she got it." Miss Flora's thin lips snapped grimly over the terse words. "But she had to take it back."

"Take it back!" cried Miss Maggie.

"Yes. And 'twas a beauty—one of them light purple stones with two pearls. Mellicent showed it to me—on the way home from the store, you know. And she was so pleased over it! 'Oh, I don't mind the saving all those years now,' she cried, 'when I see what a beautiful thing they've let me get for mother.' And she went off so happy she just couldn't keep her feet from dancing."

"I can imagine it," nodded Miss Maggie.

"Well, in an hour she was back. But what a difference! All the light and happiness and springiness were gone. She was almost crying. She still carried the little box in her hand. 'I'm takin' it back,' she choked. 'Mother doesn't like it.' 'Don't like that beautiful pin!' says I. 'What does she want?'

"'Oh, yes, she liked the pin,' said Mellicent, all teary; 'she thinks it's beautiful. But she doesn't want anything. She says she never heard of such foolish goings-on—paying all that money for a silly, useless pin. I—I told her 'twas a *present* from me, but she made me take it back. I'm on my way now back to the store. I'm to get the money, if I can. If I can't, I'm to get a credit slip. Mother says we can take it up in forks and spoons and things we need. I—I told her 'twas a present, but—' She couldn't say another word, poor child. She just turned and almost ran from the room. That was last night. She went away this morning, I suppose. I didn't see her again, so I don't know how she did come out with the store-man." "Too bad—too bad!" sympathized Miss Maggie. (Over at the table Mr. Smith had fallen to writing furiously, with vicious little jabs of his pencil.) "But Jane never did believe in present-giving. They never gave presents to each other even at Christmas. She always called it a foolish, wasteful practice, and Mellicent was always *so* unhappy Christmas morning!"

"I know it. And that's just what the trouble is. Don't you see? Jane never let 'em take even comfort, and now that they *can* take some comfort, Jane's got so out of the habit, she don't know how to begin."

"Careful, careful, Flora!" laughed Miss Maggie. "I don't think *you* can say much on that score."

"Why, Maggie Duff, I'M taking comfort," bridled Miss Flora. "Didn't I have chicken last week and turkey three weeks ago? And do I ever skimp the butter or hunt for cake-rules with one egg now? And ain't I going to Niagara and have a phonograph and move into a fine place just as soon as my mourning is up? You wait and see!"

"All right, I'll wait," laughed Miss Maggie. Then, a bit anxiously, she asked: "Did Fred go to-day?"

"Yes, looking fine as a fiddle, too. I was sweeping off the steps when he went by the house. He stopped and spoke. Said he was going in now for real work—that he'd played long enough. He said he wouldn't be good for a row of pins if he had many such weeks as this had been."

"I'm glad he realized it," observed Miss Maggie grimly. "I suppose the Gaylord young people went, too."

"Hibbard did, but Pearl doesn't go till next week. She isn't in the same school with Bess, you know. It's even grander than Bess's they say. Hattie wants to get Bess into it next year. Oh, I forgot; we've got to call her 'Elizabeth' now. Did you know that?"

Miss Maggie shook her head.

"Well, we have. Hattie says nicknames are all out now, and that 'Elizabeth' is very stylish and good form and the only proper thing to call her. She says we must call her 'Harriet,' too. I forgot that."

"And Benny 'Benjamin'?" smiled Miss Maggie.

"Yes. And Jim 'James.' But I'm afraid I shall forget—sometimes."

"I'm afraid—a good many of us will," laughed Miss Maggie.

"It all came from them Gaylords, I believe," sniffed Flora. "I don't think much of 'em; but Hattie seems to. I notice she don't put nothin' discouragin' in the way of young Gaylord and Bess. But he pays 'most as much attention to Mellicent, so far as I can see, whenever Carl Pennock will give him a chance. Did you ever see the beat of that boy? It's the money, of course. I hope Mellicent'll give him a good lesson, before she gets through with it. He deserves it," she ejaculated, as she picked up her fur neck-piece, and fastened it with a jerk.

In the doorway she paused and glanced cautiously toward Mr. Smith. Mr. Smith, perceiving the glance, tried very hard to absorb himself in the rows of names dates before him; but he could not help hearing Miss Flora's next words.

"Maggie, hain't you changed your mind a mite yet? *Won't* you let me give you some of my money? I'd so *love* to, dear!"

But Miss Maggie, with a violent shake of her head, almost pushed Miss Flora into the hall and shut the door firmly.

Mr. Smith, left alone at his table, wrote again furiously, and with vicious little jabs of his pencil.

.   .   .   .

One by one the winter days passed. At the Duffs' Mr. Smith was finding a most congenial home. He liked Miss Maggie better than ever, on closer acquaintance. The Martin girls fitted pleasantly into the household, and plainly did much to help the mistress of the house. Father Duff was still as irritable as ever, but he was not so much in evidence, for his increasing lameness was confining him almost entirely to his own room. This meant added care for Miss Maggie, but, with the help of the Martins, she still had some rest and leisure, some time to devote to the walks and talks with Mr. Smith. Mr. Smith said it was absolutely imperative, for the sake of her health, that she should have some recreation, and that it was an act of charity, anyway, that she should lighten his loneliness by letting him walk and talk with her.

Mr. Smith could not help wondering a good deal these days about Miss Maggie's financial resources. He knew from various indications that they must be slender. Yet he never heard her plead poverty or preach economy. In spite of the absence of protecting rugs and tidies, however, and in spite of the fact that she plainly conducted her life and household along the lines of the greatest possible comfort, he saw many evidences that she counted the pennies—and that she made every penny count.

He knew, for a fact, that she had refused to accept any of the Blaisdells' legacy. Jane, to be sure, had not offered any money yet (though she had offered the parlor carpet, which had been promptly refused), but Frank and James and Flora had offered money, and had urged her to take it. Miss Maggie, however would have none of it.

Mr. Smith suspected that Miss Maggie was proud, and that she regarded such a gift as savoring too much of charity. Mr. Smith wished *he* could say something to Miss Maggie. Mr. Smith was, indeed, not a little disturbed over the matter. He did try once to say something; but Miss Maggie tossed it off with a merry: "Take their money? Never! I should feel as if I were eating up some of Jane's interest, or one of Hattie's gold chairs!" After that she would not let him get near the subject. There seemed then really nothing that he could do. It was about this time, however, that Mr. Smith began to demand certain extra luxuries—honey, olives, sardines, candied fruits, and imported jellies. They were always luxuries that must be bought, not prepared in the home; and he promptly increased the price of his board—but to a sum far beyond the extra cost of the delicacies he ordered. When Miss Maggie remonstrated at the size of the increase, he pooh-poohed her objections, and declared that even that did not pay for having such a nuisance of a boarder around, with all his fussy notions. He insisted, moreover, that the family should all partake freely of the various delicacies, declaring that it seemed to take away the sting of his fussiness if they ate as he ate, and so did not make him appear singular in his tastes. Of the Blaisdells Mr. Smith saw a good deal that winter. They often came to Miss Maggie's, and occasionally he called at their homes. Mr. Smith was on excellent terms with them all. They seemed to regard him, indeed, as quite one of the family, and they asked his advice, and discussed their affairs before him with as much freedom as if he were, in truth, a member of the family.

He knew that Mrs. Hattie Blaisdell was having a very gay winter, and that she had been invited twice to the Gaylords'. He knew that James Blaisdell was happy in long evenings with his books before the fire. From Fred's mother he learned that Fred had made the most exclusive club in college, and from Fred's father he learned that the boy was already leading his class in his studies. He heard of Bessie's visits to the homes of wealthy New Yorkers, and of the trials Benny's teachers were having with Benny.

He knew something of Miss Flora's placid life in her "house of mourning" (as Bessie had dubbed the little cottage), and he heard of the "perfectly lovely times" Mellicent was having at her finishing school. He dropped in occasionally to talk over the price of beans and potatoes with

Mr. Frank Blaisdell in his bustling grocery store, and he often saw Mrs. Jane at Miss Maggie's. It was at Miss Maggie's, indeed, one day, that he heard Mrs. Jane say, as she sank wearily into a chair:—

"Well, I declare! Sometimes I think I'll never give anybody a thing again!"

Mr. Smith, at his table, was conscious of a sudden lively interest. So often, in his earlier acquaintance with Mrs. Jane, while he boarded there, had he heard her say to mission-workers, church-solicitors, and doorway beggars, alike, something similar to this; "No, I can give you nothing. I have nothing to give. I'd love to, if I could—really I would. It makes me quite unhappy to hear of all this need and suffering. I'd so love to do something! And if I were rich I would; but as it is, I can only give you my sympathy and my prayers."

Mr. Smith was thinking of this now. He had wondered several times, since the money came, as to Mrs. Jane's giving. Hence his interest now in what she was about to say.

"Why, Jane, what's the matter?" Miss Maggie was querying.

"Everything's the matter," snapped Jane. "And positively a more ungrateful set of people all around I never saw. To begin with, take the church. You know I've never been able to do anything. We couldn't afford it. And now I was so happy that I *could* do something, and I told them so; and they seemed real pleased at first. I gave two dollars apiece to the Ladies' Aid, the Home Missionary Society, and the Foreign Missionary Society— and, do you know? they hardly even thanked me! They acted for all the world as if they expected more—the grasping things! And, listen! On the way home, just as I passed the Gale girls' I heard Sue say: 'What's two dollars to her? She'll never miss it.' They meant me, of course. So you see it wasn't appreciated. Now, was it?"

"Perhaps not."

"What's the good of giving, if you aren't going to get any credit, or thanks, just because you're rich, I should like to know? And they aren't the only ones. Nothing has been appreciated," went on Mrs. Jane discontentedly. "Look at Cousin Mary Davis—*you* know how poor they've always been, and how hard it's been for them to get along. Her Carrie—Mellicent's age, you know—has had to go to work in Hooper's store. Well, I sent Mellicent's old white lace party dress to Mary. 'Twas some soiled, of course, and a little torn; but I thought she could clean it and make it over beautifully for Carrie. But, what do you think?—back it came the next day with a note from Mary saying very crisply that Carrie had no place to wear white lace dresses, and they had no time to make it over if she did. No place to wear it, indeed! Didn't I invite her to my housewarming? And didn't Hattie, too? But how are you going to help a person like that?"

"But, Jane, there must be ways—some ways." Miss Maggie's forehead was wrinkled into a troubled frown. "They need help, I know. Mr. Davis has been sick a long time, you remember."

"Yes, I know he has; and that's all the more reason, to my way of thinking, why they should be grateful for anything—*anything*! The trouble is, she wants to be helped in ways of her own choosing. They wanted Frank to take Sam, the boy,—he's eighteen now—into the store, and they wanted me to get embroidery for Nellie to do at home—she's lame, you know, but she does do beautiful work. But I couldn't do either. Frank hates relatives in the store; he says they cause all sorts of trouble with the other help; and I certainly wasn't going to ask him to take any relatives of *mine*. As for Nellie—I *did* ask Hattie if she couldn't give her some napkins to do, or something, and she gave me a dozen for her—she said Nellie'd probably do them as cheap as anybody, and maybe cheaper. But she told me not to go to the Gaylords or the Pennocks, or any of that crowd, for she wouldn't have them know for the world that we had a relative right here in town that had to take in sewing. I told her they weren't her relations nor the Blaisdells'; they were mine, and they were just as good as her folks any day, and that it was no disgrace to be poor. But, dear me! You know Hattie. What could I do? Besides, she got mad then, and took back the dozen napkins she'd given me. So I didn't have anything for poor Nellie. Wasn't it a shame?"

"I think it was." Miss Maggie's lips shut in a thin straight line.

"Well, what could I do?" bridled Jane defiantly. "Besides, if I'd taken them to her, they wouldn't have appreciated it, I know. They never appreciate anything. Why, last November, when the money came, I sent them nearly all of Mellicent's and my old summer things—and if little Tottie didn't go and say afterwards that her mamma did wish Cousin Jane wouldn't send muslins in December when they hadn't room enough to store a safety pin. Oh, of course, Mary didn't say that to *me*, but she must have said it somewhere, else Tottie wouldn't have got hold of it. 'Children and fools,' you know," she finished meaningly, as she rose to go.

Mr. Smith noticed that Miss Maggie seemed troubled that evening, and he knew that she started off early the next morning and was gone nearly all day, coming home only for a hurried luncheon. It being Saturday, the Martin girls were both there to care for Father Duff and the house. Not until some days later did Mr. Smith suspect that he had learned the reason for all this. Then a thin-faced young girl with tired eyes came to tea one evening and was introduced to him as Miss Carrie Davis. Later, when Miss Maggie had gone upstairs to put Father Duff to bed, Mr. Smith heard Carrie Davis telling Annabelle Martin all about how kind Miss Maggie had been to Nellie, finding her all that embroidery to do for that rich Mrs. Gaylord, and how wonderful it was that she had been able to get such a splendid job for Sam right in Hooper's store where she was.

Mr. Smith thought he understood then Miss Maggie's long absence on Saturday.

Mr. Smith was often running across little kindnesses that Miss Maggie had done. He began to think that Miss Maggie must be a very charitable person—until he ran across several cases that she had not helped. Then he did not know exactly what to think.

His first experience of this kind was when he met an unmistakably "down-and-out" on the street one day, begging clothing, food, anything, and telling a sorry tale of his unjust discharge from a local factory. Mr. Smith gave the man a dollar, and sent him to Miss Maggie. He happened to know that Father Duff had discarded an old suit that morning—and Father Duff and the beggar might have been taken for twins as to size. On the way home a little later he met the beggar returning, just as forlorn, and even more hungry-looking.

"Well, my good fellow, couldn't she fix you up?" questioned Mr. Smith in some surprise.

"Fix me up!" glowered the man disdainfully. "Not much she did! She didn't fix me up ter nothin'—but chin music!"

And Mr. Smith had thought Miss Maggie was so charitable!

A few days later he heard an eager-eyed young woman begging Miss Maggie for a contribution to the Pension Fund Fair in behalf of the underpaid shopgirls in Daly's. Daly's was a Hillerton department Store, notorious for its unfair treatment of its employees.

Miss Maggie seemed interested, and asked many questions. The eager-eyed young woman became even more eager-eyed, and told Miss Maggie all about the long hours, the nerve-wearing labor, the low wages—wages upon which it was impossible for any girl to live decently—wages whose meagerness sent many a girl to her ruin.

Miss Maggie listened attentively, and said, "Yes, yes, I see," several times. But in the end the eager-eyed young woman went away empty-handed and sad-eyed. And Mr. Smith frowned again.

He had thought Miss Maggie was so kind-hearted! She gave to some fairs—why not to this one? As soon as possible Mr. Smith hunted up the eager-eyed young woman and gave her ten dollars. He would have given her more, but he had learned from unpleasant experience that large gifts from unpretentious Mr. John Smith brought comments and curiosity not always agreeable.

It was not until many weeks later that Mr. Smith chanced to hear of the complete change of policy of Daly's department store. Hours were shortened, labor lightened, and wages raised. Incidentally he learned that it had all started from a crusade of women's clubs and church committees who had "got after old Daly" and threatened all sorts of publicity and unpleasantness if the wrongs were not righted at once. He learned also that the leader in the forefront of this movement had been—Maggie Duff. As it chanced, it was on that same day that a strange man accosted him on the street.

"Say, she was all right, she was, old man. I been hopin' I'd see ye some day ter tell ye."

"To tell me?" echoed Mr. Smith stupidly.

The man grinned.

"Ye don't know me, do ye? Well, I do look diff'rent, I'll own. Ye give me a dollar once, an' sent me to a lady down the street thar. Now do ye remember?"

"Oh! oh! Are *you* that man?"

"Sure I am! Well, she was all right. 'Member? I thought 'twas only chin music she was givin' me. But let me tell ye. She hunted up the wife an' kids, an' what's more, she went an' faced my boss, an' she got me my job back, too. What do ye think of that, now?"

"Why, I'm—I'm glad, of course!" Mr. Smith spoke as one in deep thought.

And all the way home Mr. Smith walked—as one in deep thought.

CHAPTER XV
IN SEARCH OF REST

June brought all the young people home again. It brought, also, a great deal of talk concerning plans for vacation. Bessie—Elizabeth—said they must all go away.

From James Blaisdell this brought a sudden and vigorous remonstrance.

"Nonsense, you've just got home!" he exclaimed. "Hillerton'll be a vacation to you all right. Besides, I want my family together again. I haven't seen a thing of my children for six months."

Elizabeth gave a silvery laugh. (Elizabeth had learned to give very silvery laughs.) She shrugged her shoulders daintily and looked at her rings.

"Hillerton? Ho! You wouldn't really doom us to Hillerton all summer, daddy."

"What's the matter with Hillerton?"

"What isn't the matter with Hillerton?" laughed the daughter again.

"But I thought we—we would have lovely auto trips," stammered her mother apologetically. "Take them from here, you know, and stay overnight at hotels around. I've always wanted to do that; and we can now, dear."

"Auto trips! Pooh!" shrugged Elizabeth. "Why, mumsey, we're going to the shore for July, and to the mountains for August. You and daddy and I. And Fred's going, too, only he'll be at the Gaylord camp in the Adirondacks, part of the time."

"Is that true, Fred?" James Blaisdell's eyes, fixed on his son, were half wistful, half accusing.

Fred stirred restlessly.

"Well, I sort of had to, governor," he apologized. "Honest, I did. There are some things a man has to do! Gaylord asked me, and—Hang it all, I don't see why you have to look at me as if I were committing a crime, dad!"

"You aren't, dear, you aren't," fluttered Fred's mother hurriedly; "and I'm sure it's lovely you've got the chance to go to the Gaylords' camp. And it's right, quite right, that we should travel this summer, as Bessie—er—Elizabeth suggests. I never thought; but, of course, you young people don't want to be hived up in Hillerton all summer!"

"Bet your life we don't, mater," shrugged Fred, carefully avoiding his father's eyes, "after all that grind."

"*Grind*, Fred?"

But Fred had turned away, and did not, apparently, hear his father's grieved question.

Mr. Smith learned all about the vacation plans a day or two later from Benny.

"Yep, we're all goin' away for all summer," he repeated, after he had told the destination of most of the family. "I don't think ma wants to, much, but she's goin' on account of Bess. Besides, she says everybody who is anybody always goes away on vacations, of course. So we've got to. They're goin' to the beach first, and I'm goin' to a boys' camp up in Vermont—Mellicent, she's goin' to a girls' camp. Did you know that?"

Mr. Smith shook his head. "Well, she is," nodded Benny. "She tried to get Bess to go—Gussie Pennock's goin'. But Bess!—my you should see her nose go up in the air! She said she wa'n't goin' where she had to wear great coarse shoes an' horrid middy-blouses all day, an' build fires an' walk miles an' eat bugs an' grasshoppers."

"Is Miss Mellicent going to do all that?" smiled Mr. Smith.

"Bess says she is—I mean, *Elizabeth*. Did you know? We have to call her that now, when we don't forget it. I forget it, mostly. Have you seen her since she came back?"

"No."

"She's swingin' an awful lot of style—Bess is. She makes dad dress up in his swallow-tail every night for dinner. An' she makes him and Fred an' me stand up the minute she comes into the room, no matter if there's forty other chairs in sight; an' we have to *stay* standin' till she sits down—an' sometimes she stands up a-purpose, just to keep *us* standing. I know she does. She says a gentleman never sits when a lady is standin' up in his presence. An' she's lecturin' us all the time on the way to eat an' talk an' act. Why, we can't even walk natural any longer. An' she says the way Katy serves our meals is a disgrace to any civilized family."

"How does Katy like that?"

"Like it! She got mad an' gave notice on the spot. An' that made ma 'most have hysterics—she did have one of her headaches—'cause good hired girls are awful scarce, she says. But Bess says, Pooh! we'll get some from the city next time that know their business, an' we're goin' away all summer, anyway, an' won't ma please call them 'maids,' as she ought to, an' not that plebeian 'hired girl.' Bess loves that word. Everything's 'plebeian' with Bess now. Oh we're havin' great times at our house since Bess—*elizabeth*—came!" grinned Benny, tossing his cap in the air, and dancing down the walk much as he had danced the first night Mr. Smith saw him a year before.

The James Blaisdells were hardly off to shore and camp when Miss Flora started on her travels. Mr. Smith learned all about her plans, too, for she came down one day to talk them over with Miss Maggie.

Miss Flora was looking very well in a soft gray and white summer silk. Her forehead had lost its lines of care, and her eyes were no longer peering for wrinkles. Miss Flora was actually almost pretty.

"How nice you look!" exclaimed Miss Maggie.

"Do I?" panted Miss Flora, as she fluttered up the steps and sank into one of the porch chairs.

"Indeed, you do!" exclaimed Mr. Smith admiringly. Mr. Smith was putting up a trellis for Miss Maggie's new rosebush. He was working faithfully, but not with the skill of accustomedness.

"I'm so glad you like it!" Miss Flora settled back into her chair and smoothed out the ruffles across her lap. "It isn't too gay, is it? You know the six months are more than up now."

"Not a bit!" exclaimed Mr. Smith.

"No, indeed!" cried Miss Maggie.

"I hoped it wasn't," sighed Miss Flora happily. "Well, I'm all packed but my dresses."

"Why, I thought you weren't going till Monday," said Miss Maggie.

"Oh, I'm not."

"But—it's only Friday now!"

Miss Flora laughed shamefacedly.

"Yes, I know. I suppose I am a little ahead of time. But you see, I ain't used to packing—not a big trunk, so—and I was so afraid I wouldn't get it done in time. I was going to put my dresses in; but Mis' Moore said they'd wrinkle awfully, if I did, and, of course, they would, when you come to think of it. So I shan't put those in till Sunday night. I'm so glad Mis' Moore's going. It'll be so nice to have somebody along that I know."

"Yes, indeed," smiled Miss Maggie.

"And she knows everything—all about tickets and checking the baggage, and all that. You know we're only going to be personally conducted to Niagara. After that we're going to New York and stay two weeks at some nice hotel. I want to see Grant's Tomb and the Aquarium, and Mis' Moore wants to go to Coney Island. She says she's always wanted to go to Coney Island just as I have to Niagara."

"I'm glad you can take her," said Miss Maggie heartily.

"Yes, and she's so pleased. You know, even if she has such a nice family, and all, she hasn't much money, and she's been awful nice to me lately. I used to think she didn't like me, too. But I must have been mistaken, of course. And 'twas so with Mis' Benson and Mis' Pennock, too. But now they've invited me there and have come to see me, and are *so* interested in my trip and all. Why, I never knew I had so many friends, Maggie. Truly I didn't!"

Miss Maggie said nothing, but, there was an odd expression on her face. Mr. Smith pounded a small nail home with an extra blow of his hammer.

"And they're all so kind and interested about the money, too," went on Miss Flora, gently rocking to and fro. "Bert Benson sells stocks and invests money for folks, you know, and Mis' Benson said he'd got some splendid-payin' ones, and he'd let me have some, and—"

"Flo, you *didn't* take any of that Benson gold-mine stock!" interrupted Miss Maggie sharply.

Mr. Smith's hammer stopped, suspended in mid-air.

"No; oh, no! I asked Mr. Chalmers and he said better not. So I didn't." Miss Maggie relaxed in her chair, and Mr. Smith's hammer fell with a gentle tap on the nail-head. "But I felt real bad about it—when Mis' Benson had been so kind as to offer it, you know. It looked sort of—of ungrateful, so."

"Ungrateful!" Miss Maggie's voice vibrated with indignant scorn. "Flora, you won't—you *won't* invest your money without asking Mr. Chalmers's advice first, will you?"

"But I tell you I didn't," retorted Miss Flora, with unusual sharpness, for her. "But it was good stock, and it pays splendidly. Jane took some. She took a lot."

"Jane!—but I thought Frank wouldn't let her."

"Oh, Frank said all right, if she wanted to, she might. I suspect he got tired of her teasing, and it did pay splendidly. Why, 'twill pay twenty-five per cent, probably, this year, Mis' Benson says. So Frank give in. You see, he felt he'd got to pacify Jane some way, I s'pose, she's so cut up about his selling out."

"Selling out!" exclaimed Miss Maggie.

"Oh, didn't you know that? Well, then I *have* got some news!" Miss Flora gave the satisfied little wriggle with which a born news-lover always prefaces her choicest bit of information. "Frank has sold his grocery stores— both of 'em."

"Why, I can't believe it!" Miss Maggie fell back with a puzzled frown.

"*Sold* them! Why, I should as soon think of his—his selling himself," cried Mr. Smith. "I thought they were inseparable."

"Well, they ain't—because he's separated 'em." Miss Flora was rocking a little faster now.

"But why?" demanded Miss Maggie.

"He says he wants a rest. That he's worked hard all his life, and it's time he took some comfort. He says he doesn't take a minute of comfort now 'cause Jane's hounding him all the time to get more money, to get more money. She's crazy to see the interest mount up, you know—Jane is. But he says he don't want any more money. He wants to *spend* money for a while. And he's going to spend it. He's going to retire from business and enjoy himself."

"Well," ejaculated Mr. Smith, "this is a piece of news, indeed!"

"I should say it was," cried Miss Maggie, still almost incredulous. "How does Jane take it?"

"Oh, she's turribly fussed up over it, as you'd know she would be. Such a good chance wasted, she thinks, when he might be making all that money earn more. You know Jane wants to turn everything into money now. Honestly, Maggie, I don't believe Jane can look at the moon nowadays without wishing it was really gold, and she had it to put out to interest!"

"Oh, Flora!" remonstrated Miss Maggie faintly.

"Well, it's so," maintained Miss Flora, "So 'tain't any wonder, of course, that she's upset over this. That's why Frank give in to her, I think, and let her buy that Benson stock. Besides, he's feeling especially flush, because he's got the cash the stores brought, too. So he told her to go ahead."

"I'm sorry about that stock," frowned Miss Maggie.

"Oh, it's perfectly safe. Mis' Benson said 'twas," comforted Miss Flora. "You needn't worry about that. And 'twill pay splendid."

"When did this happen—the sale of the store, I mean?" asked Mr. Smith. Mr. Smith was not even pretending to work now.

"Yesterday—the finish of it. I'm waiting to see Hattie. She'll be tickled to death. She's *always* hated it that Frank had a grocery store, you know; and since the money's come, and she's been going with the Gaylords and the Pennocks, and all that crowd, she's felt worse than ever. She was saying to me only last week how ashamed she was to think that her friends might see her own brother-in-law any day wearing horrid white coat, and selling molasses over the counter. My, but Hattie'll be tickled all right—or 'Harriet,' I suppose I should say, but I never can remember it."

"But what is Frank going to—to do with himself?" demanded Miss Maggie. "Why, Flora, he'll be lost without that grocery store!"

"Oh, he's going to travel, first. He says he always wanted to, and he's got a chance now, and he's going to. They're going to the Yellowstone Park and the Garden of the Gods and to California. And that's another thing that worries Jane—spending all that money for them just to ride in the cars."

"Is she going, too?" queried Mr. Smith.

"Oh, yes, she's going, too. She says she's got to go to keep Frank from spending every cent he's got," laughed Miss Flora. "I was over there last night, and they told me all about it."

"When do they go?"

"Just as soon as they can get ready. Frank's got to help Donovan, the man that's bought the store, a week till he gets the run of things, he says. Then he's going. You wait till you see him." Miss Flora got to her feet, and smoothed out the folds of her skirt. "He's as tickled as a boy with a new jack-knife. And I'm glad. Frank has been a turrible hard worker all his life. I'm glad he's going to take some comfort, same as I am."

When Miss Flora had gone, Miss Maggie turned to Mr. Smith with eyes that still carried dazed unbelief.

"*Did* Flora say that Frank Blaisdell had sold his grocery stores?"

"She certainly did! You seem surprised."

"I'm more than surprised. I'm dumfounded."

"Why? You don't think, like Mrs. Jane, that he ought not to enjoy his money, certainly?"

"Oh, no. He's got money enough to retire, if he wants to, and he's certainly worked hard enough to earn a rest."

"Then what is it?"

Miss Maggie laughed a little.

"I'm not sure I can explain. But, to me, it's—just this: while he's got plenty to retire *upon*, he hasn't got anything to—to retire *to*."

"And, pray, what do you mean by that?"

"Why, Mr. Smith, I've known that man from the time he was trading jack-knives and marbles and selling paper boxes for five pins. I remember the whipping he got, too, for filching sugar and coffee and beans from the pantry and opening a grocery store in our barn. From that time to this, that boy has always been trading *something*. He's been absolutely uninterested in anything else. I don't believe he's read a book or a magazine since his school days, unless it had something to do with business or groceries. He hasn't a sign of a fad—music, photography, collecting things—nothing. And he hates society. Jane has to fairly drag him out anywhere. Now, what I want to know is, what is the man going to do?"

"Oh, he'll find something," laughed Mr. Smith. "He's going to travel, first, anyhow."

"Yes, he's going to travel, first. And then—we'll see," smiled Miss Maggie enigmatically, as Mr. Smith picked up his hammer again.

By the middle of July the Blaisdells were all gone from Hillerton and there remained only their letters for Miss Maggie—and for Mr. Smith. Miss Maggie was very generous with her letters. Perceiving Mr. Smith's genuine interest, she read him extracts from almost every one that came. And the letters were always interesting—and usually characteristic.

Benny wrote of swimming and tennis matches, and of "hikes" and the "bully eats." Hattie wrote of balls and gowns and the attention "dear Elizabeth" was receiving from some really very nice families who were said to be fabulously rich. Neither James nor Bessie wrote at all. Fred, too, remained unheard from.

Mellicent wrote frequently—gay, breezy letters full to the brim of the joy of living. She wrote of tennis, swimming, camp-fire stories, and mountain trails: they were like Benny's letters in petticoats, Miss Maggie said.

Long and frequent epistles came from Miss Flora. Miss Flora was having a beautiful time. Niagara was perfectly lovely—only what a terrible noise it made! She was glad she did not have to stay and hear it always. She liked New York, only that was noisy, too, though Mrs. Moore did not seem to mind it. Mrs. Moore liked Coney Island, too, but Miss Flora much preferred Grant's Tomb, she said. It was so much more quiet and ladylike.

She thought some things at Coney Island were really not nice at all, and she was surprised that Mrs. Moore should enjoy them so much.

Between the lines it could be seen that in spite of all the good times, Miss Flora was becoming just the least bit homesick. She wrote Miss Maggie that it did seem queer to go everywhere, and not see a soul to bow to. It gave her such a lonesome feeling—such a lot of faces, and not one familiar one! She had tried to make the acquaintance of several people—real nice people; she knew they were by the way they looked. But they wouldn't say hardly anything to her, nor answer her questions; and they always got up and moved away very soon.

To be sure, there was one nice young man. He was lovely to them, Miss Flora said. He spoke to them first, too. It was when they were down to Coney Island. He helped them through the crowds, and told them about lots of nice things they didn't want to miss seeing. He walked with them, too, quite awhile, showing them the sights. He was very kind—he seemed so especially kind, after all those other cold-hearted people, who didn't care! That was the day she and Mrs. Moore both lost their pocketbooks, and had such an awful time getting back to New York. It was right after they had said good-bye to the nice young gentleman that they discovered that they had lost them. They were so sorry that they hadn't found it out before, Miss Flora said, for he would have helped them, she was sure. But though they looked everywhere for him, they could not find him at all, and they had to appeal to strangers, who took them right up to a policeman the first thing, which was very embarrassing, Miss Flora said. Why, she and Mrs. Moore felt as if they had been arrested, almost! Miss Maggie pursed her lips a little, when she read this letter to Mr. Smith, but she made no comment.

From Jane, also, came several letters, and from Frank Blaisdell one short scrawl.

Frank said he was having a bully time, but that he'd seen some of the most shiftless-looking grocery stores that he ever set eyes on. He asked if Maggie knew how trade was at his old store, and if Donovan was keeping it up to the mark. He said that Jane was well, only she was getting pretty tired because she *would* try to see everything at once, for fear she'd lose something, and not get her money's worth, for all the world just as she used to eat things to save them.

Jane wrote that she was having a very nice time, of course,—she couldn't help it, with all those lovely things to see; but she said she never dreamed that just potatoes, meat, and vegetables could cost so much anywhere as they did in hotels, and as for the prices those dining-cars charged—it was robbery—sheer robbery! And why an able-bodied man should be given ten cents every time he handed you your own hat, she couldn't understand.

At Hillerton, Mr. Smith passed a very quiet summer, but a very contented one. He kept enough work ahead to amuse him, but never enough to drive him. He took frequent day-trips to the surrounding towns, and when possible he persuaded Miss Maggie to go with him. Miss Maggie was wonderfully good company. As the summer advanced, however, he did not see so much of her as he wanted to, for Father Duff's increasing infirmities made more and more demands on her time.

The Martin girls were still there. Annabelle was learning the milliner's trade, and Florence had taken a clerkship for afternoons during the summer. They still helped about the work, and relieved Miss Maggie whenever possible. They were sensible, jolly girls, and Mr. Smith liked them very much.

CHAPTER XVI
THE FLY IN THE OINTMENT

In August Father Duff died. Miss Flora came home at once. James Blaisdell was already in town. Hattie was at the mountains. She wrote that she could not think of coming down for the funeral, but she ordered an expensive wreath. Frank and Jane were in the Far West, and could not possibly have arrived in time, anyway. None of the young people came.

Mr. Smith helped in every way that he could help, and Miss Maggie told him that he was a great comfort, and that she did not know what she would have done without him. Miss Flora and Mr. James Blaisdell helped, too, in every way possible, and at last the first hard sad days were over, and the household had settled back into something like normal conditions again.

Miss Maggie had more time now, and she went often to drive or for motor rides with Mr. Smith. Together they explored cemeteries for miles around; and although Miss Maggie worried sometimes because they found so little Blaisdell data, Mr. Smith did not seem to mind it at all.

In September Miss Flora moved into an attractive house on the West Side, bought some new furniture, and installed a maid in the kitchen—all under Miss Maggie's kindly supervision. In September, too, Frank and Jane Blaisdell came home, and the young people began to prepare for the coming school year.

Mr. Smith met Mrs. Hattie one day, coming out of Miss Maggie's gate. She smiled and greeted him cordially, but she looked so palpably upset over something that he exclaimed to Miss Maggie, as soon he entered the house: "What was it? *Is* anything the matter with Mrs. James Blaisdell?"

Miss Maggie smiled—but she frowned, too.

"No, oh, no—except that Hattie has discovered that a hundred thousand dollars isn't a million."

"What do you mean by that?"

"Oh, where she's been this summer she's measured up, of course, with people a great deal richer than she. And she doesn't like it. Here in Hillerton her hundred—and two-hundred-dollar dresses looked very grand to her, but she's discovered that there are women who pay five hundred and a thousand, and even more. She feels very cheap and poverty-stricken now, therefore, in her two-hundred-dollar gowns. Poor Hattie! If she only would stop trying to live like somebody else!"

"But I thought—I thought this money was making them happy," stammered Mr. Smith.

"It was—until she realized that somebody else had more," sighed Miss Maggie, with a shake of her head.

"Oh, well, she'll get over that."

"Perhaps."

"At any rate, it's brought her husband some comfort."

"Y-yes, it has; but—"

"What do you mean by that?" he demanded, when she did not finish her sentence.

"I was wondering—if it would bring him any more."

"They haven't lost it?"

"Oh, no, but they've spent a lot—and Hattie is beginning again her old talk that she *must* have more money in order to live 'even decent.' It sounds very familiar to me, and to Jim, I suspect, poor fellow. I saw him the other night, and from what he said, and what she says, I can see pretty well how things are going. She's trying to get some of her rich friends to give Jim a better position, where he'll earn more. She doesn't understand, either, why Jim can't go into the stock market and make millions, as some men do. I'm afraid she isn't always—patient. She says there are Fred and Elizabeth and Benjamin to educate, and that she's just got to have more money to tide them over till the rest of the legacy comes."

"The rest of the legacy!" exploded Mr. Smith. "Good Heavens, does that woman think that—" Mr. Smith stopped with the air of one pulling himself back from an abyss.

Miss Maggie laughed.

"I don't wonder you exclaim. It is funny—the way she takes that for granted, isn't it? Still, there are grounds for it, of course."

"Oh, are there? Do *you* think—she'll get more, then?" demanded Mr. Smith, almost savagely.

Miss Maggie laughed again.

"I don't know what to think. To my mind the whole thing was rather extraordinary, anyway, that he should have given them anything—utter strangers as they were. Still, as Hattie says, as long as he *has* recognized their existence, why, he may again of course. Still, on the other hand, he may have very reasonably argued that, having willed them a hundred thousand apiece, that was quite enough, and he'd give the rest somewhere else."

"Humph! Maybe," grunted Mr. Smith.

"And he may come back alive from South America"

"He may."

"But Hattie isn't counting on either of these contingencies, and she is counting on the money," sighed Miss Maggie, sobering again. "And Jim,— poor Jim!—I'm afraid he's going to find it just as hard to keep caught up now—as he used to."

"Humph!" Mr. Smith frowned. He did not speak again. He stood looking out of the window, apparently in deep thought.

Miss Maggie, with another sigh, turned and went out into the kitchen.

The next day, on the street, Mr. Smith met Mellicent Blaisdell. She was with a tall, manly-looking, square-jawed young fellow whom Mr. Smith had never seen before. Mellicent smiled and blushed adorably. Then, to his surprise, she stopped him with a gesture.

"Mr. Smith, I know it's on the street, but I—I want Mr. Gray to meet you, and I want you to meet Mr. Gray. Mr. Smith is—is a very good friend of mine, Donald."

Mr. Smith greeted Donald Gray with a warm handshake and a keen glance into his face. The blush, the hesitation, the shy happiness in Mellicent's eyes had been unmistakable. Mr. Smith felt suddenly that Donald Gray was a man he very much wanted to know—a good deal about. He chatted affably for a minute. Then he went home and straight to Miss Maggie.

"Who's Donald Gray, please?" he demanded.

Miss Maggie laughed and threw up her hands.

"Oh, these children!" "But who is he?"

"Well, to begin with, he's devoted to Mellicent."

"You don't have to tell me that. I've seen him—and Mellicent."

"Oh!" Miss Maggie smiled appreciatively.

"What I want to know is, who is he?"

"He's a young man whom Mellicent met this summer. He plays the violin, and Mellicent played his accompaniments in a church entertainment. That's where she met him first. He's the son of a minister near their camp, where the girls went to church. He's a fine fellow, I guess. He's hard hit—that's sure. He came to Hillerton at once, and has gone to work in Hammond's real estate office. So you see he's in earnest."

"I should say he was! I liked his appearance very much."

"Yes, I did—but her mother doesn't."

"What do you mean? She—objects?"

"Decidedly! She says he's worse than Carl Pennock—that he hasn't got any money, not *any* money."

"Money!" ejaculated Mr. Smith, in genuine amazement. "You don't mean that she's really letting money stand in the way if Mellicent cares for him? Why, it was only a year ago that she herself was bitterly censuring Mrs. Pennock for doing exactly the same thing in the case of young Pennock and Mellicent."

"I know," nodded Miss Maggie. "But—she seems to have forgotten that."

"Shoe's on the other foot this time."

"It seems to be."

"Hm-m!" muttered Mr. Smith.

"I don't think Jane has done much yet, by way of opposition. You see they've only reached home, and she's just found out about it. But she told me she shouldn't let it go on, not for a moment. She has other plans for Mellicent."

"Shall I be—meddling in what isn't my business, if I ask what they are?" queried Mr. Smith diffidently. "You know I am very much interested in—Miss Mellicent."

"Not a bit. I'm glad to have you. Perhaps you can suggest—a way out for us," sighed Miss Maggie. "The case is just this: Jane wants Mellicent to marry Hibbard Gaylord."

"Shucks! I've seen young Gray only once, but I'd give more for his little finger than I would for a cartload of Gaylords!" flung out Mr. Smith.

"So would I," approved Miss Maggie. "But Jane—well, Jane feels otherwise. To begin with, she's very much flattered at Gaylord's attentions to Mellicent—the more so because he's left Bessie—I beg her pardon, 'Elizabeth'—for her."

"Then Miss Elizabeth is in it, too?"

"Very much in it. That's one of the reasons why Hattie is so anxious for more money. She wants clothes and jewels for Bessie so she can keep pace with the Gaylords. You see there's a wheel within a wheel here."

"I should say there was!"

"As near as I can judge, young Gaylord is Bessie's devoted slave—until Mellicent arrives; then he has eyes only for *her*, which piques Bessie and her mother not a little. They were together more or less all summer and I think Hattie thought the match was as good as made. Now, once in Hillerton, back he flies to Mellicent."

"And—Mellicent?"

Miss Maggie's eyes became gravely troubled.

"I don't understand Mellicent. I think—no, I *know* she cares for young Gray; but—well, I might as well admit it, she is ready any time to flirt outrageously with Hibbard Gaylord, or—or with anybody else, for that matter. I saw her flirting with you at the party last Christmas!" Miss Maggie's face showed a sudden pink blush.

Mr. Smith gave a hearty laugh.

"Don't you worry, Miss Maggie. If she'll flirt with young Gaylord *and others*, it's all right. There's safety in numbers, you know."

"But I don't like to have her flirt at all, Mr. Smith."

"It isn't flirting. It's just her bottled-up childhood and youth bubbling over. She can't help bubbling, she's been repressed so long. She'll come out all right, and she won't come out hand in hand with Hibbard Gaylord. You see if she does."

Miss Maggie shook her head and sighed. "You don't know Jane. Jane will never give up. She'll be quiet, but she'll be firm. With one hand she'll keep Gray away, and with the other she'll push Gaylord forward. Even Mellicent herself won't know how it's done. But it'll be done, and I tremble for the consequences."

"Hm-m!" Mr. Smith's eyes had lost their twinkle now. To himself he muttered: "I wonder if maybe—I hadn't better take a hand in this thing myself."

"You said—I didn't understand what you said," murmured Miss Maggie doubtfully.

"Nothing—nothing, Miss Maggie," replied the man. Then, with businesslike alertness, he lifted his chin. "How long do you say this has been going on?"

"Why, especially since they all came home two weeks ago. Jane knew nothing of Donald Gray till then."

"Where does Carl Pennock come in?"

Miss Maggie gave a gesture of despair.

"Oh, he comes in anywhere that he can find a chance; though, to do her justice, Mellicent doesn't give him—many chances."

"What does her father say to all this? How does he like young Gray?"

Miss Maggie gave another gesture of despair.

"He says nothing—or, rather, he laughs, and says: 'Oh, well, it will come out all right in time. Young folks will be young folks!'"

"But does he like Gray? He knows him, of course."

"Oh, yes, he likes him. He's taken him to ride in his car once, to my knowledge."

"His car! Then Mr. Frank Blaisdell has—a car?"

"Oh, yes, he's just been learning to run it. Jane says he's crazy over it, and that he's teasing her to go all the time. She says he wants to be on the move somewhere every minute. He's taken up golf, too. Did you know that?"

"Well, no, I—didn't."

"Oh yes, he's joined the Hillerton Country Club, and he goes up to the links every morning for practice."

"I can't imagine it—Frank Blaisdell spending his mornings playing golf!"

"You forget," smiled Miss Maggie. "Frank Blaisdell is a retired business man. He has begun to take some pleasure in life now."

"Humph!" muttered Mr. Smith, as he turned to go into his own room.

Mr. Smith called on the Frank Blaisdells that evening. Mr. Blaisdell took him out to the garage (very lately a barn), and showed him the shining new car. He also showed him his lavish supply of golf clubs, and told him what a "bully time" he was having these days. He told him, too, all about his Western trip, and said there was nothing like travel to broaden a man's outlook. He said a great deal about how glad he was to get out of the old grind behind the counter—but in the next breath he asked Mr. Smith if he had ever seen a store run down as his had done since he left it. Donovan didn't know any more than a cat how such a store should be run, he said.

When they came back from the garage they found callers in the living-room. Carl Pennock and Hibbard Gaylord were chatting with Mellicent. Almost at once the doorbell rang, too, and Donald Gray came in with his violin and a roll of music. Mellicent's mother came in also. She greeted all the young men pleasantly, and asked Carl Pennock to tell Mr. Smith all about his fishing trip. Then she sat down by young Gray and asked him many questions about his music. She was *so* interested in violins, she said.

Gray waxed eloquent, and seemed wonderfully pleased—for about five minutes; then Mr. Smith saw that his glance was shifting more and more frequently and more and more unhappily to Mellicent and Hibbard Gaylord, talking tennis across the room.

Mr. Smith apparently lost interest in young Pennock's fish story then. At all events, another minute found him eagerly echoing Mrs. Blaisdell's interest in violins—but with this difference: violins in the abstract with her became A violin in the concrete with him; and he must hear it at once.

Mrs. Jane herself could not have told exactly how it was done, but she knew that two minutes later young Gray and Mellicent were at the piano, he, shining-eyed and happy, drawing a tentative bow across the strings: she, no less shining-eyed and happy, giving him "A" on the piano.

Mr. Smith enjoyed the music very much—so much that he begged for another selection and yet another. Mr. Smith did not appear to realize that Messrs. Pennock and Gaylord were passing through sham interest and frank boredom to disgusted silence. Equally oblivious was he of Mrs. Jane's efforts to substitute some other form of entertainment for the violin-playing. He shook hands very heartily, however, with Pennock and Gaylord when they took their somewhat haughty departure, a little later, and, strange to say, his interest in the music seemed to go with their going; for at once then he turned to Mr. and Mrs. Frank Blaisdell with a very animated account of some Blaisdell data he had found only the week before.

He did not appear to notice that the music of the piano had become nothing but soft fitful snatches with a great deal of low talk and laughter between. He seemed interested only that Mr. Blaisdell, and especially Mrs. Blaisdell, should know the intimate history of one Ephraim Blaisdell, born in 1720, and his ten children and forty-nine grandchildren. He talked of various investments then, and of the weather. He talked of the Blaisdells' trip, and of the cost of railroad fares and hotel life. He talked—indeed, Mrs. Jane told her husband after he left that Mr. Smith had talked of everything under the sun, and that she nearly had a fit because she could not get one minute to herself to break in upon Mellicent and that horrid Gray fellow at the piano. She had not supposed Mr. Smith could talk like that. She had never remembered he was such a talker!

The young people had a tennis match on the school tennis court the next day. Mr. Smith told Miss Maggie that he thought he would drop around there. He said he liked very much to watch tennis games.

Miss Maggie said yes, that she liked to watch tennis games, too. If this was just a wee bit of a hint, it quite failed of its purpose, for Mr. Smith did not offer to take her with him. He changed the subject, indeed, so abruptly, that Miss Maggie bit her lip and flushed a little, throwing a swift glance into his apparently serene countenance.

Miss Maggie herself, in the afternoon, with an errand for an excuse, walked slowly by the tennis court. She saw Mr. Smith at once—but he did not seem at all interested in the playing. He had his back to the court, in fact. He was talking very animatedly with Mellicent Blaisdell. He was still talking with her—though on the opposite side of the court—when Miss Maggie went by again on her way home.

Miss Maggie frowned and said something just under her breath about "that child—flirting as usual!" Then she went on, walking very fast, and without another glance toward the tennis ground. But a little farther on Miss Maggie's step lagged perceptibly, and her head lost its proud poise. Miss Maggie, for a reason she could not have explained herself, was feeling suddenly old, and weary, and very much alone.

To the image in the mirror as she took off her hat a few minutes later in her own hall, she said scornfully:

"Well, why shouldn't you feel old? You are old. *You are old!*" Miss Maggie had a habit of talking to herself in the mirror—but never before had she said anything like this to herself.

An hour later Mr. Smith came home to supper.

"Well, how did the game go?" queried Miss Maggie, without looking up from the stocking she was mending.

"Game? Go? Oh! Why, I don't remember who did win finally," he answered. Nor did it apparently occur to him that for one who was so greatly interested in tennis, he was curiously uninformed.

It did occur to Miss Maggie, however.

The next day Mr. Smith left the house soon after breakfast, and, contrary to his usual custom, did not mention where he was going. Miss Maggie was surprised and displeased. More especially was she displeased because she *was* displeased. As if it mattered to her where he went, she told herself scornfully.

The next day and the next it was much the same. On the third day she saw Jane.

"Where's Mr. Smith?" demanded Jane, without preamble, glancing at the vacant chair by the table in the corner.

Miss Maggie, to her disgust, could feel the color burning in her cheeks; but she managed to smile as if amused.

"I don't know, I'm sure. I'm not Mr. Smith's keeper, Jane."

"Well, if you were I should ask you to keep him away from Mellicent," retorted Mrs. Jane tartly.

"What do you mean?"

"I mean he's been hanging around Mellicent almost every day for a week."

Miss Maggie flushed painfully.

"Nonsense, Jane! He's more than twice her age. Mr. Smith is fifty if he's a day."

"I'm not saying he isn't," sniffed Jane, her nose uptilted. "But I do say, 'No fool like an old fool'!"

"Nonsense!" scorned Miss Maggie again. "Mr. Smith has always been fond of Mellicent, and—and interested in her. But I don't believe he cares for her—that way."

"Then why does he come to see her and take her auto-riding, and hang around her every minute he gets a chance?" snapped Jane. "I know how he acts at the house, and I hear he scarcely left her side at the tennis match the other day."

"Yes, I—" Miss Maggie did not finish her sentence. A slow change came to her countenance. The flush receded, leaving her face a bit white.

"I wonder if the man really thinks he stands any chance," spluttered Jane, ignoring Miss Maggie's unfinished sentence. "Why, he's worse than that Donald Gray. He not only hasn't got the money, but he's old, as well."

"Yes, we're all—getting old, Jane." Miss Maggie tossed the words off lightly, and smiled as she uttered them. But after Mrs. Jane had gone, she went to the little mirror above the mantel and gazed at herself long and fixedly.

"Well, what if he does? It's nothing to you, Maggie Duff!" she muttered under her breath. Then resolutely she turned away, picked up her work, and fell to sewing very fast.

Two days later Mellicent went back to school. Bessie went, too. Fred and Benny had already gone. To Miss Maggie things seemed to settle back into their old ways again then. With Mr. Smith she took drives and motor-rides, enjoying the crisp October air and the dancing sunlight on the reds and browns and yellows of the autumnal foliage. True, she used to wonder sometimes if the end always justified the means—it seemed an expensive business to hire an automobile to take them fifty miles and back, and all to verify a single date. And she could not help noticing that Mr. Smith appeared to have many dates that needed verifying—dates that were located in very diverse parts of the surrounding country. Miss Maggie also could not help noticing that Mr. Smith was getting very little new material for his Blaisdell book these days, though he still worked industriously over the old, re-tabulating, and recopying. She knew this, because she helped him do it—though she was careful to let him know that she recognized the names and dates as old acquaintances.

To tell the truth, Miss Maggie did not like to admit, even to herself, that Mr. Smith must be nearing the end of his task. She did not like to think of the house—after Mr. Smith should have gone. She told herself that he was just the sort of homey boarder that she liked, and she wished she might keep him indefinitely.

She thought so all the more when the long evenings of November brought a new pleasure; Mr. Smith fell into the way of bringing home books to read aloud; and she enjoyed that very much. They had long talks, too, over the books they read. In one there was an old man who fell in love with a young girl, and married her. Miss Maggie, as certain parts of this story were read, held her breath, and stole furtive glances into Mr. Smith's face. When it was finished she contrived to question with careful casualness, as to his opinion of such a marriage.

Mr. Smith's answer was prompt and unequivocal. He said he did not believe that such a marriage should take place, nor did he believe that in real life, it would result in happiness. Marriage should be between persons of similar age, tastes, and habits, he said very decidedly. And Miss Maggie blushed and said yes, yes, indeed! And that night, when Miss Maggie gazed at herself in the glass, she looked so happy—that she appeared to be almost as young as Mellicent herself!

CHAPTER XVII
AN AMBASSADOR OF CUPID'S

Christmas again brought all the young people home for the holidays. It brought, also, a Christmas party at James Blaisdell's home. It was a very different party, however, from the housewarming of a year before.

To begin with, the attendance was much smaller; Mrs. Hattie had been very exclusive in her invitations this time. She had not invited "everybody who ever went anywhere." There were champagne, and cigarettes for the ladies, too.

As before, Mr. Smith and Miss Maggie went together. Miss Maggie, who had not attended any social gathering since Father Duff died, yielded to Mr. Smith's urgings and said that she would go to this. But Miss Maggie wished afterward that she had not gone—there were so many, many features about that party that Miss Maggie did not like.

She did not like the champagne nor the cigarettes. She did not like Bessie's showy, low-cut dress, nor her supercilious airs. She did not like the look in Fred's eyes, nor the way he drank the champagne. She did not like Jane's maneuvers to bring Mellicent and Hibbard Gaylord into each other's company—nor the way Mr. Smith maneuvered to get Mellicent for himself.

Of all these, except the very last, Miss Maggie talked with Mr. Smith on the way home—yet it was the very last that was uppermost in her mind, except perhaps, Fred. She did speak of Fred; but because that, too, was so much to her, she waited until the last before she spoke of it.

"You saw Fred, of course," she began then.

"Yes." Short as the word was, it carried a volume of meaning to Miss Maggie's fearful ears. She turned to him quickly.

"Mr. Smith, it—it isn't true, is it?"

"I'm afraid it is."

"You saw him—drinking, then?"

"Yes. I saw some, and I heard—more. It's just as I feared. He's got in with Gaylord and the rest of his set at college, and they're a bad lot—drinking, gambling—no good."

"But Fred wouldn't—gamble, Mr. Smith! Oh, Fred wouldn't do that. And he's so ambitious to get ahead! Surely he'd know he couldn't get anywhere in his studies, if—if he drank and gambled!"

"It would seem so."

"Did you see his father? I saw him only a minute at the first, and he didn't look well a bit, to me."

"Yes, I saw him. I found him in his den just as I did last year. He didn't look well to me, either."

"Did he say anything about—Fred?"

"Not a word—and that's what worries me the most. Last year he talked a lot about him, and was so proud and happy in his coming success. This time he never mentioned him; but he looked—bad."

"What did he talk about?"

"Oh, books, business:—nothing in particular. And he wasn't interested in what he did say. He was very different from last year."

"Yes, I know. He is different," sighed Maggie. "He's talked with me quite a lot about—about the way they're living. He doesn't like—so much fuss and show and society."

Mr. Smith frowned.

"But I thought—Mrs. Hattie would get over all that by this time, after the newness of the money was worn off."

"I hoped she would. But—she doesn't. It's worse, if anything," sighed Miss Maggie, as they ascended the steps at her own door.

Mr. Smith frowned again.

"And Miss Bessie—" he began disapprovingly, then stopped. "Now, Miss Mellicent—" he resumed, in a very different voice.

But Miss Maggie was not apparently listening. With a rather loud rattling of the doorknob she was pushing open the door.

"Why, how hot it is! Did I leave that damper open?" she cried, hurrying into the living-room.

And Mr. Smith, hurrying after, evidently forgot to finish his sentence.

Miss Maggie did not attend any more of the merrymakings of that holiday week. But Mr. Smith did. It seemed to Miss Maggie, indeed, that Mr. Smith was away nearly every minute of that long week—and it *was* a long week to Miss Maggie. Even the Martin girls were away many of the evenings. Miss Maggie told herself that that was why the house seemed so lonesome.

But though Miss Maggie did not participate in the gay doings, she heard of them. She heard of them on all sides, except from Mr. Smith—and on all sides she heard of the devotion of Mr. Smith to Miss Mellicent. She concluded that this was the reason why Mr. Smith himself was so silent.

Miss Maggie was shocked and distressed. She was also very much puzzled. She had supposed that Mr. Smith understood that Mellicent and young Gray cared for each other, and she had thought that Mr. Smith even approved of the affair between them. Now to push himself on the scene in this absurd fashion and try "to cut everybody out," as it was vulgarly termed—she never would have believed it of Mr. Smith in the world. And she was disappointed, too. She liked Mr. Smith very much. She had considered him to be a man of good sense and good judgment. And had he not himself said, not so long ago, that he believed lovers should be of the same age, tastes, and habits? And yet, here now he was—

And there could be no mistake about it. Everybody was saying the same thing. The Martin girls brought it home as current gossip. Jane was highly exercised over it, and even Harriet had exclaimed over the "shameful flirtation Mellicent was carrying on with that man old enough to be her father!" No, there was no mistake. Besides, did she not see with her own eyes that Mr. Smith was gone every day and evening, and that, when he was at home at meal time, he was silent and preoccupied, and not like himself at all?

And it was such a pity—she had thought so much of Mr. Smith! It really made her feel quite ill.

And Miss Maggie looked ill on the last evening of that holiday week when, at nine o'clock, Mr. Smith found her sitting idle-handed before the stove in the living-room.

"Why, Miss Maggie, what's the matter with you?" cried the man, in very evident concern. "You don't look like yourself to-night!"

Miss Maggie pulled herself up hastily.

"Nonsense! I—I'm perfectly well. I'm just—tired, I guess. You're home early, Mr. Smith." In spite of herself Miss Maggie's voice carried a tinge of something not quite pleasant.

Mr. Smith, however, did not appear to notice it.

"Yes, I'm home early for once, thank Heaven!" he half groaned, as he dropped himself into a chair.

"It has been a strenuous week for you, hasn't it?" Again the tinge of something not quite pleasant in Miss Maggie's voice.

"Yes, but it's been worth it."

"Of course!"

Mr. Smith turned deliberately and looked at Miss Maggie. There was a vague questioning in his eyes. Obtaining, apparently, however, no satisfactory answer from Miss Maggie's placid countenance, he turned away and began speaking again.

"Well, anyway, I've accomplished what I set out to do."

"You-you've *already* accomplished it?" faltered Miss Maggie. She was gazing at him now with startled, half-frightened eyes.

"Yes. Why, Miss Maggie, what's the matter? What makes you look so—so queer?"

"Queer? Nonsense! Why, nothing—nothing at all," laughed Miss Maggie nervously, but very gayly. "I may have been a little—surprised, for a moment; but I'm very glad—very."

"Glad?"

"Why, yes, for—for you. Isn't one always glad when—when a love affair is—is all settled?"

"Oh, then you suspected it." Mr. Smith smiled pleasantly, but without embarrassment. "It doesn't matter, of course, only—well, I had hoped it wasn't too conspicuous."

"Oh, but you couldn't expect to hide a thing like that, Mr. Smith," retorted Miss Maggie, with what was very evidently intended for an arch smile. "I heard it everywhere—everywhere."

"The mischief you did!" frowned Mr. Smith, looking slightly annoyed. "Well, I suppose I couldn't expect to keep a thing like that entirely in the dark. Still, I don't believe the parties themselves—quite understood. Of course, Pennock and Gaylord knew that they were kept effectually away, but I don't believe they realized just how systematically it was done. Of course, Gray understood from the first."

"Poor Mr. Gray! I—I can't help being sorry for him."

"*Sorry* for him!"

"Certainly; and I should think *you* might give him a little sympathy," rejoined Miss Maggie spiritedly. "You *know* how much he cared for Mellicent."

Mr. Smith sat suddenly erect in his chair.

"Cared for her! Sympathy! Why, what in the world are you talking about? Wasn't I doing the best I could for them all the time? Of *course*, it kept *him* away from her, too, just as it did Pennock and Gaylord; but *he* understood. Besides, he *had* her part of the time. I let him in whenever it was possible."

"Let him in!" Miss Maggie was sitting erect now. "Whatever in the world are *you* talking about? Do you mean to say you were doing this *for* Mr. Gray, all the time?"

"Why, of course! Whom else should I do it for? You didn't suppose it was for Pennock or Gaylord, did you? Nor for—" He stopped short and stared at Miss Maggie in growing amazement and dismay. "You didn't— you *didn't* think—I was doing that—for *myself?*"

"Well, of course, I—I—" Miss Maggie was laughing and blushing painfully, but there was a new light in her eyes. "Well, anyway, everybody said you were!" she defended herself stoutly.

"Oh, good Heavens!" Mr. Smith leaped to his feet and thrust his hands into his pockets, as he took a nervous turn about the room. "For myself, indeed! as if, in my position, I'd—How perfectly absurd!" He wheeled and faced her irritably. "And you believed that? Why, I'm not a marrying man. I don't like—I never saw the woman yet that I—" With his eyes on Miss Maggie's flushed, half-averted face, he stopped again abruptly. "Well, I'll be—" Even under his breath he did not finish his sentence; but, with a new, quite different expression on his face, he resumed his nervous pacing of the room, throwing now and then a quick glance at Miss Maggie's still averted face.

"It *was* absurd, of course, wasn't it?" Miss Maggie stirred and spoke lightly, with the obvious intention of putting matters back into usual conditions again. "But, come, tell me, just what did you do, and how? I'm so interested—indeed, I am!"

"Eh? What?" Mr. Smith spoke as if he was thinking of something else entirely. "Oh—*that.*" Mr. Smith sat down, but he did not go on speaking at once. His eyes frowningly regarded the stove.

"You said—you kept Pennock and Gaylord away," Miss Maggie hopefully reminded him.

"Er—yes. Oh, I—it was really very simple—I just monopolized Mellicent myself, when I couldn't let Donald have her. That's all. I saw very soon that she couldn't cope with her mother alone. And Gaylord—well, I've no use for that young gentleman."

"But you like—Donald?"

"Very much. I've been looking him up for some time. He's all right."

"I'm glad."

"Yes." Mr. Smith spoke abstractedly, without enthusiasm. Plainly Mr. Smith was still thinking of something else.

Miss Maggie asked other questions—Miss Maggie was manifestly interested—and Mr. Smith answered them, but still without enthusiasm. Very soon he said good-night and went to his own room.

For some days after this, Mr. Smith did not appear at all like himself. He seemed abstracted and puzzled. Miss Maggie, who still felt self-conscious and embarrassed over her misconception of his attentions to Mellicent, was more talkative than usual in her nervous attempt to appear perfectly natural. The fact that she often found his eyes fixed thoughtfully upon her, and felt them following her as she moved about the room, did not tend to make her more at ease. At such times she talked faster than ever—usually, if possible, about some member of the Blaisdell family: Miss Maggie had learned that Mr. Smith was always interested in any bit of news about the Blaisdells.

It was on such an occasion that she told him about Miss Flora and the new house.

"I don't know, really, what I am going to do with her," she said. "I wonder if perhaps you could help me."

"Help you?—about Miss Flora?"

"Yes. Can you think of any way to make her contented?"

"*Contented!* Why, I thought—Don't tell me *she* isn't happy!" There was a curious note of almost despair in Mr. Smith's voice. "Hasn't she a new house, and everything nice to go with it?"

Miss Maggie laughed. Then she sighed.

"Oh, yes—and that's what's the trouble. They're *too* nice. She feels smothered and oppressed—as if she were visiting somewhere, and not at home. She's actually afraid of her maid. You see, Miss Flora has always lived very simply. She isn't used to maids—and the maid knows it, which, if you ever employed maids, you would know is a terrible state of affairs."

"Oh, but she—she'll get used to that, in time." "Perhaps," conceded Miss Maggie, "but I doubt it. Some women would, but not Miss Flora. She is too inherently simple in her tastes. 'Why, it's as bad as always living in a hotel!' she wailed to me last night. 'You know on my trip I was so afraid always I'd do something that wasn't quite right, before those awful waiters in the dining-rooms, and I was anticipating so much getting home where I could act natural—and here I've got one in my own house!'"

Mr. Smith frowned, but he laughed, too.

"Poor Miss Flora! But why doesn't she dismiss the lady?"

"She doesn't dare to. Besides, there's Hattie. She says Hattie is always telling her what is due her position, and that she must do this and do that. She's being invited out, too, to the Pennocks' and the Bensons'; and they're worse than the maid, she declares. She says she loves to 'run in' and see people, and she loves to go to places and spend the day with her sewing; but that these things where you go and stand up and eat off a jiggly plate, and see everybody, and not really see *anybody*, are a nuisance and an abomination."

"Well, she's about right there," chuckled Mr. Smith.

"Yes, I think she is," smiled Miss Maggie; "but that isn't telling me how to make her contented."

"Contented! Great Scott!" snapped Mr. Smith, with an irritability that was as sudden as it was apparently causeless. "I didn't suppose you had to tell any woman on this earth how to be contented—with a hundred thousand dollars!"

"It would seem so, wouldn't it?"

Something in Miss Maggie's voice sent Mr. Smith's eyes to her face in a keen glance of interrogation.

"You mean—you'd like the chance to prove it? That you wish *you* had that hundred thousand?"

"Oh, I didn't say—that," twinkled Miss Maggie mischievously, turning away.

It was that same afternoon that Mr. Smith met Mrs. Jane Blaisdell on the street.

"You're just the man I want to see," she accosted him eagerly.

"Then I'll turn and walk along with you, if I may," smiled Mr. Smith. "What can I do for you?"

"Well, I don't know as you can do anything," she sighed; "but somebody's got to do something. Could you—*do* you suppose you could interest my husband in this Blaisdell business of yours?"

Mr. Smith gave a start, looking curiously disconcerted.

"B-Blaisdell business?" he stammered. "Why, I—I thought he was—er—interested in motoring and golf."

"Oh, he was, for a time; but it's too cold for those now, and he got sick of them, anyway, before it did come cold, just as he does of everything. Well, yesterday he asked a question—something about Father Blaisdell's mother; and that gave me the idea. *Do* you suppose you could get him interested in this ancestor business? Oh, I wish you could! It's so nice and quiet, and it *can't* cost much—not like golf clubs and caddies and gasoline, anyway. Do you think you could?"

"Why, I—I don't know, Mrs. Blaisdell," murmured Mr. Smith, still a little worriedly. "I—I could show him what I have found, of course."

"Well, I wish you would, then. Anyway, *something's* got to be done," she sighed. "He's nervous as a witch. He can't keep still a minute. And he isn't a bit well, either. He ate such a lot of rich food and all sorts of stuff on our trip that he got his stomach all out of order; and now he can't eat anything, hardly."

"Humph! Well, if his stomach's knocked out I pity him," nodded Mr. Smith. "I've been there."

"Oh, have you? Oh, yes, I remember. You did say so when you first came, didn't you? But, Mr. Smith *please*, if you know any of those health fads, don't tell them to my husband. Don't, I beg of you! He's tried dozens of them until I'm nearly wild, and I've lost two hired girls already. One day it'll be no water, and the next it'll be all he can drink; and one week he won't eat anything but vegetables, and the next he won't touch a thing but meat and—is it fruit that goes with meat or cereals? Well, never mind. Whatever it is, he's done it. And lately he's taken to inspecting every bit of meat and groceries that comes into the house. Why, he spends half his time in the kitchen, nosing 'round the cupboards and refrigerator; and, of course, *no* girl will stand that! That's why I'm hoping, oh, I *am* hoping that you can do *something* with him on that ancestor business. There, here is the Bensons', where I've got to stop—and thank you ever so much, Mr. Smith, if you will."

"All right, I'll try," promised Mr. Smith dubiously, as he lifted his hat. But he frowned, and he was still frowning when he met Miss Maggie at the Duff supper-table half an hour later.

"Well, I've found another one who wants me to tell how to be contented, though afflicted with a hundred thousand dollars," he greeted her gloweringly.

"Is that so?" smiled Miss Maggie.

"Yes.—*can't* a hundred thousand dollars bring any one satisfaction?"

Miss Maggie laughed, then into her eyes came the mischievous twinkle that Mr. Smith had learned to watch for.

"Don't blame the poor money," she said then demurely. "Blame—the way it is spent!"

CHAPTER XVIII
JUST A MATTER OF BEGGING

True to his promise, Mr. Smith "tried" Mr. Frank Blaisdell on "the ancestor business" very soon. Laboriously he got out his tabulated dates and names and carefully he traced for him several lines of descent from remote ancestors. Painstakingly he pointed out a "Submit," who had no history but the bare fact of her marriage to one Thomas Blaisdell, and a "Thankful Marsh," who had eluded his every attempt to supply her with parents. He let it be understood how important these missing links were, and he tried to inspire his possible pupil with a frenzied desire to go out and dig them up. He showed some of the interesting letters he had received from various Blaisdells far and near, and he spread before him the genealogical page of his latest "Transcript," and explained how one might there stumble upon the very missing link he was looking for.

But Mr. Frank Blaisdell was openly bored. He said he didn't care how many children his great-grandfather had, nor what they died of; and as for Mrs. Submit and Miss Thankful, the ladies might bury themselves in the "Transcript," or hide behind that wall of dates and names till doomsday, for all he cared. *He* shouldn't disturb 'em. He never did like figures, he said, except figures that represented something worth while, like a day's sales or a year's profits.

And speaking of grocery stores, had Mr. Smith ever seen a store run down as his old one had since he sold out? For that matter, something must have got into all the grocery stores; for a poorer lot of goods than those delivered every day at his home he never saw. It was a disgrace to the trade.

He said a good deal more about his grocery store—but nothing whatever more about his Blaisdell ancestors; so Mr. Smith felt justified in considering his efforts to interest Mr. Frank Blaisdell in the ancestor business a failure. Certainly he never tried it again.

It was in February that a certain metropolitan reporter, short for feature articles, ran up to Hillerton and contributed to his paper, the following Sunday, a write-up on "The Blaisdells One Year After," enlarging on the fine new homes, the motor cars, and the luxurious living of the three families.

And it was three days after this article was printed that Miss Flora appeared at Miss Maggie's, breathless with excitement.

"Just see what I've got in the mail this morning!" she cried to Miss Maggie, and to Mr. Smith, who had opened the door for her.

With trembling fingers she took from her bag a letter, and a small picture evidently cut from a newspaper.

"There, see," she panted, holding them out. "It's a man in Boston, and these are his children. There are seven of them. He wrote me a beautiful letter. He said he knew I must have a real kind heart, and he's in terrible trouble. He said he saw in the paper about the wonderful legacy I'd had, and he told his wife he was going to write to me, to see if I wouldn't help them—if only a little, it would aid them that much."

"He wants money, then?" Miss Maggie had taken the letter and the picture rather gingerly in her hands. Mr. Smith had gone over to the stove suddenly—to turn a damper, apparently, though a close observer might have noticed that he turned it back to its former position almost at once.

"Yes," palpitated Miss Flora. "He's sick, and he lost his position, and his wife's sick, and two of the children, and one of 'em's lame, and another's blind. Oh, it was such a pitiful story, Maggie! Why, some days they haven't had enough to eat—and just look at me, with all my chickens and turkeys and more pudding every day than I can stuff down!"

"Did he give you any references?"

"References! What do you mean? He didn't ask me to *hire* him for anything."

"No, no, dear, but I mean—did he give you any references, to show that he was—was worthy and all right," explained Miss Maggie patiently.

"Of course he didn't! Why, he didn't need to. He told me himself how things were with him," rebuked Miss Flora indignantly. "It's all in the letter there. Read for yourself."

"But he really ought to have given you *some* reference, dear, if he asked you for money."

"Well, I don't want any reference. I believe him. I'd be ashamed to doubt a man like that! And *you* would, after you read that letter, and look into those blessed children's faces. Besides, he never thought of such a thing—I know he didn't. Why, he says right in the letter there that he never asked for help before, and he was so ashamed that he had to now."

Mr. Smith made a sudden odd little noise in his throat. Perhaps he got choked. At all events, he was seized with a fit of coughing just then.

Miss Maggie turned over the letter in her hand.

"Where does he tell you to send the money?"

"It's right there—Box four hundred and something; and I got a money order, just as he said."

"You *got* one! Do you mean that you've already sent this money?" cried Miss Maggie.

"Why, yes, of course. I stopped at the office on the way down here."

"And you sent—a money order?"

"Yes. He said he would rather have that than a check."

"I don't doubt it! You don't seem to have—delayed any."

"Of course I didn't delay! Why, Maggie, he said he *had* to have it at once. He was going to be turned out—*turned out* into the streets! Think of those seven little children in the streets! Wait, indeed! Why, Maggie, what can you be thinking of?"

"I'm thinking you've been the easy victim of a professional beggar, Flora," retorted Miss Maggie, with some spirit, handing back the letter and the picture.

"Why, Maggie, I never knew you to be so—so unkind," charged Miss Flora, her eyes tearful. "He can't be a professional beggar. He *said* he wasn't—that he never begged before in his life."

Miss Maggie, with a despairing gesture, averted her face.

Miss Flora turned to Mr. Smith.

"Mr. Smith, you—*you* don't think so, do you?" she pleaded.

Mr. Smith grew very red—perhaps because he had to stop to cough again.

"Well, Miss Flora, I—I'm sorry, but I'm afraid I shall have to agree with Miss Maggie here, to some extent."

"But you didn't read the letter. You don't know how beautifully he talked."

"You told me; and you say yourself that he gave you only a post-office box for an address. So you see you couldn't look him up very well."

"I don't need to!" Miss Flora threw back her head a little haughtily. "And I'm glad I don't doubt my fellow men and women as you and Maggie

Duff do! If either of you *knew* what you're talking about, I wouldn't say anything. But you don't. You *can't know* anything about this man, and you didn't ever get letters like this, either of you, of course. But, anyhow, I don't care if he ain't worthy. I wouldn't let those children suffer; and I—I'm glad I sent it. I never in my life was so happy as I was on the way here from the post-office this morning."

Without waiting for a reply, she turned away majestically; but at the door she paused and looked back at Miss Maggie.

"And let me tell you that, however good or bad this particular man may be, it's given me an idea, anyway," she choked. The haughtiness was all gone now "I know now why it hasn't seemed right to be so happy. It's because there are so many other folks in the world that *aren't* happy. Why, my chicken and turkey would choke me now if I didn't give some of it to— to all these others. And I'm going to—*I'm going to!*" she reiterated, as she fled from the room.

As the door shut crisply, Miss Maggie turned and looked at Mr. Smith. But Mr. Smith had crossed again to the stove and was fussing with the damper. Miss Maggie, after a moment's hesitation, turned and went out into the kitchen, without speaking.

Mr. Smith and Miss Maggie saw very little of Miss Flora after this for some time. But they heard a good deal about her. They heard of her generous gifts to families all over town.

A turkey was sent to every house on Mill Street, without exception, and so much candy given to the children that half of them were made ill, much to the distress of Miss Flora, who, it was said, promptly sent a physician to undo her work. The Dow family, hard-working and thrifty, and the Nolans, notorious for their laziness and shiftlessness, each received a hundred dollars outright. The Whalens, always with both hands metaphorically outstretched for alms, were loud in their praises of Miss Flora's great kindness of heart; but the Davises (Mrs. Jane Blaisdell's impecunious relatives) had very visible difficulty in making Miss Flora understand that gifts bestowed as she bestowed them were more welcome unmade.

Every day, from one quarter or another, came stories like these to the ears of Miss Maggie and Mr. Smith. But Miss Flora was seen very seldom. Then one day, about a month later, she appeared as before at the Duff cottage, breathless and agitated; only this time, plainly, she had been crying.

"Why, Flora, what in the world is the matter?" cried Miss Maggie, as she hurried her visitor into a comfortable chair and began to unfasten her wraps.

"I'll tell you in a minute. I came on purpose to tell you. But I want Mr. Smith, too. Oh, he ain't here, is he?" she lamented, with a disappointed glance toward the vacant chair by the table in the corner. "I thought maybe he could help me, some way. I won't go to Frank, or Jim. They've—they've said so many things. Oh, I did so hope Mr. Smith was here!"

"He is here, dear. He's in his room. He just came in. I'll call him," comforted Miss Maggie, taking off Miss Flora's veil and hat and smoothing back her hair. "But you don't want him to find you crying like this, Flora. What is it, dear?"

"Yes, yes, I know, but I'm not crying—I mean, I won't any more. And I'll tell you just as soon as you get Mr. Smith. It's only that I've been—so silly, I suppose. Please get Mr. Smith."

"All right, dear."

Miss Maggie, still with the disturbed frown between her eyebrows, summoned Mr. Smith. Then together they sat down to hear Miss Flora's story.

"It all started, of course, from—from that day I brought the letter here—from that man in Boston with seven children, you know."

"Yes, I remember," encouraged Miss Maggie.

"Well, I—I did quite a lot of things after that. I was so glad and happy to discover I could do things for folks. It seemed to—to take away the wickedness of my having so much, you know; and so I gave food and money, oh, lots of places here in town—everywhere, 'most, that I could find that anybody needed it."

"Yes, I know. We heard of the many kind things you did, dear." Miss Maggie had the air of one trying to soothe a grieved child.

"But they didn't turn out to be kind—all of 'em," quavered Miss Flora. "Some of 'em went wrong. I don't know why. I *tried* to do 'em all right!"

"Of course you did!"

"I know; but 'tain't those I came to talk about. It's the others—the letters."

"Letters?"

"Yes. I got 'em—lots of 'em—after the first one—the one you saw. First I got one, then another and another, till lately I've been getting 'em every day, 'most, and some days two or three at a time."

"And they all wanted—money, I suppose," observed Mr. Smith, "for their sick wives and children, I suppose."

"Oh, not for children always—though it was them a good deal. But it was for different things—and such a lot of them! I never knew there could be so many kinds of such things. And I was real pleased, at first,—that I could help, you know, in so many places."

"Then you always sent it—the money?" asked Mr. Smith.

"Oh, yes. Why, I just had to, the way they wrote; I wanted to, too. They wrote lovely letters, and real interesting ones, too. One man wanted a warm coat for his little girl, and he told me all about what hard times they'd had. Another wanted a brace for his poor little crippled boy, and *he* told me things. Why, I never s'posed folks could have such awful things, and live! One woman just wanted to borrow twenty dollars while she was so sick. She didn't ask me to give it to her. She wasn't a beggar. Don't you suppose I'd send her that money? Of course I would! And there was a poor blind man—he wanted money to buy a Bible in raised letters; and of *course* I wouldn't refuse that! Some didn't beg; they just wanted to sell things. I bought a diamond ring to help put a boy through school, and a ruby pin of a man who needed the money for bread for his children. And there was—oh, there was lots of 'em—too many to tell."

"And all from Boston, I presume," murmured Mr. Smith.

"Oh, no,—why, yes, they were, too, most of 'em, when you come to think of it. But how did you know?"

"Oh, I—guessed it. But go on. You haven't finished."

"No, I haven't finished," moaned Miss Flora, almost crying again. "And now comes the worst of it. As I said, at first I liked it—all these letters—and I was so glad to help. But they're coming so fast now I don't know what to do with 'em. And I never saw such a lot of things as they want—pensions and mortgages, and pianos, and educations, and wedding dresses, and clothes to be buried in, and—and there were so many, and—and so queer, some of 'em, that I began to be afraid maybe they weren't quite honest, all of 'em, and of course I *can't* send to such a lot as there are now, anyway, and I was getting so worried. Besides, I got another one of those awful proposals from those dreadful men that want to marry me. As if I didn't know *that* was for my money! Then to-day, this morning, I—I got the worst of all." From her bag she took an envelope and drew out a small picture of several children, cut apparently from a newspaper. "Look at that. Did you ever see that before?" she demanded.

Miss Maggie scrutinized the picture.

"Why, no,—yes, it's the one you brought us a month ago, isn't it?"

Miss Flora's eyes flashed angrily.

"Indeed, it ain't! The one I showed you before is in my bureau drawer at home. But I got it out this morning, when this one came, and compared them; and they're just exactly alike—*exactly*!"

"Oh, he wrote again, then,—wants more money, I suppose," frowned Miss Maggie.

"No, he didn't. It ain't the same man. This man's name is Haley, and that one was Fay. But Mr. Haley says this is a picture of his children, and he says that the little girl in the corner is Katy, and she's deaf and dumb; but Mr. Fay said her name was Rosie, and that she was *lame*. And all the others—their names ain't the same, either, and there ain't any of 'em blind. And, of course, I know now that—that one of those men is lying to me. Why, they cut them out of the same newspaper; they've got the same reading on the back! And I—I don't know what to believe now. And there are all those letters at home that I haven't answered yet; and they keep coming—why, I just dread to see the postman turn down our street. And one man—he wrote twice. I didn't like his first letter and didn't answer it; and now he says if I don't send him the money he'll tell everybody everywhere what a stingy t-tight-wad I am. And another man said he'd come and *take* it if I didn't send it; and you *know* how afraid of burglars I am! Oh what shall I do, what shall I do?" she begged piteously.

Mr. Smith said a sharp word behind his teeth.

"Do?" he cried then wrathfully. "First, don't you worry another bit, Miss Flora. Second, just hand those letters over to me—every one of them. I'll attend to 'em!"

"To *you*?" gasped Miss Flora. "But—how can you?"

"Oh, I'll be your secretary. Most rich people have to have secretaries, you know."

"But how'll you know how to answer *my* letters?" demanded Miss Flora dubiously. "Have you ever been—a secretary?"

"N-no, not exactly a secretary. But—I've had some experience with similar letters," observed Mr. Smith dryly.

Miss Flora drew a long sigh.

"Oh, dear! I wish you could. Do you think you can? I hoped maybe you could help me some way, but I never thought of that—your answering 'em, I mean. I supposed everybody had to answer their own letters. How'll you know what I want to say?"

Mr. Smith laughed a little.

"I shan't be answering what *you* want to say—but what _I_ want to say. In this case, Miss Flora, I exceed the prerogatives of the ordinary secretary just a bit, you see. But you can count on one thing—I shan't be spending any money for you."

"You won't send them anything, then?"

"Not a red cent."

Miss Flora looked distressed.

"But, Mr. Smith, I want to send some of 'em something! I want to be kind and charitable."

"Of course you do, dear," spoke up Miss Maggie. "But you aren't being either kind or charitable to foster rascally fakes like that," pointing to the picture in Miss Flora's lap.

"Are they *all* fakes, then?"

"I'd stake my life on most of 'em," declared Mr. Smith. "They have all the earmarks of fakes, all right."

Miss Flora stirred restlessly.

"But I was having a beautiful time giving until these horrid letters began to come."

"Flora, do you give because *you* like the sensation of giving, and of receiving thanks, or because you really want to help somebody?" asked Miss Maggie, a bit wearily.

"Why, Maggie Duff, I want to help people, of course," almost wept Miss Flora.

"Well, then, suppose you try and give so it will help them, then," said Miss Maggie. "One of the most risky things in the world, to my way of thinking, is a present of—cash. Don't you think so, Mr. Smith?"

"Er—ah—w-what? Y-yes, of course," stammered Mr. Smith, growing suddenly, for some unapparent reason, very much confused. "Yes—yes, I do." As Mr. Smith finished speaking, he threw an oddly nervous glance into Miss Maggie's face.

But Miss Maggie had turned back to Miss Flora.

"There, dear," she admonished her, "now, you do just as Mr. Smith says. Just hand over your letters to him for a while, and forget all about them. He'll tell you how he answers them, of course. But you won't have to worry about them any more. Besides they'll soon stop coming,—won't they, Mr. Smith?"

"I think they will. They'll dwindle to a few scattering ones, anyway,—after I've handled them for a while."

"Well, I should like that," sighed Miss Flora. "But—can't I give anything anywhere?" she besought plaintively.

"Of course you can!" cried Miss Maggie. "But I would investigate a little, first, dear. Wouldn't you, Mr. Smith? Don't you believe in investigation?"

Once again, before he answered, Mr. Smith threw a swiftly questioning glance into Miss Maggie's face.

"Yes, oh, yes; I believe in—investigation," he said then. "And now, Miss Flora," he added briskly, as Miss Flora reached for her wraps, "with your kind permission I'll walk home with you and have a look at—my new job of secretarying."

CHAPTER XIX
STILL OTHER FLIES

It was when his duties of secretaryship to Miss Flora had dwindled to almost infinitesimal proportions that Mr. Smith wished suddenly that he were serving Miss Maggie in that capacity, so concerned was he over a letter that had come to Miss Maggie in that morning's mail.

He himself had taken it from the letter-carrier's hand and had placed it on Miss Maggie's little desk. Casually, as he did so, he had noticed that it bore a name he recognized as that of a Boston law firm; but he had given it no further thought until later, when, as he sat at his work in the living-room, he had heard Miss Maggie give a low cry and had looked up to find her staring at the letter in her hand, her face going from red to white and back to red again.

"Why, Miss Maggie, what is it?" he cried, springing to his feet.

As she turned toward him he saw that her eyes were full of tears.

"Why, it—it's a letter telling me—" She stopped abruptly, her eyes on his face.

"Yes, yes, tell me," he begged. "Why, you are—*crying*, dear!" Mr. Smith, plainly quite unaware of the caressing word he had used, came nearer, his face aglow with sympathy, his eyes very tender.

The red surged once more over Miss Maggie's face. She drew back a little, though manifestly with embarrassment, not displeasure.

"It's—nothing, really it's nothing," she stammered. "It's just a letter that—that surprised me."

"But it made you cry!"

"Oh, well, I—I cry easily sometimes." With hands that shook visibly, she folded the letter and tucked it into its envelope. Then with a carelessness that was a little too elaborate, she tossed it into her open desk. Very plainly, whatever she had meant to do in the first place, she did not now intend to disclose to Mr. Smith the contents of that letter.

"Miss Maggie, please tell me—was it bad news?"

"Bad? Why, of course not!" She laughed gayly.

Mr. Smith thought he detected a break very like a sob in the laugh.

"But maybe I could—help you," he pleaded.

She shook her head.

"You couldn't—indeed, you couldn't!"

"Miss Maggie, was it—money matters?"

He had his answer in the telltale color that flamed instantly into her face—but her lips said:—

"It was—nothing—I mean, it was nothing that need concern you." She hurried away then to the kitchen, and Mr. Smith was left alone to fume up and down the room and frown savagely at the offending envelope tip-tilted against the ink bottle in Miss Maggie's desk, just as Miss Maggie's carefully careless hand had thrown it.

Miss Maggie had several more letters from the Boston law firm, and Mr. Smith knew it—though he never heard Miss Maggie cry out at any of the other ones. That they affected her deeply, however, he was certain. Her very evident efforts to lead him to think that they were of no consequence would convince him of their real importance to her if nothing else had done so. He watched her, therefore, covertly, fearfully, longing to help her, but not daring to offer his services.

That the affair had something to do with money matters he was sure. That she would not deny this naturally strengthened him in this belief. He came in time, therefore, to formulate his own opinion: she had lost money— perhaps a good deal (for her), and she was too proud to let him or any one else know it.

He watched then all the more carefully to see if he could detect any *new* economies or new deprivations in her daily living. Then, because he could not discover any such, he worried all the more: if she *had* lost that money, she ought to economize, certainly. Could she be so foolish as to carry her desire for secrecy to so absurd a length as to live just exactly as before when she really could not afford it?

It was at about this time that Mr. Smith requested to have hot water brought to his room morning and night, for which service he insisted, in spite of Miss Maggie's remonstrances, on paying three dollars a week extra.

There came a strange man to call one day. He was a member of the Boston law firm. Mr. Smith found out that much, but no more. Miss Maggie was almost hysterical after his visit. She talked very fast and laughed a good deal at supper that night; yet her eyes were full of tears nearly all the time, as Mr. Smith did not fail to perceive.

"And I suppose she thinks she's hiding it from me—that her heart is breaking!" muttered Mr. Smith savagely to himself, as he watched Miss Maggie's nervous efforts to avoid meeting his eyes. "I vow I'll have it out of her. I'll have it out—to-morrow!"

Mr. Smith did not "have it out" with Miss Maggie the following day, however. Something entirely outside of himself sent his thoughts into a new channel.

He was alone in the Duff living-room, and was idling over his work, at his table in the corner, when Mrs. Hattie Blaisdell opened the door and hurried in, wringing her hands. Her face was red and swollen from tears.

"Where's Maggie? I want Maggie! Isn't Maggie here?" she implored.

Mr. Smith sprang to his feet and hastened toward her.

"Why, Mrs. Blaisdell, what is it? No, she isn't here. I'm so sorry! Can't I do—anything?"

"Oh, I don't know—I don't know," moaned the woman, flinging herself into a chair. "There can't anybody do anything, I s'pose; but I've got to have somebody. I can't stay there in that house—I can't—I can't—I can't!"

"No, no, of course not. And you shan't," soothed the man. "And she'll be here soon, I'm sure—Miss Maggie will. But just let me help you off with your things," he urged, somewhat awkwardly trying to unfasten her heavy wraps. "You'll be so warm here."

"Yes, I know, I know." Impatiently she jerked off the rich fur coat and tossed it into his arms; then she dropped into the chair again and fell to wringing her hands. "Oh, what shall I do, what shall I do?"

"But what is it?" stammered Mr. Smith helplessly. "Can't I do—something? Can't I send for—for your husband?"

At the mention of her husband, Mrs. Blaisdell fell to weeping afresh.

"No, no! He's gone—to Fred, you know."

"To—Fred?"

"Yes, yes, that's what's the matter. Oh, Fred, Fred, my boy!"

"Fred! Oh, Mrs. Blaisdell, I'm so sorry! But what—is it?"

The woman dropped her hands from her face and looked up wildly, half defiantly.

"Mr. Smith, *you* know Fred. You liked him, didn't you? He isn't bad and wicked, is he? And they can't shut him up if—if we pay it back—all of it that he took? They won't take my boy—to *prison*?"

"To *prison—Fred!*"

At the look of horror on Mr. Smith's face, she began to wring her hands again.

"You don't know, of course. I'll have to tell you—I'll have to," she moaned.

"But, my dear woman,—not unless you want to."

"I do want to—I do want to! I've *got* to talk—to somebody. It's this way." With a visible effort she calmed herself a little and forced herself to talk more coherently. "We got a letter from Fred. It came this morning. He wanted, some money—quick. He wanted seven hundred dollars and forty-two cents. He said he'd got to have it—if he didn't, he'd go and *kill* himself. He said he'd spent all of his allowance, every cent, and that's what made him take it—this other money, in the first place."

"You mean—money that didn't belong to him?" Mr. Smith's voice was a little stern.

"Yes; but you mustn't blame him, you mustn't blame him, Mr. Smith. He said he owed it. It was a—a debt of honor. Those were his very words."

"Oh! A debt of honor, was it?" Mr. Smith's lips came together grimly.

"Yes; and—Oh, Maggie, Maggie, what shall I do? What shall I do?" she broke off wildly, leaping to her feet as Miss Maggie pushed open the door and hurried in.

"Yes, I know. Don't worry. We'll find something to do." Miss Maggie, white-faced, but with a cheery smile, was throwing off her heavy coat and her hat. A moment later she came over and took Mrs. Hattie's trembling hands in both her own. "Now, first, tell me all about it, dear."

"You *know*, then?"

"Only a little," answered Miss Maggie, gently pushing the other back into her chair. "I met Frank. Jim telephoned him something, just before he left. But I want the whole story. Now, what is it?" "I was just telling Mr. Smith." She began to wring her hands again, but Miss Maggie caught and held them firmly. "You see, Fred, he was treasurer of some club, or society, or something; and—and he—he needed some money to—to pay a man, and he took that—the money that belonged to the club, you know, and he thought he could pay it back, little by little. But something happened—I don't know what—a new treasurer, or something: anyhow, it was going to be found out—that he'd taken it. It was going to be found out to-morrow, and so he wrote the letter to his father. And Jim's gone. But he looked so— oh, I never saw him look so white and terrible. And I'm so afraid—of what he'll do—to Fred. My boy—my boy!"

"Is Jim going to give him the money?" asked Miss Maggie.

"Yes, oh, yes. Jim drew it out of the bank. Fred said he must have cash. And he's going to give it to him. Oh, they can't shut him up—they *can't* send him to prison *now*, can they?"

"Hush, dear! No, they won't send him to prison. If Jim has gone with the money, Fred will pay it back and nobody will know it. But, Hattie, Fred *did* it, just the same."

"I—I know it."

"And, Hattie, don't you see? Something will have to be done. Don't you see where all this is leading? Fred has been gambling, hasn't he?"

"I—I'm afraid so."

"And you know he drinks."

"Y-yes. But he isn't going to, any more. He said he wasn't. He wrote a beautiful letter. He said if his father would help him out of this scrape, he'd never get into another one, and he'd *show* him how much he appreciated it."

"Good! I'm glad to hear that," cried Miss Maggie. "He'll come out all right, yet."

"Of course he will!" Mr. Smith, over at the window, blew his nose vigorously. Mr. Smith had not sat down since Miss Maggie's entrance. He had crossed to the window, and had stood looking out—at nothing—all through Mrs. Hattie's story.

"You do think he will, don't you?" choked Mrs. Hattie, turning from one to the other piteously. "He said he was ashamed of himself; that this thing had been an awful lesson to him, and he promised—oh, he promised lots of things, if Jim would only go up and help him out of this. He'd never, never have to again. But he will, I know he will, if that Gaylord fellow stays there. The whole thing was his fault—I know it was. I hate him! I hate the whole family!"

"Why, Hattie, I thought you liked them!"

"I don't. They're mean, stuck-up things, and they snub me awfully. Don't you suppose I know when I'm being snubbed? And that Gaylord girl—she's just as bad, and she's making my Bessie just like her. I got Bess into the same school with her, you know, and I was so proud and happy. But I'm not—any longer. Why, my Bess, my own daughter, actually looks down on us. She's ashamed of her own father and mother—and she shows it. And it's that Gaylord girl that's done it, too, I believe. I thought I—I was training my daughter to be a lady—a real lady; but I never meant to train her to look down on—on her own mother!"

"I'm afraid Bessie—needs something of a lesson," commented Miss Maggie tersely. "But Bessie will be older, one of these days, Hattie, and then she'll—know more."

"But that's what I've been trying to teach her—'more,' something more all the time, Maggie," sighed Mrs. Hattie, wiping her eyes. "And I've tried to remember and call her Elizabeth, too.—but I can't. But, somehow, to-day, nothing seems of any use, any way. And even if she learns more and more, I don't see as it's going to do any good. I haven't got *any* friends now. I'm not fine enough yet, it seems, for Mrs. Gaylord and all that crowd. They don't want me among them, and they show it. And all my old friends are so envious and jealous since the money came that *they* don't want me, and *they* show it; so I don't feel comfortable anywhere."

"Never mind, dear, just stop trying to live as you think other folks want you to live, and live as *you* want to, for a while."

Mrs. Hattie smiled faintly, wiped her eyes again, and got to her feet.

"You talk just like Jim. He's always saying that."

"Well, just try it," smiled Miss Maggie, helping her visitor into the luxurious fur coat. "You've no idea how much more comfort you'll take."

"Would I?" Mrs. Hattie's eyes were wistful, but almost instantly they showed an alert gleam of anger.

"Well, anyhow, I'm not going to try to do what those Gaylords do any longer. And—and you're *sure* Fred won't have to go to prison?"

"I'm very sure," nodded Miss Maggie.

"All right, then. I can go home now with some comfort. You always make me feel better, Maggie, and you, too, Mr. Smith. I'm much obliged to you. Good-bye."

"Good-bye," said Mr. Smith.

"Good-bye," said Miss Maggie. "Now, go home and go to bed, and don't worry any more or you'll have one of your headaches."

As the door closed behind her visitor, Miss Maggie turned and sank into a chair. She looked worn and white, and utterly weary.

"I hope she won't meet Frank or Jane anywhere." She sighed profoundly.

"Why? What do you mean? Do you think they'd blame her—about this unfortunate affair of Fred's?"

Miss Maggie sighed again.

"I wasn't thinking of that. I was thinking of another matter. I just came from Frank's, and—"

"Yes?" Something in her face sent a questioning frown to Mr. Smith's own countenance.

"Do you remember hearing Flora say that Jane had bought a lot of the Benson gold-mine stock?"

"Yes."

"Well, Benson has failed; and they've just found out that that gold-mine stock is worth—about two cents on a dollar."

"Two cents! And how much—"

"About forty thousand dollars," said Miss Maggie wearily.

Mr. Smith sat down.

"Well, I'll be—"

He did not finish his sentence.

CHAPTER XX
FRANKENSTEIN: BEING A LETTER
FROM JOHN SMITH TO EDWARD D.
NORTON, ATTORNEY AT LAW

My dear Ned:—Wasn't there a story written once about a fellow who created some sort of a machine man without any soul that raised the very dickens and all for him? Frank—Frankenstein?—I guess that was it. Well, I've created a Frankenstein creature—and I'm dead up against it to know what to do with him.

Ned, what in Heaven's name am I going to do with Mr. John Smith? Mr. John Smith, let me tell you, is a very healthy, persistent, insistent, important person, with many kind friends, a definite position in the world, and no small degree of influence. Worse yet (now prepare for a stunning blow, Ned!), Mr. Smith has been so inconsiderate as to fall in love. Yes, he has. And he has fallen in love as absolutely and as idiotically as if he were twenty-one instead of fifty-two. Now, will you kindly tell me how Mr. John Smith is going to fade away into nothingness? And, even if he finds the way to do that, shall he, before fading, pop the question for Mr. Stanley G. Fulton, or shall he trust to Mr. Stanley G. Fulton's being able to win for himself the love Mr. John Smith fondly hopes is his?

Seriously, joking aside, I'm afraid I've made a mess of things, not only for myself, but for everybody else.

First, my own future. I'll spare you rhapsodies, Ned. They say, anyway, that there's no fool like an old fool. But I will admit that that future looks very dark to me if I am not to have the companionship of the little woman, Maggie Duff. Oh, yes, it's "Poor Maggie." You've probably guessed as much. As for Miss Maggie herself, perhaps it's conceited, but I believe she's not entirely indifferent to Mr. John Smith. How she'll like Mr. Stanley G. Fulton I have my doubts; but, alas! I have no doubts whatever as to what her opinion will be of Mr. Stanley G. Fulton's masquerading as Mr. John Smith! And I don't envy Mr. Stanley G. Fulton the job he's got on his hands to put himself right with her, either. But there's one thing he can be sure of, at least; if she does care for Mr. John Smith, it wasn't Mr. Stanley G. Fulton's money that was the bait.

Poor Maggie! (There! you see already I have adopted the Hillerton vernacular.) But I fear Miss Maggie is indeed "poor" now. She has had several letters that I don't like the looks of, and a call from a villainous-looking man from Boston—one of your craft, I believe (begging your pardon). I think she's lost some money, and I don't believe she had any extra to lose. She's as proud as Lucifer, however, and she's determined no one shall find out she's lost any money, so her laugh is gayer than ever. But I know, just the same. I can hear something in her voice that isn't laughter.

Jove! Ned, what a mess I *have* made of it! I feel more than ever now like the boy with his ear to the keyhole. These people are my friends—or, rather, they are Mr. John Smith's friends. As for being mine—who am I, Smith, or Fulton? Will they be Fulton's friends, after they find he is John Smith? Will they be Smith's friends, even, after they find he is Fulton? Pleasant position I am in! What?

Oh, yes, I can hear you say that it serves me right, and that you warned me, and that I was deaf to all remonstrances. It does. You did. I was. Now, we'll waste no more time on that. I've admitted all you could say. I've acknowledged my error, and my transgression is ever before me. I built the box, I walked into it, and I deliberately shut the cover down. But now I want to get out. I've got to get out—some way. I can't spend the rest of my natural existence as John Smith, hunting Blaisdell data—though sometimes I think I'd be willing to, if it's the only way to stay with Miss Maggie. I tell you, that little woman can make a home out of—

But I couldn't stay with Miss Maggie. John Smith wouldn't have money enough to pay his board, to say nothing of inviting Miss Maggie to board with him, would he? The opening of Mr. Stanley G. Fulton's last will and testament on the first day of next November will effectually cut off Mr. John Smith's source of income. There is no provision in the will for Mr. John Smith. Smith would have to go to work. I don't think he'd like that. By the way, I wonder: do you suppose John Smith could earn—his salt, if he was hard put to it? Very plainly, then, something has got to be done about getting John Smith to fade away, and Stanley G. Fulton to appear before next November.

And I had thought it would be so easy! Early this summer John Smith was to pack up his Blaisdell data, bid a pleasant adieu to Hillerton, and betake himself to South America. In due course, after a short trip to some obscure Inca city, or down some little-known river, Mr. Stanley G. Fulton would arrive at some South American hotel from the interior, and would take immediate passage for the States, reaching Chicago long before November first.

There would be a slight flurry, of course, and a few annoying interviews and write-ups; but Mr. Stanley G. Fulton always was known to keep his affairs to himself pretty well, and the matter would soon be put down as merely another of the multi-millionaire's eccentricities. The whole thing would then be all over, and well over. But—nowhere had there been taken into consideration the possibilities of—a Maggie Duff. And now, to me, that same Maggie Duff is the only thing worth considering—anywhere. So there you are!

And even after all this, I haven't accomplished what I set out to do—that is, find the future possessor of the Fulton millions (unless Miss Maggie—bless her!—says "yes." And even then, some one will have to have them after us). I have found out one thing, though. As conditions are now, I should not want either Frank, or James, or Flora to have them—not unless the millions could bring them more happiness than these hundred thousand apiece have brought.

Honest, Ned, that miserable money has made more—But, never mind. It's too long a story to write. I'll tell you when I see you—if I ever do see you. There's still the possibility, you know, that Mr. Stanley G. Fulton is lost in darkest South America, and of course John Smith *can* go to work!

I believe I won't sign any name—I haven't got any name—that I feel really belongs to me now. Still I might—yes, I will sign it

"Frankenstein."

CHAPTER XXI
SYMPATHIES MISPLACED

The first time Mr. Smith saw Frank Blaisdell, after Miss Maggie's news of the forty-thousand-dollar loss, he tried, somewhat awkwardly, to express his interest and sympathy. But Frank Blaisdell cut him short.

"That's all right, and I thank you," he cried heartily. "And I know most folks would think losing forty thousand dollars was about as bad as it could be. Jane, now, is all worked up over it; can't sleep nights, and has gone back to turning down the gas and eating sour cream so's to save and help make it up. But me—I call it the best thing that ever happened."

"Well, really," laughed Mr. Smith; "I'm sure that's a very delightful way to look at it—if you can."

"Well, I can; and I'll tell you why. It's put me back where I belong—behind the counter of a grocery store. I've bought out the old stand. Oh, I had enough left for that, and more! Closed the deal last night. Gorry, but I was glad to feel the old floor under my feet again!"

"But I thought you—you were tired of work, and—wanted to enjoy yourself," stammered Mr. Smith.

Frank Blaisdell laughed.

"Tired of work—wanted to enjoy myself, indeed! Yes, I know I did say something like that. But, let me tell you this, Mr. Smith. Talk about work!—I never worked so hard in my life as I have the last ten months trying to enjoy myself. How these folks can stand gadding 'round the country week in and week out, feeding their stomachs on a French dictionary instead of good United States meat and potatoes and squash, and spending their days traipsing off to see things they ain't a mite interested in, and their nights trying to get rested so they can go and see some more the next day, I don't understand."

Mr. Smith chuckled.

"I'm afraid these touring agencies wouldn't like to have you write their ads for them, Mr. Blaisdell!"

"Well, they hadn't better ask me to," smiled the other grimly. "But that ain't all. Since I come back I've been working even harder trying to enjoy myself here at home—knockin' silly little balls over a ten-acre lot in a game a healthy ten-year-old boy would scorn to play."

"But how about your new car? Didn't you enjoy riding in that?" bantered Mr. Smith.

"Oh, yes, I enjoyed the riding well enough; but I didn't enjoy hunting for punctures, putting on new tires, or burrowing into the inside of the critter to find out why she didn't go! And that's what I was doing most of the time. I never did like machinery. It ain't in my line."

He paused a moment, then went on a little wistfully:—

"I suspect, Mr. Smith, there ain't anything in my line but groceries. It's all I know. It's all I ever have known. If—if I had my life to live over again, I'd do different, maybe. I'd see if I couldn't find out what there was in a picture to make folks stand and stare at it an hour at a time when you could see the whole thing in a minute—and it wa'n't worth lookin' at, anyway, even for a minute. And music, too. Now, I like a good tune what is a tune; but them caterwaulings and dirges that that chap Gray plays on that fiddle of his—gorry, Mr. Smith, I'd rather hear the old barn door at home squeak any day. But if I was younger I'd try to learn to like 'em. I would! Look at Flora, now. She can set by the hour in front of that phonygraph of hers, and not know it!"

"Yes, I know," smiled Mr. Smith.

"And there's books, too," resumed the other, still wistfully. "I'd read books—if I could stay awake long enough to do it—and I'd find out what there was in 'em to make a good sensible man like Jim Blaisdell daft over 'em—and Maggie Duff, too. Why, that little woman used to go hungry sometimes, when she was a girl, so she could buy a book she wanted. I know she did. Why, I'd 'a' given anything this last year if I could 'a' got interested—really interested, readin'. I could 'a' killed an awful lot of time that way. But I couldn't do it. I bought a lot of 'em, too, an' tried it; but I expect I didn't begin young enough. I tell ye, Mr. Smith, I've about come to the conclusion that there ain't a thing in the world so hard to kill as time. I've tried it, and I know. Why, I got so I couldn't even kill it *eatin'*—though I 'most killed myself *tryin'* to! An' let me tell ye another thing. A full stomach ain't in it with bein' hungry an' knowing a good dinner's coming. Why, there was whole weeks at a time back there that I didn't know the meaning of the word 'hungry.' You'd oughter seen the jolt I give one o' them waiter-chaps one day when he comes up with his paper and his pencil and asks me what I wanted. 'Want?' says I. 'There ain't but one thing on this earth I want, and you can't give it to me. I want to *want* something. I'm tired of bein' so blamed satisfied all the time!'"

"And what did—Alphonso say to that?" chuckled Mr. Smith appreciatively.

"Alphonso? Oh, the waiter-fellow, you mean? Oh, he just stared a minute, then mumbled his usual 'Yes, sir, very good, sir,' and shoved that confounded printed card of his a little nearer to my nose. But, there! I guess you've heard enough of this, Mr. Smith. It's only that I was trying to tell you why I'm actually glad we lost that money. It's give me back my man's job again."

"Good! All right, then. I won'twaste any more sympathy on you," laughed Mr. Smith.

"Well, you needn't. And there's another thing. I hope it'll give me back a little of my old faith in my fellow-man."

"What do you mean by that?"

"Just this. I won't suspect every man, woman, and child that says a civil word to me now of having designs on my pocketbook. Why, Mr. Smith, you wouldn't believe it, if I told you, the things that's been done and said to get a little money out of me. Of course, the open gold-brick schemes I knew enough to dodge, 'most of 'em (unless you count in that darn Benson mining stock), and I spotted the blackmailers all right, most generally. But I *was* flabbergasted when a *woman* tackled the job and began to make love to me—actually make love to me!—one day when Jane's back was turned. Gorry! *Do* I look such a fool as that, Mr. Smith? Well, anyhow, there won't be any more of that kind, nor anybody after my money now, I guess," he finished with a sage wag of his head as he turned away.

To Miss Maggie that evening Mr. Smith said, after recounting the earlier portion of the conversation: "So you see you were right, after all. I shall have to own it up. Mr. Frank Blaisdell had plenty to retire upon, but nothing to retire to. But I'm glad—if he's happy now."

"And he isn't the only one that that forty-thousand-dollar loss has done a good turn to," nodded Miss Maggie. "Mellicent has just been here. You know she's home from school. It's the Easter vacation, anyway, but she isn't going back. It's too expensive." Miss Maggie spoke with studied casualness, but there was an added color in her cheeks—Miss Maggie always flushed a little when she mentioned Mellicent's name to Mr. Smith, in spite of her indignant efforts not to do so.

"Oh, is that true?"

"Yes. Well, the Pennocks had a dance last night, and Mellicent went. She said she had to laugh to see Mrs. Pennock's efforts to keep Carl away from her—the loss of the money is known everywhere now, and has been greatly exaggerated, I've heard. She said that even Hibbard Gaylord had the air of one trying to let her down easy. Mellicent was immensely amused."

"Where was Donald Gray?"

"Oh, he wasn't there. He doesn't move in the Pennock crowd much. But Mellicent sees him, and—and everything's all right there, now. That's why Mellicent is so happy."

"You mean—Has her mother given in?"

"Yes. You see, Jane was at the dance, too, and she saw Carl, and she saw Hibbard Gaylord. And she was furious. She told Mellicent this morning that she had her opinion of fellows who would show so plainly as Carl Pennock and Hibbard Gaylord did that it was the money they were after."

"I'm afraid—Mrs. Jane has changed her shoes again," murmured Mr. Smith, his eyes merry.

"Has changed—oh!" Miss Maggie's puzzled frown gave way to a laugh. "Well, yes, perhaps the shoe is on the other foot again. But, anyway, she doesn't love Carl or Hibbard any more, and she does love Donald Gray. He *hasn't* let the loss of the money make any difference to him, you see. He's been even more devoted, if anything. She told Mellicent this morning that he was a very estimable young man, and she liked him very much. Perhaps you see now why Mellicent is—happy."

"Good! I'm glad to know it," cried Mr. Smith heartily. "I'm glad—" His face changed suddenly. His eyes grew somber. "I'm glad the *loss* of the money brought them some happiness—if the possession of it didn't," he finished moodily, turning to go to his own room. At the hall door he paused and looked back at Miss Maggie, standing by the table, gazing after him with troubled eyes. "Did Mellicent say—whether Fred was there?" he asked.

"Yes. She said he wasn't there. He didn't come home for this vacation at all. She said she didn't know why. I suspect Mellicent doesn't know anything about that wretched affair of his."

"We'll hope not. So the young gentleman didn't show up at all?"

"No, nor Bessie. She went home with a Long Island girl. Hattie didn't go to the Pennocks' either. Hattie has—has been very different since this affair of Fred's. I think it frightened her terribly—it was so near a tragedy; the boy threatened to kill himself, you know, if his father didn't help him out."

"But his father *did* help him out!" flared the man irritably.

"Yes, I know he did; and I'm afraid he found things in a pretty bad mess—when he got there," sighed Miss Maggie. "It was a bad mess all around."

"You are exactly right!" ejaculated Mr. Smith with sudden and peculiar emphasis. "It is, indeed, a bad mess all around," he growled as he disappeared through the door.

Behind him, Miss Maggie still stood motionless, looking after him with troubled eyes.

As the spring days grew warmer, Miss Maggie had occasion many times to look after Mr. Smith with troubled eyes. She could not understand him at all. One day he would be the old delightful companion, genial, cheery, generously donating a box of chocolates to the center-table bonbon dish or a dozen hothouse roses to the mantel vase. The next, he would be nervous, abstracted, almost irritable. Yet she could see no possible reason for the change.

Sometimes she wondered fearfully if Mellicent could have anything to do with it. Was it possible that he had cared for Mellicent, and to see her now so happy with Donald Gray was more than he could bear? It did not seem credible. There was his own statement that he had devoted himself to her solely and only to help keep the undesirable lovers away and give Donald Gray a chance.

Besides, had he not said that he was not a marrying man, anyway? To be sure, that seemed a pity—a man so kind and thoughtful and so delightfully companionable! But then, it was nothing to her, of course—only she did hope he was not feeling unhappy over Mellicent!

Miss Maggie wished, too, that Mr. Smith would not bring flowers and candy so often. It worried her. She felt as if he were spending too much money—and she had got the impression in some way that he did not have any too much money to spend. And there were the expensive motor trips, too—she feared Mr. Smith *was* extravagant. Yet she could not tell him so, of course. He never seemed to realize the value of a dollar, anyway, and he very obviously did not know how to get the most out of it. Look at his foolish generosity in regard to the board he paid her!

Miss Maggie wondered sometimes if it might not be worry over money matters that was making him so nervous and irritable on occasions now. Plainly he was very near the end of his work there in Hillerton. He was not getting so many letters on Blaisdell matters from away, either. For a month now he had done nothing but a useless repetition of old work; and of late, a good deal of the time, he was not even making that pretense of being busy.

For days at a time he would not touch his records. That could mean but one thing, of course; his work was done. Yet he seemed to be making no move toward departure. Not that she wanted him to go. She should miss him very much when he went, of course. But she did not like to feel that he was staying simply because he had nowhere to go and nothing to do. Miss Maggie did not believe in able-bodied men who had nowhere to go and nothing to do—and she wanted very much to believe in Mr. Smith.

She had been under the impression that he was getting the Blaisdell material together for a book, and that he was intending to publish it himself. He had been very happy and interested. Now he was unhappy and uninterested. His book must be ready, but he was making no move to publish it. To Miss Maggie this could mean but one thing: some financial reverses had made it impossible for him to carry out his plans, and had left him stranded with no definite aim for the future.

She was so sorry!—but there seemed to be nothing that she could do. She *had* tried to help by insisting that he pay less for his board; but he had not only scouted that idea, but had brought her more chocolates and flowers than ever—for all the world as if he had divined her suspicions and wished to disprove them.

That Mr. Smith was trying to keep something from her, Miss Maggie was sure. She was the more sure, perhaps, because she herself had something that she was trying to keep from Mr. Smith—and she thought she recognized the symptoms.

Meanwhile April budded into May, and May blossomed into June; and June brought all the Blaisdells together again in Hillerton.

CHAPTER XXII
WITH EVERY JIM A JAMES

Two days after Fred Blaisdell had returned from college, his mother came to see Miss Maggie. Mr. Smith was rearranging the books on Miss Maggie's shelves and trying to make room for the new ones he had brought her through the winter. When Mrs. Hattie came in, red-eyed and flushed-faced, he ceased his work at once and would have left the room, but she stopped him with a gesture.

"No, don't go. You know all about it, anyway,—and I'd just as soon you knew the rest. So you can keep right to work. I just came down to talk things over with Maggie. I—I'm sure I don't know w-what I'm going to do—when I can't."

"But you always can, dear," soothed Miss Maggie cheerily, handing her visitor a fan and taking a chair near her.

Mr. Smith, after a moment's hesitation, turned quietly back to his bookshelves.

"But I can't," choked Mrs. Hattie. "I—I'm going away."

"Away? Where? What do you mean?" cried Miss Maggie. "Not to— live!"

"Yes. That's what I came to tell you."

"Why, Hattie Blaisdell, where are you going?"

"To Plainville—next month."

"Plainville? Oh, well, cheer up! That's only forty miles from here. I guess we can still see each other. Now, tell me, what does all this mean?"

"Well, of course, it began with Fred—his trouble, you know."

"But I thought Jim fixed that all up, dear."

"Oh, he did. He paid the money, and nobody there at college knew a thing about it. But there were—other things. Fred told us some of them night before last. He says he's ashamed of himself, but that he believes there's enough left in him to make a man of him yet. But he says he can't do it—there."

"You mean—he doesn't want to go back to college?" Miss Maggie's voice showed her disappointment.

"Oh, he wants to go to college—but not there."

"Oh," nodded Miss Maggie. "I see."

"He says he's had too much money to spend—and that 'twouldn't be easy not to spend it—if he was back there, in the old crowd. So he wants to go somewhere else." "Well, that's all right, isn't it?"

"Y-yes, oh, yes. Jim says it is. He's awfully happy over it, and—and I guess I am."

"Of course you are! But now, what is this about Plainville?" "Oh, that grew out of it—all this. Mr. Hammond is going to open a new office in Plainville and he's offered Jim—James—no, *Jim*—I'm not going to call him 'James' any more!—the chance to manage it."

"Well, that's fine, I'm sure."

"Yes, of course that part is fine—splendid. He'll get a bigger salary, and all that, and—and I guess I'm glad to go, anyway—I don't like Hillerton any more. I haven't got any friends here, Maggie. Of course, I wouldn't have anything to do with the Gaylords now, after what's happened,—that boy getting my boy to drink and gamble, and—and everything. And yet—*you* know how I've strained every nerve for years, and worked and worked to get where my children could—*could* be with them!"

"It didn't pay, did it, Hattie?"

"I guess it didn't! They're perfectly horrid—every one of them, and I hate them!"

"Oh, Hattie, Hattie!"

"Well, I do. Look at what they've done to Fred, and Bessie, too! I shan't let *her* be with them any more, either. There aren't any folks here we can be with now. That's why I don't mind going away. All our friends that we used to know don't like us any more, they're so jealous on account of the money. Oh, yes, I know you think I'm to blame for that," she went on aggrievedly. "I can see you do, by your face. Jim says so, too. And maybe I am. But it was just so I could get ahead. I did so want to *be* somebody!"

"I know, Hattie." Miss Maggie looked as if she would like to say something more—but she did not say it.

Over at the bookcase Mr. Smith was abstractedly opening and shutting the book in his hand. His gaze was out the window near him. He had not touched the books on the shelves for some time.

"And look at how I've tried and see what it has come to—Bessie so high-headed and airy she makes fun of us, and Fred a gambler and a drunkard, and 'most a thief. And it's all that horrid hundred thousand dollars!"

The book in Mr. Smith's hand slipped to the floor with a bang; but no one was noticing Mr. Smith.

"Oh, Hattie, don't blame the hundred thousand dollars," cried Miss Maggie.

"Jim says it was, and Fred does, too. They talked awfully. Fred said it was all just the same kind of a way that I'd tried to make folks call Jim 'James.' He said I'd been trying to make every single 'Jim' we had into a 'James,' until I'd taken away all the fun of living. And I suppose maybe he's right, too." Mrs. Hattie sighed profoundly. "Well, anyhow, I'm not going to do it any more. There isn't any fun in it, anyway. It doesn't make any difference how hard I tried to get ahead, I always found somebody else a little 'aheader' as Benny calls it. So what's the use?"

"There isn't any use—in that kind of trying, Hattie."

"No, I suppose there isn't. Jim said I was like the little boy that they asked what would make him the happiest of anything in the world, and he answered, 'Everything that I haven't got.' And I suppose I have been something like that. But I don't see as I'm any worse than other folks. Everybody goes for money; but I'm sure I don't see why—if it doesn't make them any happier than it has me! Well, I must be going." Mrs. Hattie rose wearily. "We shall begin to pack the first of the month. It looks like a mountain to me, but Jim and Fred say they'll help, and—"

Mr. Smith did not hear any more, for Miss Maggie and her guest had reached the hall and had closed the door behind them. But when Miss Maggie returned, Mr. Smith was pacing up and down the room nervously.

"Well," he demanded with visible irritation, as soon as she appeared, "will you kindly tell me if there is anything—desirable—that that confounded money has done?"

Miss Maggie looked up in surprise.

"You mean—Jim Blaisdell's money?" she asked.

"I mean all the money—I mean the three hundred thousand dollars that those three people received. Has it ever brought any good or happiness—anywhere?"

"Oh, yes, I know," smiled Miss Maggie, a little sadly. "But—" Her countenance changed abruptly. A passionate earnestness came to her eyes. "Don't blame the money—blame the *spending* of it! The money isn't to blame. The dollar that will buy tickets to the movies will just as quickly buy a good book; and if you're hungry, it's up to you whether you put your money into chocolate eclairs or roast beef. Is the *money* to blame that goes for a whiskey bill or a gambling debt instead of for shoes and stockings for the family?"

"Why, n-no." Mr. Smith had apparently lost his own irritation in his amazement at hers. "Why, Miss Maggie, you—you seem worked up over this matter."

"I am worked up. I'm always worked up—over money. It's been money, money, money, ever since I could remember! We're all after it, and we all want it, and we strain every nerve to get it. We think it's going to bring us happiness. But it won't—unless we do our part. And there are some things that even money can't buy. Besides, it isn't the money that does the things, anyway,—it's the man behind the money. What do you think money is good for, Mr. Smith?"

Mr. Smith, now thoroughly dazed, actually blinked his eyes at the question, and at the vehemence with which it was hurled into his face.

"Why, Miss Maggie, it—it—I—I—"

"It isn't good for anything unless we can exchange it for something we want, is it?"

"Why, I—I suppose we can *give* it—"

"But even then we're exchanging it for something we want, aren't we? We want to make the other fellow happy, don't we?"

"Well, yes, we do." Mr. Smith spoke with sudden fervor. "But it doesn't always work that way. Look at the case right here. Now, very likely this—er—Mr. Fulton thought those three hundred thousand dollars were going to make these people happy. Personification of happiness—that woman was, a few minutes ago, wasn't she?" Mr. Smith had regained his air of aggrieved irritation.

"No, she wasn't. But that wasn't the money's fault. It was her own. She didn't know how to spend it. And that's just what I mean when I say we've got to do our part—money won't buy happiness, unless we exchange it for the things that will bring happiness. If we don't know how to get any happiness out of five dollars, we won't know how to get it out of five hundred, or five thousand, or five hundred thousand, Mr. Smith. I don't mean that we'll get the same amount out of five dollars, of course,—though I've seen even that happen sometimes!—but I mean that we've got to know how to spend five dollars—and to make the most of it."

"I reckon—you're right, Miss Maggie."

"I know I'm right, and 'tisn't the money's fault when things go wrong. Money's all right. I love money. Oh, yes, I know—we're taught that the love of money is the root of all evil. But I don't think it should be so—necessarily. I think money's one of the most wonderful things in the world. It's more than a trust and a gift—it's an opportunity, and a test. It brings out what's strongest in us, every time. And it does that whether it's five dollars or five hundred thousand dollars. If—if we love chocolate eclairs and the movies better than roast beef and good books, we're going to buy them, whether they're chocolate eclairs and movies on five dollars, or or—champagne suppers and Paris gowns on five hundred thousand dollars!"

"Well, by—by Jove!" ejaculated Mr. Smith, rather feebly.

Miss Maggie gave a shamefaced laugh and sank back in her chair.

"You don't know what to think of me, of course; and no wonder," she sighed. "But I've felt so bad over this—this money business right here under my eyes. I love them all, every one of them. And *you* know how it's been, Mr. Smith. Hasn't it worked out to prove just what I say? Take Hattie this afternoon. She said that Fred declared she'd been trying to make every one of her 'Jims' a 'James,' ever since the money came. But he forgot that she did that very same thing before it came. All her life she's been trying to make five dollars look like ten; so when she got the hundred thousand, it wasn't six months before she was trying to make that look like two hundred thousand."

"I reckon you're right."

"Jane is just the opposite. Jane used to buy ingrain carpets and cheap chairs and cover them with mats and tidies to save them."

"You're right she did!"

Miss Maggie laughed appreciatively.

"They got on your nerves, too, didn't they? Such layers upon layers of covers for everything! It brought me to such a pass that I went to the other extreme. I wouldn't protect *anything*—which was very reprehensible, of course. Well, now she has pretty dishes and solid silver—but she hides them in bags and boxes, and never uses them except for company. She doesn't take any more comfort with them than she did with the ingrain carpets and cheap chairs. Of course, that's a little thing. I only mentioned it to illustrate my meaning. Jane doesn't know how to play. She never did. When you can't spend five cents out of a hundred dollars for pleasure without wincing, you needn't expect you're going to spend five dollars out of a hundred thousand without feeling the pinch," laughed Miss Maggie.

"And Miss Flora? You haven't mentioned her," observed Mr. Smith, a little grimly.

Miss Maggie smiled; then she sighed.

"Poor Flora—and when she tried so hard to quiet her conscience because she had so much money! But *you* know how that was. *You* helped her out of that scrape. And she's so grateful! She told me yesterday that she hardly ever gets a begging letter now."

"No; and those she does get she investigates," asserted Mr. Smith. "So the fakes don't bother her much these days. And she's doing a lot of good, too, in a small way."

"She is, and she's happy now," declared Miss Maggie, "except that she still worries a little because she is so happy. She's dismissed the maid and does her own work—I'm afraid Miss Flora never was cut out for a fine-lady life of leisure, and she loves to putter in the kitchen. She says it's such a relief, too, not to keep dressed up in company manners all the time, and not to have that horrid girl spying 'round all day to see if she behaves proper. But Flora's a dear."

"She is! and I reckon it worked the best with her of any of them."

"*Worked?*" hesitated Miss Maggie.

"Er—that is, I mean, perhaps she's made the best use of the hundred thousand," stammered Mr. Smith. "She's been—er—the happiest."

"Why, y-yes, perhaps she has, when you come to look at it that way."

"But you wouldn't—er—advise this Mr. Fulton to leave her—his twenty millions?"

"Mercy!" laughed Miss Maggie, throwing up both hands. "She'd faint dead away at the mere thought of it."

"Humph! Yes, I suppose so." Mr. Smith turned on his heel and resumed his restless pacing up and down the room. From time to time he glanced furtively at Miss Maggie. Miss Maggie, her hands idly resting in her lap, palms upward, was gazing fixedly at nothing.

"Of just what—are you thinking?" he demanded at last, coming to a pause at her side.

"I was thinking—of Mr. Stanley G. Fulton," she answered, not looking up.

"Oh, you were!" There was an odd something in Mr. Smith's voice.

"Yes. I was wondering—about those twenty millions."

"Oh, you were!" The odd something had increased, but Miss Maggie's eyes were still dreamily fixed on space.

"Yes. I was wondering what he had done with them."

"Had done with them!"

"Yes, in the letter, I mean." She looked up now in faint surprise. "Don't you remember? There was a letter—a second letter to be opened in two years' time. They said that that was to dispose of the remainder of the property—his last will and testament."

"Oh, yes, I remember," assented Mr. Smith, turning on his heel again. "Then you think—Mr. Fulton is—dead?" Mr. Smith was very carefully not meeting Miss Maggie's eyes.

"Why, yes, I suppose so." Miss Maggie turned back to her meditative gazing at nothing. "The two years are nearly up, you know,—I was talking with Jane the other day—just next November."

"Yes, I know." The words were very near a groan, but at once Mr. Smith hurriedly repeated, "I know—I know!" very lightly, indeed, with an apprehensive glance at Miss Maggie.

"So it seems to me if he were alive that he'd be back by this time. And so I was wondering—about those millions," she went on musingly. "What do *you* suppose he has done with them?" she asked, with sudden animation, turning full upon him.

"Why, I—I—How should I know?" stuttered Mr. Smith, a swift crimson dyeing his face.

Miss Maggie laughed merrily.

"You wouldn't, of course—but that needn't make you look as if I'd intimated that *you* had them! I was only asking for your opinion, Mr. Smith," she twinkled, with mischievous eyes.

"Of course!" Mr. Smith laughed now, a little precipitately. "But, indeed, Miss Maggie, you turned so suddenly and the question was so unexpected that I felt like the small boy who, being always blamed for everything at home that went wrong, answered tremblingly, when the teacher sharply demanded, 'Who made the world?' 'Please, ma'am, I did; but I'll never do it again!'"

"And now," said Mr. Smith, when Miss Maggie had done laughing at his little story, "suppose I turn the tables on you? What do *you* think Mr. Fulton has done—with that money?"

"I don't know what to think." Miss Maggie shifted her position, her face growing intently interested again. "I've been trying to remember what I know of the man."

"What you—*know* of him!" cried Mr. Smith, with startled eyes.

"Yes, from the newspaper and magazine accounts of him. Of course, there was quite a lot about him at the time the money came; and Flora let me read some things she'd saved, in years gone. Flora was always interested in him, you know."

"Well, what did you find?"

"Why, not much, really, about the man. Besides, very likely what I did find wasn't true. Oh, he was eccentric. Everything mentioned that. But I was trying to find out how he'd spent his money himself. I thought that might give me a clue—about the will, I mean."

"Oh, I see."

"Yes; but I didn't find much. In spite of his reported eccentricities, he seems to me to have done nothing very extraordinary."

"Oh, indeed!" murmured Mr. Smith.

"He doesn't seem to have been very bad."

"No?" Mr. Smith's eyebrows went up.

"Nor very good either, for that matter."

"Sort of a—nonentity, perhaps." Mr. Smith's lips snapped tight shut.

Miss Maggie laughed softly.

"Perhaps—though I suppose he couldn't really be that—not very well—with twenty millions, could he? But I mean, he wasn't very bad, nor very good. He didn't seem to be dissipated, or mixed up in any scandal, or to be recklessly extravagant, like so many rich men. On the other hand, I couldn't find that he'd done any particular good in the world. Some charities were mentioned, but they were perfunctory, apparently, and I don't believe, from the accounts, that he ever really *interested* himself in any one—that he ever really cared for—any one."

"Oh, you don't!" If Miss Maggie had looked up, she would have met a most disconcerting expression in the eyes bent upon her. But Miss Maggie did not look up.

"No," she proceeded calmly. "Why, he didn't even have a wife and children to stir him from his selfishness. He had a secretary, of course, and he probably never saw half his begging letters. I can imagine his tossing them aside with a languid 'Fix them up, James,—give the creatures what they want, only don't bother me.'"

"He *never* did!" stormed Mr. Smith; then, hastily: "I'm sure he never did. You wrong him. I'm sure you wrong him."

"Maybe I do," sighed Miss Maggie. "But when I think of what he might do—Twenty millions! I can't grasp it. Can you? But he didn't do—anything—worth while with them, so far as I can see, when he was living, so that's why I can't imagine what his will may be. Probably the same old perfunctory charities, however, with the Chicago law firm instead of 'James' as disburser—unless, of course, Hattie's expectations are fulfilled, and he divides them among the Blaisdells here."

"You think—there's something worth while he *might* have done with those millions, then?" pleaded Mr. Smith, a sudden peculiar wistfulness in his eyes.

"Something he *might* have done with them!" exclaimed Miss Maggie. "Why, it seems to me there's no end to what he might have done—with twenty millions."

"What would *you* do?"

"I?—do with twenty millions?" she breathed.

"Yes, you." Mr. Smith came nearer, his face working with emotion. "Miss Maggie, if a man with twenty millions—that is, could you love a man with twenty millions, if—if Mr. Fulton should ask you—if _I_ were Mr. Fulton—if—" His countenance changed suddenly. He drew himself up with a cry of dismay. "Oh, no—no—I've spoiled it all now. That isn't what I meant to say first. I was going to find out—I mean, I was going to tell—Oh, good Heavens, what a—That confounded money—again!"

Miss Maggie sprang to her feet.

"Why, Mr. Smith, w-what—" Only the crisp shutting of the door answered her. With a beseeching look and a despairing gesture Mr. Smith had gone.

Once again Miss Maggie stood looking after Mr. Smith with dismayed eyes. Then, turning to sit down, she came face to face with her own image in the mirror.

"Well, now you've done it, Maggie Duff," she whispered wrathfully to the reflection in the glass. "And you've broken his heart! He was—was going to say something—I know he was. And you? You've talked money, money, *money* to him for an hour. You said you *loved* money; and you told what you'd do—if you had twenty millions of dollars. And you know—you *know* he's as poor as Job's turkey, and that just now he's more than ever plagued over—money! And yet you—Twenty millions of dollars! As if that counted against—"

With a little sobbing cry Miss Maggie covered her face with her hands and sat down, helplessly, angrily.

CHAPTER XXIII
REFLECTIONS—MIRRORED AND OTHERWISE

Miss Maggie was still sitting in the big chair with her face in her hands when the door opened and Mr. Smith came in. He was very white.

Miss Maggie, dropping her hands and starting up at his entrance, caught a glimpse of his face in the mirror in front of her. With a furtive, angry dab of her fingers at her wet eyes, she fell to rearranging the vases and photographs on the mantel.

"Oh, back again, Mr. Smith?" she greeted him, with studied unconcern.

Mr. Smith shut the door and advanced determinedly.

"Miss Maggie, I've got to face this thing out, of course. Even if I had—made a botch of things at the very start, it didn't help any to—to run away, as I did. And I was a coward to do it. It was only because I—I—But never mind that. I'm coming now straight to the point. Miss Maggie, will you—marry me?"

The photograph in Miss Maggie's hand fell face down on the shelf. Miss Maggie's fingers caught the edge of the mantel in a convulsive grip. A swift glance in the mirror before her disclosed Mr. Smith's face just over her shoulder, earnest, pleading, and still very white. She dropped her gaze, and turned half away. She did not want to meet Mr. Smith's eyes just then. She tried to speak, but only a half-choking little breath came.

Then Mr. Smith spoke again.

"Miss Maggie, please don't say no—yet. Let me—explain—about how I came here, and all that. But first, before I do that, let me tell you how—how I love you—how I have loved you all these long months. I *think* I loved you from the first time I saw you. Whatever comes, I want you to know that. And if you could care for me a little—just a little, I'm sure I could make it more—in time, so you would marry me. And we would be so happy! Don't you believe I'd try to make you happy—dear?"

"Yes, oh, yes," murmured Miss Maggie, still with her head turned away.

"Good! Then all you've got to say is that you'll let me try. And we will be happy, dear! Why, until I came here to this little house, I didn't know what living, real living, was. And I *have* been, just as you said, a selfish old thing."

Miss Maggie, with a start of surprise, faced the image in the mirror; but Mr. Smith was looking at her, not at her reflection, so she did not meet his ayes.

"Why, I never—" she stammered.

"Yes, you did, a minute ago. Don't you remember? Oh, of course you didn't realize—everything, and perhaps you wouldn't have said it if you'd known. But you said it—and you meant it, and I'm glad you said it. And, dear little woman, don't you see? That's only another reason why you should say yes. You can show me how not to be selfish."

"But, Mr. Smith, I—I—" stammered Miss Maggie, still with puzzled eyes.

"Yes, you can. You can show me how to make life really worth while, for me, and for—for lots of others. And *now* I have some one to care for. And, oh, little woman, I—I care so much, it can't be that you—you don't care—any!"

Miss Maggie caught her breath and turned away again.

"Don't you care—a little?"

The red crept up Miss Maggie's neck to her forehead but still she was silent.

"If I could only see your eyes," pleaded the man. Then, suddenly, he saw Miss Maggie's face in the mirror. The next moment Miss Maggie herself turned a little, and in the mirror their eyes met—and in the mirror Mr. Smith found his answer. "You *do* care—a *little!*" he breathed, as he took her in his arms.

"But I don't!" Miss Maggie shook her head vigorously against his coat-collar.

"What?" Mr. Smith's clasp loosened a little.

"I care—a *great deal*," whispered Miss Maggie to the coat-collar, with shameless emphasis.

"You—darling!" triumphed the man, bestowing a rapturous kiss on the tip of a small pink ear—the nearest point to Miss Maggie's lips that was available, until, with tender determination, he turned her face to his.

A moment later, blushing rosily, Miss Maggie drew herself away.

"There, we've been quite silly enough—old folks like us."

"We're not silly. Love is never silly—not real love like ours. Besides, we're only as old as we feel. Do you feel old? I don't. I've lost—*years* since this morning. And you know I'm just beginning to live—really live, anyway! I feel—twenty-one."

"I'm afraid you act it," said Miss Maggie, with mock severity.

"*You* would—if you'd been through what _I_ have," retorted Mr. Smith, drawing a long breath. "And when I think what a botch I made of it, to begin with—You see, I didn't mean to start off with that, first thing; and I was so afraid that—that even if you did care for John Smith, you wouldn't for me—just at first. But you do, dear!" At arms' length he held her off, his hands on her shoulders. His happy eyes searching her face saw the dawn of the dazed, question.

"Wouldn't care for *you* if I did for John Smith! Why, you *are* John Smith. What do you mean?" she demanded, her eyes slowly sweeping him from head to foot and back again. "What *do* you mean?"

"*Miss Maggie!*" Instinctively his tongue went back to the old manner of address, but his hands still held her shoulders. "You don't mean—you can't mean that—that you didn't understand—that you *don't* understand that I am—Oh, good Heavens! Well, I have made a mess of it this time," he groaned. Releasing his hold on her shoulders, he turned and began to tramp up and down the room. "Nice little John-Alden-Miles-Standish affair this is now, upon my word! Miss Maggie, have I got to—to propose to you all over again for—for another man, now?"

"For—*another man!* I—I don't think I understand you." Miss Maggie had grown a little white.

"Then you don't know—you didn't understand a few minutes ago, when I—I spoke first, when I asked you about—about those twenty millions—"

She lifted her hand quickly, pleadingly.

"Mr. Smith, please, don't let's bring money into it at all. I don't care—I don't care a bit if you haven't got any money."

Mr. Smith's jaw dropped.

"If I *haven't* got any money!" he ejaculated stupidly.

"No! Oh, yes, I know, I said I loved money." The rich red came back to her face in a flood. "But I didn't mean—And it's just as much of a test and an opportunity when you *don't* have money—more so, if anything. I didn't mean it—that way. I never thought of—of how you might take it—as if I *wanted* it. I don't. Indeed, I don't! Oh, can't you—understand?"

"Understand! Good Heavens!" Mr. Smith threw up both his hands. "And I thought I'd given myself away! Miss Maggie." He came to her and stood close, but he did not offer to touch her. "I thought, after I'd said what I did about—about those twenty millions that you understood—that you knew I was—Stanley Fulton himself."

"That you were—who?" Miss Maggie stood motionless, her eyes looking straight into his, amazed incredulous.

"Stanley Fulton. I am Stanley Fulton. My God! Maggie, don't look at me like that. I thought—I had told you. Indeed, I did!"

She was backing away now, slowly, step by step. Anger, almost loathing, had taken the place of the amazement and incredulity in her eyes.

"And *you* are Mr. Fulton?"

"Yes, yes! But—"

"And you've been here all these months—yes, years—under a false name, pretending to be what you weren't—talking to us, eating at our tables, winning our confidence, letting us talk to you about yourself, even pretending that—Oh, how could you?" Her voice broke.

"Maggie, dearest," he begged, springing toward her, "if you'll only let me—"

But she stopped him peremptorily, drawing herself to her full height.

"I am *not* your dearest," she flamed angrily. "I did not give my love—to *you*."

"Maggie!" he implored.

But she drew back still farther.

"No! I gave it to John Smith—gentleman, I supposed. A man—poor, yes, I believed him poor; but a man who at least had a right to his *name*! I didn't give it to Mr. Stanley G. Fulton, spy, trickster, who makes life itself a masquerade for *sport*! I do not know Mr. Stanley G. Fulton, and—I do not wish to." The words ended in a sound very like a sob; but Miss Maggie, with her head still high, turned her back and walked to the window.

The man, apparently stunned for a moment, stood watching her, his eyes grieved, dismayed, hopeless. Then, white-faced, he turned and walked toward the door. With his hand almost on the knob he slowly wheeled about and faced the woman again. He hesitated visibly, then in a dull, lifeless voice he began to speak.

"Miss Maggie, before John Smith steps entirely out of your life, he would like to say just this, please, not on justification, but on explanation of— —of Stanley G. Fulton. Fulton did not intend to be a spy, or a trickster, or to make life a masquerade for—sport. He was a lonely old man—he felt old. He had no wife or child. True, he had no one to care for, but—he had no one to care for *him*, either. Remember that, please. He did have a great deal of money—more than he knew what to do with. Oh, he tried—various ways of spending it. Never mind what they were. They are not worth speaking of here. They resulted, chiefly, in showing him that he wasn't—as wise as he might be in that line, perhaps."

The man paused and wet his lips. At the window Miss Maggie still stood, with her back turned as before.

"The time came, finally," resumed the man, "when Fulton began to wonder what would become of his millions when he was done with them. He had a feeling that he would like to will a good share of them to some of his own kin; but he had no nearer relatives than some cousins back East, in—Hillerton."

Miss Maggie at the window drew in her breath, and held it suspended, letting it out slowly.

"He didn't know anything about these cousins," went on the man dully, wearily, "and he got to wondering what they would do with the money. I think he felt, as you said to-day that you feel, that one must know how to spend five dollars if one would get the best out of five thousand. So Fulton felt that, before he gave a man fifteen or twenty millions, he would like to know—what he would probably do with them. He had seen so many cases where sudden great wealth had brought—great sorrow.

"And so then he fixed up a little scheme; he would give each one of these three cousins of his a hundred thousand dollars apiece, and then, unknown to them, he would get acquainted with them, and see which of them would be likely to make the best use of those twenty millions. It was a silly scheme, of course,—a silly, absurd foolishness from beginning to end. It—"

He did not finish his sentence. There was a rush of swift feet, a swish of skirts, then full upon him there fell a whirlwind of sobs, clinging arms, and incoherent ejaculations.

"It wasn't silly—it wasn't silly. It was perfectly splendid! I see it all now. I see it all! I understand. Oh, I think it was—*wonderful*! And I—I'm so *ashamed*!"

Later—very much later, when something like lucid coherence had become an attribute of their conversation, as they sat together upon the old sofa, the man drew a long breath and said:—

"Then I'm quite forgiven?"

"There is nothing to forgive."

"And you consider yourself engaged to *both* John Smith and Stanley G. Fulton?"

"It sounds pretty bad, but—yes," blushed Miss Maggie.

"And you must love Stanley G. Fulton just exactly as well—no, a little better, than you did John Smith."

"I'll—try to—if he's as lovable." Miss Maggie's head was at a saucy tilt.

"He'll try to be; but—it won't be all play, you know, for you. You've got to tell him what to do with those twenty millions. By the way, what *will* you do with them?" he demanded interestedly.

Miss Maggie looked up, plainly startled.

"Why, yes, that's so. You—you—if you're Mr. Fulton, you *have* got— And I forgot all about—those twenty millions. And they're *yours*, Mr. Smith!"

"No, they're not Mr. Smith's," objected the man. "They belong to Fulton, if you please. Furthermore, *can't* you call me anything but that abominable 'Mr. Smith'? My name is Stanley. You might—er—abbreviate it to—er— 'Stan,' now."

"Perhaps so—but I shan't," laughed Miss Maggie,—"not yet. You may be thankful I have wits enough left to call you anything—after becoming engaged to two men all at once."

"And with having the responsibility of spending twenty millions, too."

"Oh, yes, the money!" Her eyes began to shine. She drew another long breath. "Oh, we can do so much with that money! Why, only think what is needed right *here*—better milk for the babies, and a community house, and the streets cleaner, and a new carpet for the church, and a new hospital with—"

"But, see here, aren't you going to spend some of that money on yourself?" he demanded. "Isn't there something *you* want?"

She gave him a merry glance.

"Myself? Dear me, I guess I am! I'm going to Egypt, and China, and Japan—with you, of course; and books—oh, you never saw such a lot of books as I shall buy. And—oh, I'll spend heaps on just my selfish self—you see if I don't! But, first,—oh, there are so many things that I've so wanted to do, and it's just come over me this minute that *now* I can do them! And you *know* how Hillerton needs a new hospital." Her eyes grew luminous and earnest again. "And I want to build a store and run it so the girls can *live*, and a factory, too, and decent homes for the workmen, and a big market, where they can get their food at cost; and there's the playground for the children, and—"

But Mr. Smith was laughing, and lifting both hands in mock despair.

"Look here," he challenged, "I *thought* you were marrying *me*, but—*are* you marrying me or that confounded money?"

Miss Maggie laughed merrily.

"Yes, I know; but you see—" She stopped short. An odd expression came to her eyes.

Suddenly she laughed again, and threw into his eyes a look so merry, so whimsical, so altogether challenging, that he demanded:—

"Well, what is it now?"

"Oh, it's so good, I have—half a mind to tell you."

"Of course you'll tell me. Where are you going?" he asked discontentedly.

Miss Maggie had left the sofa, and was standing, as if half-poised for flight, midway to the door.

"I think—yes, I will tell you," she nodded, her cheeks very pink; "but I wanted to be—over here to tell it."

"'Way over there?"

"Yes, 'way over here. Do you remember those letters I got awhile ago, and the call from the Boston; lawyer, that I—I wouldn't tell you about?"

"I should say I did!"

"Well; you know you—you thought they—they had something to do with—my money; that I—I'd lost some."

"I did, dear."

"Well, they—they did have something to do—with money."

"I knew they did!" triumphed the man. "Oh, why wouldn't you tell me then—and let me help you some way?"

She shook her head nervously and backed nearer the door. He had half started from his seat.

"No, stay there. If you don't—I won't tell you."

He fell back, but with obvious reluctance.

"Well, as I said, it did have something to do—with my money; but just now, when you asked me if I—I was marrying you or your money—"

"But I was in fun—you know I was in fun!" defended the man hotly.

"Oh, yes, I knew that," nodded Miss Maggie. "But it—it made me laugh and remember—the letters. You see, they weren't as you thought. They didn't tell me of—of money lost. They told me of money—gained."

"Gained?"

"Yes. That father's Cousin George in Alaska had died and left me—fifty thousand dollars."

"But, my dear woman, why in Heaven's name wouldn't you tell me that?"

"Because." Miss Maggie took a step nearer the door. "You see, I thought you were poor—very poor, and I—I wouldn't even own up to it myself, but I knew, in my heart, that I was afraid, if you heard I had this money, you wouldn't—you wouldn't—ask me to—to—"

She was blushing so adorably now that the man understood and leaped to his feet.

"Maggie, you—darling!"

But the door had shut—Miss Maggie had fled.

CHAPTER XXIV
THAT MISERABLE MONEY

In the evening, after the Martin girls had gone to their rooms, Miss Maggie and Mr. Smith faced the thing squarely.

"Of course," he began with a sigh, "I'm really not out of the woods at all. Blissfully happy as I am, I'm really deeper in the woods than ever, for now I've got you there with me, to look out for. However successfully John Smith might dematerialize into nothingness—Maggie Duff can't."

"No, I know she can't," admitted Miss Maggie soberly.

"Yet if she marries John Smith she'll have to—and if she doesn't marry him, how's Stanley G. Fulton going to do his courting? He can't come here."

"But he must!" Miss Maggie looked up with startled eyes. "Why, Mr. Smith, you'll *have* to tell them—who you are. You'll have to tell them right away."

The man made a playfully wry face.

"I shall be glad," he observed, "when I shan't have to be held off at the end of a 'Mr.'! However, we'll let that pass—until we settle the other matter. Have you given any thought as to *how* I'm going to tell Cousin Frank and Cousin James and Cousin Flora that I am Stanley G. Fulton?"

"No—except that you must do it," she answered decidedly. "I don't think you ought to deceive them another minute—not another minute."

"Hm-m." Mr. Smith's eyes grew reflective. "And had you thought—as to what would happen when I did tell them?"

"Why, n-no, not particularly, except that—that they naturally wouldn't like it, at first, and that you'd have to explain—just as you did to me—why you did it."

"And do you think they'll like it any better—when I do explain? Think!"

Miss Maggie meditated; then, a little tremulously she drew in her breath. She lifted startled eyes to his face.

"Why, you'd have to tell them that—that you did it for a test, wouldn't you?"

"If I told the truth—yes."

"And they'd know—they couldn't help knowing—that they had failed to meet it adequately."

"Yes. And would that help matters any—make things any happier, all around?"

"No—oh, no," she frowned despairingly.

"Would it do anybody any *real* good, now? Think of that."

"N-no," she admitted reluctantly, "except that—that you'd be doing right."

"But *would* I be doing right? And another thing—aside from the mortification, dismay, and anger of my good cousins, have you thought what I'd be bringing on you?"

"*Me!*"

"Yes. In less than half a dozen hours after the Blaisdells knew that Mr. John Smith was Stanley G. Fulton, Hillerton would know it. And in less than half a dozen more hours, Boston, New York, Chicago,—to say nothing of a dozen lesser cities,—would know it—if there didn't happen to be anything bigger on foot. Headlines an inch high would proclaim the discovery of the missing Stanley G. Fulton, and the fine print below would tell everything that happened, and a great deal that didn't happen, in the carrying-out of the eccentric multi-millionaire's extraordinary scheme of testing his relatives with a hundred thousand dollars apiece to find a suitable heir. Your picture would adorn the front page of the yellowest of yellow journals, and—"

"*My* picture! Oh, no, no!" gasped Miss Maggie.

"Oh, yes, yes," smiled the man imperturbably. "You'll be in it, too. Aren't you the affianced bride of Mr. Stanley G. Fulton? I can see them now: 'In Search of an Heir and Finds a Wife.'—'Charming Miss Maggie Duff Falls in Love with Plain John Smith,' and—"

"Oh, no, no," moaned Miss Maggie, shrinking back as if already the lurid headlines were staring her in the face.

Mr. Smith laughed.

"Oh, well, it might not be so bad as that, of course. But you never can tell. Undoubtedly there are elements for a pretty good story in the case, and some man, with nothing more important to write up, is bound to make the most of it somewhere. Then other papers will copy. There's sure to be unpleasant publicity, my dear, if the truth once leaks out."

"But what—what *had* you planned to do?" she faltered, shuddering again.

"Well, I *had* planned something like this: pretty quick, now, Mr. Smith was to announce the completion of his Blaisdell data, and, with properly grateful farewells, take his departure from Hillerton. He would go to South America. There he would go inland on some sort of a simple expedition with a few native guides and carriers, but no other companion. Somewhere in the wilderness he would shed his beard and his name, and would emerge in his proper person of Stanley G. Fulton and promptly take passage for the States. Of course, upon the arrival in Chicago of Mr. Stanley G. Fulton, there would be a slight flurry at his appearance, and a few references to the hundred-thousand-dollar gifts to the Eastern relatives, and sundry speculations as to the why and how of the exploring trip. There would be various rumors and alleged interviews; but Mr. Stanley G. Fulton never was noted for his communicativeness, and, after a very short time, the whole thing would be dismissed as probably another of the gentleman's well-known eccentricities. And there it would end."

"Oh, I see," murmured Miss Maggie, in very evident relief. "That would be better—in some ways; only it does seem terrible not to—to tell them who you are."

"But we have just proved that to do that wouldn't bring happiness anywhere, and would bring misery everywhere, haven't we?"

"Y-yes."

"Then why do it?—particularly as by not doing it I am not defrauding anybody in the least. No; that part isn't worrying me a bit now—but there is one point that does worry me very much."

"What do you mean? What is it?"

"Yourself. My scheme gets Stanley G. Fulton back to life and Chicago very nicely; but it doesn't get Maggie Duff there worth a cent! Maggie Duff can't marry Mr. John Smith in Hillerton and arrive in Chicago as the wife of Stanley G. Fulton, can she?"

"N-no, but he—he can come back and get her—if he wants her." Miss Maggie blushed.

"If he wants her, indeed!" (Miss Maggie blushed all the more at the method and the fervor of Mr. Smith's answer to this.) "Come back as Mr. Stanley G. Fulton, you mean?" went on Mr. Smith, smiling at Miss Maggie's hurried efforts to smooth her ruffled hair. "Too risky, my dear! He'd look altogether too much like—like Mr. John Smith."

"But your beard will be gone—I wonder how I shall like you without a beard." She eyed him critically.

Mr. Smith laughed and threw up his hands with a doleful shrug.

"That's what comes of courting as one man and marrying as another," he groaned. Then, sternly: "I'll warn you right now, Maggie Duff, that Stanley G. Fulton is going to be awfully jealous of John Smith if you don't look out."

"He should have thought of that before," retorted Miss Maggie, her eyes mischievous. "But, tell me, wouldn't you *ever* dare to come—in your proper person?"

"Never!—or, at least, not for some time. The beard would be gone, to be sure; but there'd be all the rest to tattle—eyes, voice, size, manner, walk—everything; and smoked glasses couldn't cover all that, you know. Besides, glasses would be taboo, anyway. They'd only result in making me look more like John Smith than ever. John Smith, you remember, wore smoked glasses for some time to hide Mr. Stanley G. Fulton from the ubiquitous reporter. No, Mr. Stanley G. Fulton can't come to Hillerton. So, as Mahomet can't go to the mountain, the mountain must come to Mahomet."

"Meaning—?" Miss Maggie's eyes were growing dangerously mutinous.

"That you will have to come to Chicago—yes."

"And court you? No, sir—thank you!"

Mr. Smith chuckled softly.

"I love you with your head tilted that way." (Miss Maggie promptly tilted it the other.) "Or that, either, for that matter," continued Mr. Smith genially. "However, speaking of courting—Mr. Fulton will do that, all right, and endeavor to leave nothing lacking, either as to quantity or quality. Think, now. Don't you know any one in Chicago? Haven't you got some friend that you can visit?"

"No!" Miss Maggie's answer was prompt and emphatic—too prompt and too emphatic for unquestioning acceptance.

"Oh, yes, you have," asserted the man cheerfully. "I don't know her name—but she's there. She's waving a red flag from your face this minute! Now, listen. Well, turn your head away, if you like—if you can listen better that way," he went on tranquilly paying no attention to her little gasp. "Well, all you have to do is to write the lady you're coming, and go. Never mind who she is—Mr. Stanley G. Fulton will find a way to meet her. Trust him for that! Then he'll call and meet you—and be so pleased to see you! The rest will be easy. There'll be a regular whirlwind courtship then—calls, dinners, theaters, candy, books, flowers! Then Mr. Stanley G. Fulton will propose marriage. You'll be immensely surprised, of course, but you'll accept. Then we'll get married," he finished with a deep sigh of satisfaction. "*Mr. Smith!*" ejaculated Miss Maggie faintly.

"Say, *can't* you call me anything—" he began wrathfully, but interrupted himself. "However, it's better that you don't, after all. Because I've got to be 'Mr. Smith' as long as I stay here. But you wait till you meet Mr. Stanley G. Fulton in Chicago! Now, what's her name, and where does she live?"

Miss Maggie laughed in spite of herself, as she said severely: "Her name, indeed! I'm afraid Mr. Stanley G. Fulton is so in the habit of having his own way that he forgets he is still Mr. John Smith. However, there *is* an old schoolmate," she acknowledged demurely.

"Of course there is! Now, write her at once, and tell her you're coming."

"But she—she may not be there."

"Then get her there. She's *got* to be there. And, listen. I think you'd better plan to go pretty soon after I go to South America. Then you can be there when Mr. Stanley G. Fulton arrives in Chicago and can write the news back here to Hillerton. Oh, they'll get it in the papers, in time, of course; but I think it had better come from you first. You see—the reappearance on this earth of Mr. Stanley G. Fulton is going to be of—of some moment to them, you know. There is Mrs. Hattie, for instance, who is counting on the rest of the money next November."

"Yes, I know, it will mean a good deal to them, of course. Still, I don't believe Hattie is really expecting the money. At any rate, she hasn't said anything about it very lately—perhaps because she's been too busy bemoaning the pass the present money has brought them to."

"Yes, I know," frowned Mr. Smith, with a gloomy sigh. "That miserable money!"

"No, no—I didn't mean to bring that up," apologized Miss Maggie quickly, with an apprehensive glance into his face. "And it wasn't miserable money a bit! Besides, Hattie has—has learned her lesson, I'm sure, and she'll do altogether differently in the new home. But, Mr. Smith, am I never to—to come back here? Can't we come back—ever?"

"Indeed we can—some time, by and by, when all this has blown over, and they've forgotten how Mr. Smith looks. We can come back then. Meanwhile, you can come alone—a *very* little. I shan't let you leave me very much. But I understand; you'll have to come to see your friends. Besides, there are all those playgrounds for the babies and cleaner milk for the streets, and—"

"Cleaner milk for the streets, indeed!"

"Eh? What? Oh, yes, it *was* the milk for the babies, wasn't it?" he teased. "Well, however that may be you'll have to come back to superintend all those things you've been wanting to do so long. But"—his face grew a little wistful—"you don't want to spend too much time here. You know— Chicago has a few babies that need cleaner milk."

"Yes, I know, I know!" Her face grew softly luminous as it had grown earlier in the afternoon.

"So you can bestow some of your charity there; and—"

"It isn't charity," she interrupted with suddenly flashing eyes. "Oh, how I hate that word—the way it's used, I mean. Of course, the real charity means love. Love, indeed! I suppose it was *love* that made John Daly give one hundred dollars to the Pension Fund Fair—after he'd jewed it out of those poor girls behind his counters! And Mrs. Morse went around everywhere telling how kind dear Mr. Daly was to give so much to charity! *Charity*! Nobody wants charity—except a few lazy rascals like those beggars of Flora's! But we all want our *rights*. And if half the world gave the other half its rights there wouldn't *be* any charity, I believe."

"Dear, dear! What have we here? A rabid little Socialist?" Mr. Smith held up both hands in mock terror. "I shall be petitioning her for my bread and butter, yet!"

"Nonsense! But, honestly, Mr. Smith, when I think of all that money"— her eyes began to shine again—"and of what we can do with it, I—I just can't believe it's so!"

"But you aren't expecting that twenty millions are going to right all the wrongs in the world, are you?" Mr. Smith's eyes were quizzical.

"No, oh, no; but we can help *some* that we know about. But it isn't that I just want to *give*, you know. We must get behind things—to the causes. We must—"

"We must make the Mr. Dalys pay more to their girls before they pay anything to pension funds, eh?" laughed Mr. Smith, as Miss Maggie came to a breathless pause.

"Exactly!" nodded Miss Maggie earnestly. "Oh, can't you *see* what we can do—with that twenty million dollars?"

Mr. Smith, his gaze on Miss Maggie's flushed cheeks and shining eyes, smiled tenderly. Then with mock severity he frowned.

"I see—that I'm being married for my money—after all!" he scolded.

"Pooh!" sniffed Miss Maggie, so altogether bewitchingly that Mr. Smith gave her a rapturous kiss.

CHAPTER XXV
EXIT MR. JOHN SMITH

Early in July Mr. Smith took his departure from Hillerton. He made a farewell call upon each of the Blaisdell families, and thanked them heartily for all their kindness in assisting him with his Blaisdell book.

The Blaisdells, one and all, said they were very sorry to have him go. Miss Flora frankly wiped her eyes, and told Mr. Smith she could never, never thank him enough for what he had done for her. Mellicent, too, with shy eyes averted, told him she should never forget what he had done for her—and for Donald.

James and Flora and Frank—and even Jane!—said that they would like to have one of the Blaisdell books, when they were published, to hand down in the family. Flora took out her purse and said that she would pay for hers now; but Mr. Smith hastily, and with some evident embarrassment, refused the money, saying that he could not tell yet what the price of the book would be.

All the Blaisdells, except Frank, Fred, and Bessie, went to the station to see Mr. Smith off. They said they wanted to. They told him he was just like one of the family, anyway, and they declared they hoped he would come back soon. Frank telephoned him that he would have gone, too, if he had not had so much to do at the store.

Mr. Smith seemed pleased at all this attention—he seemed, indeed, quite touched; but he seemed also embarrassed—in fact, he seemed often embarrassed during those last few days at Hillerton.

Miss Maggie Duff did not go to the station to see Mr. Smith off. Miss Flora, on her way home, stopped at the Duff cottage and reproached Miss Maggie for the delinquency.

"Nonsense! Why should I go?" laughed Miss Maggie.

"Why *shouldn't* you?" retorted Miss Flora. "All the rest of us did, 'most."

"Well, that's all right. You're Blaisdells—but I'm not, you know."

"You're just as good as one, Maggie Duff! Besides, hasn't that man boarded here for over a year, and paid you good money, too?"

"Why, y-yes, of course."

"Well, then, I don't think it would have hurt you any to show him this last little attention. He'll think you don't like him, or—or are mad about something, when all the rest of us went."

"Nonsense, Flora!"

"Well, then, if—Why, Maggie Duff, you're *blushing*!" she broke off, peering into Miss Maggie's face in a way that did not tend to lessen the unmistakable color that was creeping to her forehead. "You *are* blushing! I declare, if you were twenty years younger, and I didn't know better, I should say that—" She stopped abruptly, then plunged on, her countenance suddenly alight with a new idea. "*Now* I know why you didn't go to the station, Maggie Duff! That man proposed to you, and you refused him!" she triumphed.

"Flora!" gasped Miss Maggie, her face scarlet.

"He did, I know he did! Hattie always said it would be a match—from the very first, when he came here to your house."

"*Flora!*" gasped Miss Maggie again, looking about her very much as if she were meditating flight.

"Well, she did—but I didn't believe it. Now I know. You refused him—now, didn't you?"

"Certainly not!" Miss Maggie caught her breath a little convulsively.

"Honest?"

"Flora! Stop this silly talk right now. I have answered you once. I shan't again."

"Hm-m." Miss Flora fell back in her chair. "Well, I suppose you didn't, then, if you say so. And I don't need to ask if you accepted him. You didn't, of course, or you'd have been there to see him off. And he wouldn't have gone then, anyway, probably. So he didn't ask you, I suppose. Well, I never did believe, like Hattie did, that—"

"Flora," interrupted Miss Maggie desperately, "*Will* you stop talking in that absurd way? Listen, I did not care to go to the station to-day. I am very busy. I am going away next week. I am going—to Chicago."

"To *chicago*—you!" Miss Flora came erect in her chair.

"Yes, for a visit. I'm going to see my old classmate, Nellie Maynard—Mrs. Tyndall."

"Maggie!"

"What's the matter?"

"Why, n-nothing. It's lovely, of course, only—only I—I'm so surprised! You never go anywhere."

"All the more reason why I should, then. It's time I did," smiled Miss Maggie. Miss Maggie was looking more at ease now.

"When are you going?"

"Next Wednesday. I heard from Nellie last night. She is expecting me then."

"How perfectly splendid! I'm so glad! And I do hope you can *do* it, and that it won't peter out at the last minute, same's most of your good times do. Poor Maggie! And you've had such a hard life—and your boarder leaving, too! That'll make a lot of difference in your pocketbook, won't it? But, Maggie, you'll have to have some new clothes."

"Of course. I've been shopping this afternoon. I've got to have—oh, lots of things."

"Of course you have. And, Maggie,"—Miss Flora's face grew eager,—"please, *please*, won't you let me help you a little—about those clothes? And get some nice ones—some real nice ones, for once. You *know* how I'd love to! Please, Maggie, there's a good girl!"

"Thank you, no, dear," refused Miss Maggie, shaking her head with a smile. "But I appreciate your kindness just the same—indeed, I do!"

"If you wouldn't be so horrid proud," pouted Miss Flora.

But Miss Maggie stopped her with a gesture.

"No, no,—listen! I—I have something to tell you. I was going to tell you soon, anyway, and I'll tell it now. I *have* money, dear,—lots of it now."

"You *have* money!"

"Yes. Father's Cousin George died two months ago."

"The rich one, in Alaska?"

"Yes; and to father's daughter he left—fifty thousand dollars."

"*Mag*-gie!"

"And I never even *saw* him! But he loved father, you know, years ago, and father loved him."

"But had you ever heard from him—late years?"

"Not much. Father was very angry because he went to Alaska in the first place, you know, and they haven't ever written very often."

"Fifty thousand! And you've got it now?"

"Not yet—all of it. They sent me a thousand—just for pin money, they said. The lawyer's written several times, and he's been here once. I believe it's all to come next month."

"Oh, I'm so glad, Maggie," breathed Flora. "I'm so glad! I don't know of anybody I'd rather see take a little comfort in life than you!"

At the door, fifteen minutes later, Miss Flora said again how glad she was; but she added wistfully:—

"I'm sure I don't know, though, what I'm going to do all summer without you. Just think how lonesome we'll be—you gone to Chicago, Hattie and Jim and all their family moved to Plainville, and even Mr. Smith gone, too! And I think we're going to miss Mr. Smith a whole lot, too. He was a real nice man. Don't you think so, Maggie?"

"Indeed, I do think he was a very nice man!" declared Miss Maggie. "Now, Flora, I shall want you to go shopping with me lots. Can you?"

And Miss Flora, eagerly entering into Miss Maggie's discussion of frills and flounces, failed to notice that Miss Maggie had dropped the subject of Mr. Smith somewhat hastily.

Hillerton had much to talk about during those summer days. Mr. Smith's going had created a mild discussion—the "ancestor feller" was well known and well liked in the town. But even his departure did not arouse the interest that was bestowed upon the removal of the James Blaisdells to Plainville; and this, in turn, did not cause so great an excitement as did the news that Miss Maggie Duff had inherited fifty thousand dollars and had gone to Chicago to spend it. And the fact that nearly all who heard this promptly declared that they hoped she *would* spend a good share of it—in Chicago, or elsewhere—on herself, showed pretty well just where Miss Maggie Duff stood in the hearts of Hillerton.

. . . . . .

It was early in September that Miss Flora had the letter from Miss Maggie. Not but that she had received letters from Miss Maggie before, but that the contents of this one made it at once, to all the Blaisdells, "the letter."

Miss Flora began to read it, gave a little cry, and sprang to her feet. Standing, her breath suspended, she finished it. Five minutes later, gloves half on and hat askew, she was hurrying across the common to her brother Frank's home.

"Jane, Jane," she panted, as soon as she found her sister-in-law. "I've had a letter from Maggie. Mr. Stanley G. Fulton has come back. *He's come back!*"

"Come back! Alive, you mean? Oh, my goodness gracious! What'll Hattie do? She's just been living on having that money. And us, with all we've lost, too! But, then, maybe we wouldn't have got it, anyway. My stars! And Maggie wrote you? Where's the letter?"

"There! And I never thought to bring it," ejaculated Miss Flora vexedly. "But, never mind! I can tell you all she said. She didn't write much. She said it would be in all the Eastern papers right away, of course, but she wanted to tell us first, so we wouldn't be so surprised. He's just come. Walked into his lawyer's office without a telegram, or anything. Said he didn't want any fuss made. Mr. Tyndall brought home the news that night in an 'Extra'; but that's all it told—just that Mr. Stanley G. Fulton, the multi-millionaire who disappeared nearly two years ago on an exploring trip to South America, had come back alive and well. Then it told all about the two letters he left, and the money he left to us, and all that, Maggie said; and it talked a lot about how lucky it was that he got back just in time before the other letter had to be opened next November. But it didn't say any more about his trip, or anything. The morning papers will have more, Maggie said, probably."

"Yes, of course, of course," nodded Jane, rolling the corner of her upper apron nervously. (Since the forty-thousand-dollar loss Jane had gone back to her old habit of wearing two aprons.) "Where *do* you suppose he's been all this time? Was he lost or just exploring?"

"Maggie said it wasn't known—that the paper didn't say. It was an 'Extra' anyway, and it just got in the bare news of his return. But we'll know, of course. The papers here will tell us. Besides, Maggie'll write again about it, I'm sure. Poor Maggie! I'm so glad she's having such a good time!"

"Yes, of course, of course," nodded Jane again nervously. "Say, Flora, I wonder—do you suppose *we'll* ever hear from him? He left us all that money—he knows that, of course. He can't ask for it back—the lawyer said he couldn't do that! Don't you remember? But, I wonder—do you suppose we ought to write him and—and thank him?"

"Oh, mercy!" exclaimed Miss Flora, aghast. "Mercy me, Jane! I'd be scared to death to do such a thing as that. Oh, you don't think we've got to do *that*?" Miss Flora had grown actually pale.

Jane frowned.

"I don't know. We'd want to do what was right and proper, of course. But I don't see—" She paused helplessly.

Miss Flora gave a sudden hysterical little laugh.

"Well, I don't see how we're going to find out what's proper, in this case," she giggled. "We can't write to a magazine, same as I did when I wanted to know how to answer invitations and fix my knives and forks on the table. We *can't* write to them, 'cause nothing like this ever happened before, and they wouldn't know what to say. How'd we look writing, 'Please, dear Editor, when a man wills you a hundred thousand dollars and then comes to life again, is it proper or not proper to write and thank him?' They'd think we was crazy, and they'd have reason to! For my part, I—"

The telephone bell rang sharply, and Jane rose to answer it. She was gone some time. When she came back she was even more excited.

"It was Frank. He's heard it. It was in the papers to-night."

"Did it tell anything more?"

"Not much, I guess. Still, there was some. He's going to bring it home. It's 'most supper-time. Why don't you wait?" she questioned, as Miss Flora got hastily to her feet.

Miss Flora shook her head.

"I can't. I left everything just as it was and ran, when I got the letter. I'll get a paper myself on the way home. I'm going to call up Hattie, too, on the long distance. My, it's 'most as exciting as it was when it first came,—the money, I mean,—isn't it?" panted Miss Flora as she hurried away.

The Blaisdells bought many papers during the next few days. But even by the time that the Stanley G. Fulton sensation had dwindled to a short paragraph in an obscure corner of a middle page, they (and the public in general) were really little the wiser, except for these bare facts:—

Stanley G. Fulton had arrived at a South American hotel, from the interior, had registered as S. Fulton, frankly to avoid publicity, and had taken immediate passage to New York. Arriving at New York, still to avoid publicity, he had not telegraphed his attorneys, but had taken the sleeper for Chicago, and had fortunately not met any one who recognized him until his arrival in that city. He had brought home several fine specimens of Incan textiles and potteries: and he declared that he had had a very enjoyable and profitable trip. Beyond that he would say nothing. He did not care to talk of his experiences, he said.

For a time, of course, his return was made much of. Fake interviews and rumors of threatened death and disaster in impenetrable jungles made frequent appearance; but in an incredibly short time the flame of interest died from want of fuel to feed upon; and, as Mr. Stanley G. Fulton himself had once predicted, the matter was soon dismissed as merely another of the multi-millionaire's well-known eccentricities.

All of this the Blaisdells heard from Miss Maggie in addition to seeing it in the newspapers. But very soon, from Miss Maggie, they began to learn more. Before a fortnight had passed, Miss Flora received another letter from Chicago that sent her flying as before to her sister-in-law.

"Jane, Jane, Maggie's *met him*!" she cried, breathlessly bursting into the kitchen where Jane was paring the apples that she would not trust to the maid's more wasteful knife.

"Met him! Met who?"

"Mr. Fulton. She's *talked* with him! She wrote me all about it."

"*Our* Mr. Fulton?"

"Yes."

"*Flora!*" With a hasty twirl of a now reckless knife, Jane finished the last apple, set the pan on the table before the maid, and hurried her visitor into the living-room. "Now, tell me quick—what did she say? Is he nice? Did she like him? Did he know she belonged to us?"

"Yes—yes—everything," nodded Miss Flora, sinking into a chair. "She liked him real well, she said and he knows all about that she belongs to us. She said he was real interested in us. Oh, I hope she didn't tell him about— Fred!"

"And that awful gold-mine stock," moaned Jane. "But she wouldn't—I know she wouldn't!"

"Of course she wouldn't," cried Miss Flora. "'Tisn't like Maggie one bit! She'd only tell the nice things, I'm sure. And, of course, she'd tell him how pleased we were with the money!"

"Yes, of course, of course. And to think she's met him—really met him!" breathed Jane. "Mellicent!" She turned an excited face to her daughter, who had just entered the room. "What do you think? Aunt Flora's just had a letter from Aunt Maggie, and she's met Mr. Fulton—actually *talked* with him!"

"Really? Oh, how perfectly splendid! Is he nice? Did she like him?"

Miss Flora laughed.

"That's just what your mother asked. Yes, he's real nice, your Aunt Maggie says, and she likes him very much."

"But how'd she do it? How'd she happen to meet him?" demanded Jane.

"Well, it seems he knew Mr. Tyndall, and Mr. Tyndall brought him home one night and introduced him to his wife and Maggie; and since then he's been very nice to them. He's taken them out in his automobile, and taken them to the theater twice."

"That's because she belongs to us, of course," nodded Jane wisely.

"Yes, I suppose so," agreed Flora. "And I think it's very kind of him."

"Pooh!" sniffed Mellicent airily. "_I_ think he does it because he *wants* to. You never did appreciate Aunt Maggie. I'll warrant she's nicer and sweeter and—and, yes, *prettier* than lots of those old Chicago women. Aunt Maggie looked positively *handsome* that day she left here last July. She looked so—so absolutely happy! Probably he *likes* to take her to places. Anyhow, I'm glad she's having one good time before she dies."

"Yes, so am I, my dear. We all are," sighed Miss Flora. "Poor Maggie!"

"I only wish he'd marry her and—and give her a good time all her life," avowed Mellicent, lifting her chin.

"Marry her!" exclaimed two scornful voices.

"Well, why not? She's good enough for him," bridled Mellicent. "Aunt Maggie's good enough for anybody!"

"Of course she is, child!" laughed Miss Flora. "Maggie's a saint—if ever there was one."

"Yes, but I shouldn't call her a *marrying* saint," smiled Jane.

"Well, I don't know about that," frowned Miss Flora thoughtfully. "Hattie always declared there'd be a match between her and Mr. Smith, you know."

"Yes. But there wasn't one, was there?" twitted Jane. "Well, then, I shall stick to my original statement that Maggie Duff is a saint, all right, but not a marrying one—unless some one marries her now for her money, of course."

"As if Aunt Maggie'd stand for that!" scoffed Mellicent. "Besides, she wouldn't have to! Aunt Maggie's good enough to be married for herself."

"There, there, child, just because you are a love-sick little piece of romance just now, you needn't think everybody else is," her mother reproved her a little sharply.

But Mellicent only laughed merrily as she disappeared into her own room.

"Speaking of Mr. Smith, I wonder where he is, and if he'll ever come back here," mused Miss Flora, aloud. "I wish he would. He was a very nice man, and I liked him."

"Goodness, Flora, *you* aren't, getting romantic, too, are you?" teased her sister-in-law.

"Nonsense, Jane!" ejaculated Miss Flora sharply, buttoning up her coat. "I'm no more romantic than—than poor Maggie herself is!"

Two weeks later, to a day, came Miss Maggie's letter announcing her engagement to Mr. Stanley G. Fulton, and saying that she was to be married in Chicago before Christmas.

CHAPTER XXVI
REENTER MR. STANLEY G. FULTON

In the library of Mrs. Thomas Tyndall's Chicago home Mr. Stanley G. Fulton was impatiently awaiting the appearance of Miss Maggie Duff. In a minute she came in, looking charmingly youthful in her new, well-fitting frock.

The man, quickly on his feet at her entrance, gave her a lover's ardent kiss; but almost instantly he held her off at arms' length.

"Why, dearest, what's the matter?" he demanded.

"W-what do you mean?"

"You look as if—if something had happened—not exactly a bad something, but—What is it?"

Miss Maggie laughed softly.

"That's one of the very nicest things about you, Mr. Stanley-G.-Fulton-John-Smith," she sighed, nestling comfortably into the curve of his arm, as they sat down on the divan;—"that you *notice* things so. And it seems so good to me to have somebody—*notice.*"

"Poor lonely little woman! And to think of all these years I've wasted!"

"Oh, but I shan't be lonely any more now. And, listen—I'll tell you what made me look so funny. I've had a letter from Flora. You know I wrote them—about my coming marriage."

"Yes, yes," eagerly. "Well, what did they say?"

Miss Maggie laughed again.

"I believe—I'll let you read the letter for yourself, Stanley. It tells some things, toward the end that I think you'll like to know," she said, a little hesitatingly, as she held out the letter she had brought into the room with her.

"Good! I'd like to read it," cried Fulton, whisking the closely written sheets from the envelope.

My Dear Maggie (Flora had written): Well, mercy me, you have given us a surprise this time, and no mistake! Yet we're all real glad, Maggie, and we hope you'll be awfully happy. You deserve it, all right. Poor Maggie! You've had such an awfully hard time all your life!

Well, when your letter came, we were just going out to Jim's for an old-fashioned Thanksgiving dinner, so I took it along with me and read it to them all. I kept it till we were all together, too, though I most bursted with the news all the way out.

Well, you ought to have heard their tongues wag! They were all struck dumb first, for a minute, all except Mellicent. She spoke up the very first thing, and clapped her hands.

"There," she cried. "What did I tell you? I knew Aunt Maggie was good enough for anybody!"

To explain that I'll have to go back a little. We were talking one day about you—Jane and Mellicent and me—and we said you were a saint, only not a marrying saint. But Mellicent thought you were, and it seems she was right. Oh, of course, we'd all thought once Mr. Smith might take a fancy to you, but we never dreamed of such a thing as this—Mr. Stanley G. Fulton! Sakes alive—I can hardly sense it yet!

Jane, for a minute, forgot how rich he was, and spoke right up real quick—"It's for her money, of course. I *knew* some one would marry her for that fifty thousand dollars!" But she laughed then, right off, with the rest of us, at the idea of a man worth twenty millions marrying *anybody* for fifty thousand dollars.

Benny says there ain't any man alive good enough for his Aunt Maggie, so if Mr. Fulton gets to being too high-headed sometimes, you can tell him what Benny says.

But we're all real pleased, honestly, Maggie, and of course we're terribly excited. We're so sorry you're going to be married out there in Chicago. Why can't you make him come to Hillerton? Jane says she'd be glad to make a real nice wedding for you—and when Jane says a thing like that, you can know how much she's really saying, for Jane's feeling awfully poor these days, since they lost all that money, you know.

And we'd all like to see Mr. Fulton, too—"Cousin Stanley," as Hattie always calls him. Please give him our congratulations—but there, that sounds funny, doesn't it? (But the etiquette editors in the magazines say we must always give best wishes to the bride and congratulations to the groom.) Only it seems funny here, to congratulate that rich Mr. Fulton on marrying you. Oh, dear! I didn't mean it that way, Maggie. I declare, if that sentence wasn't 'way in the middle of this third page, and so awfully hard for me to write, anyway, I'd tear up this sheet and begin another. But, after all, you'll understand, I'm sure. You *know* we all think the world of you, Maggie, and that I didn't mean anything against *you*. It's just that—that Mr. Fulton is—is such a big man, and all—But you know what I meant.

Well, anyway, if you can't come here to be married, we hope you'll bring him here soon so we can see him, and see you, too. We miss you awfully, Maggie,—truly we do, especially since Jim's folks went, and with Mr. Smith gone, too, Jane and I are real lonesome.

Jim and Hattie like real well where they are. They've got a real pretty home, and they're the biggest folks in town, so Hattie doesn't have to worry for fear she won't live quite so fine as her neighbors—though really I think Hattie's got over that now a good deal. That awful thing of Fred's sobered her a lot, and taught her who her real friends were, and that money ain't everything.

Fred is doing splendidly now, just as steady as a clock. It does my soul good to see him and his father together. They are just like chums. And Bessie—she isn't near so disagreeable and airy as she was. Hattie took her out of that school and put her into another where she's getting some real learning and less society and frills and dancing. Jim is doing well, and I think Hattie's real happy. Oh, of course, when we first heard that Mr. Fulton had got back, I think she was kind of disappointed. You know she always did insist we were going to have the rest of that money if he didn't show up. But she told me just Thanksgiving Day that she didn't know but 'twas just as well, after all, that they didn't have the money, for maybe Fred'd go wrong again, or it would strike Benny this time. Anyhow, however much money she had, she said, she'd never let her children spend so much again, and she'd found out money didn't bring happiness, always, anyway.

Mellicent and Donald are going to be married next summer. Donald don't get a very big salary yet, but Mellicent says she won't mind a bit going back to economizing again, now that for once she's had all the chocolates and pink dresses she wanted. What a funny girl she is—but she's a dear girl, just the same, and she's settled down real sensible now. She and Donald are as happy as can be, and even Jane likes Donald real well now.

Jane's gone back to her tidies and aprons and skimping on everything. She says she's got to, to make up that forty thousand dollars. But she enjoys it, I believe. Honestly, she acts 'most as happy trying to save five cents as Frank does earning it in his old place behind the counter. And that's saying a whole lot, as you know. Jane knows very well she doesn't have to pinch that way. They've got lots of the money left, and Frank's business is better than ever. But she just likes to.

You complain because I don't tell you anything about myself in my letters, but there isn't anything to tell. I am well and happy, and I've just thought up the nicest thing to do. Mary Hicks came home from Boston sick last September, and she's been here at my house ever since. Her own home ain't no place for a sick person, you know, with all those children, and they're awfully poor, too. So I took her here with me. She's a real nice girl. She works in a department store and was all played out, but she's picked up wonderfully here and is going back next week.

Well, she was telling me about a girl that works with her at the same counter, and saying how she wished she had a place like this to go to for a rest and change, so I'm going to do it—give them one, I mean, she and the other girls. Mary says there are a dozen girls that she knows right there that are half-sick, but would get well in a minute if they only had a few weeks of rest and quiet and good food. So I'm going to take them, two at a time, so they'll be company for each other. Mary is going to fix it up for me down there, and pick out the girls, and she says she knows the man who owns the store will be glad to let them off, for they are all good help, and he's been afraid he'd lose them. He'd offered them a month off, besides their vacation, but they couldn't take it, because they didn't have any place to go or money to pay. Of course, that part will be all right now. And I'm so glad and excited I don't know what to do. Oh, I do hope you'll tell Mr. Fulton some time how happy he's made me, and how perfectly splendid that money's been for me.

Well, Maggie, this is a long letter, and I must close. Tell me all about the new clothes you are getting, and I hope you will get a lot.

Lovingly yours,
Flora.

P.S. Does Mr. Fulton look like his pictures? You know I've got one. F.

P.S. again. Maggie Duff, for pity's sake, never, never tell that man that I ever went into mourning for him and put flowers before his picture. I'd be mortified to death!

"Bless her heart!" With a smile Mr. Fulton folded the letter and handed it back to Miss Maggie.

"I didn't feel that I was betraying confidences—under the circumstances," murmured Miss Maggie.

"Hardly!"

"And there was a good deal in the letter that I *did* want you to see," added Miss Maggie.

"Hm-m; the congratulations, for one thing, of course," twinkled the man. "Poor Maggie!"

"I wanted you to see how really, in the end, that money was not doing so much harm, after all," asserted Miss Maggie, with some dignity, shaking her head at him reprovingly. "I thought you'd be *glad*, sir!"

"I am glad. I'm so glad that, when I come to make my will now, I shouldn't wonder if I remembered them all again—a little—that is, if I have anything left to will," he teased shamelessly. "Oh, by the way, that makes me think. I've just been putting up a monument to John Smith."

"Stanley!" Miss Maggie's voice carried genuine shocked distress.

"But, my dear Maggie, something was due the man," maintained Fulton, reaching for a small flat parcel near him and placing it in Miss Maggie's hands.

"But—oh, Stanley, how could you?" she shivered, her eyes on the words the millionaire had penciled on the brown paper covering of the parcel.

Sacred to the memory of John Smith.

"Open it," directed the man.

With obvious reluctance Miss Maggie loosened the paper covers and peered within. The next moment she gave a glad cry.

In her hands lay a handsome brown leather volume with gold letters, reading:—

The Blaisdell Family
By
John Smith

"And you—did that?" she asked, her eyes luminous.

"Yes. I shall send a copy each to Frank and Jim and Miss Flora, of course. That's the monument. I thought it due—Mr. John Smith. Poor man, it's the least I can do for him—and the most—unless—" He hesitated with an unmistakable look of embarrassment.

"Yes," prompted Miss Maggie eagerly. "Yes!"

"Well, unless—I let you take me to Hillerton one of these days and see if—if Stanley G. Fulton, with your gracious help, can make peace for John Smith with those—er—cousins of mine. You see, I still feel confoundedly like that small boy at the keyhole, and I'd like—to open that door! Could we do it, do you think?"

"Do it? Of course we could! And, oh, Stanley, it's the one thing needed to make me perfectly happy," she sighed blissfully.